My War

My War

'LIFE IS FOR LIVING'

Brian Walpole
with David Levell

ABC
Books

Published by ABC Books for the
AUSTRALIAN BROADCASTING CORPORATION
GPO Box 9994 Sydney NSW 2001

Copyright © Brian Walpole 2004

First published 2004

ISBN 0 7333 1463 5

Design and Typesetting Reno Design / Graham Rendoth R24019
Typeset in Berthold Garamond, Frutiger, Pelican
Colour reproduction by Colorwize Studio, Adelaide
Printed and bound in Australia by Griffin Press, Adelaide

5 4 3 2 1

PREFACE

I met Brian Walpole in June 2003, when I was conducting videotaped interviews with a wide range of Australian World War II veterans for the 'Australians At War' film archive. As we set about shifting furniture and arranging the camera and lights in Brian's flat, his first question was most unexpected. Instead of the usual comments about the technical gear, he said, 'Do you know any literary agents?'

Brian explained that he'd recently finished writing a memoir of his life during the war, a project which had occupied the past couple of years. As it happened, I knew a very good agent indeed. Pleased to do a favour for a likeable and enthusiastic gentleman, I put Brian in touch with Selwa Anthony. Her expert eye quickly detected in his manuscript a strong and unusual story, one with a distinctive Australian flavour. All it needed was some editing to knock it into shape for a publisher, and so I found myself immersed in one of the most fascinating tales I've ever come across in my career as a writer and television producer. Carl Harrison-Ford, Mark Macleod and Brigitta Doyle, who made valuable contributions to this process, have my grateful thanks.

Although modestly insisting that he's no author, there's no doubt Brian is a gifted storyteller with excellent recall of detail and a wry, distinctively Australian sense of humour. He offers a unique and honest insight into what went through the mind of a young Australian of the 1940s facing the challenges and pressures of an often ruthless and desperate war. Brian's firsthand account is full of youthful verve and energy. The voice isn't as much that of an eighty-year-old man reflecting on incidents long past as it is the voice of a digger in his early twenties, reaching across the decades to take you to the very heart of an adventure as it unfolds.

'Life is for Living' is not only the subtitle of this book; it's Brian's motto throughout.

Dwelling on the past isn't really his style, so we must thank his friends for urging him to put on paper what is perhaps one of the most extraordinary individual experiences an Australian soldier ever had during the Second World War.

David Levell

PROLOGUE

Almost sixty years later, I remember the Japanese commanding officer as if it was yesterday. At first he was cowed, but when he realised that Bujang wasn't going to cut off his head, his sneering arrogance returned. He was Kempeitai – Japanese secret police – feared even by his own side. Neatly pressed jungle greens. White scarf. Highly polished black jackboots. The treatment he had dished out to POWs and local indigenous people was beyond belief: four years of murder, torture, bashings and starvation.

I remember the lady, too. Her name was Lena. An attractive nurse in her twenties, she was absolutely covered in filth and wore clothes so shredded they were barely even rags. She had been forced to clean gutters and forbidden to wash, so the worst of scarecrows was respectable by comparison. The look on her face was utterly desperate. Her father hadn't survived their long captivity and now, a month after Japan's unconditional surrender, she was to be put to death along with all the other prisoners of war, on the very day of the Japanese withdrawal from the Sarawak town of Simanggang.

The war was over, but that didn't stop the Japanese officer attempting to ambush and massacre us as we came into Simanggang to accept his surrender. And he had no intention of letting his prisoners live to bear witness to his atrocities. But he was my prisoner now. Twenty-one of us had taken possession of Simanggang: twenty headhunters from the jungles along the Rejang River, and me, the twenty-two-year-old kid from Melbourne. It was the culmination of one of the strangest operations Australia undertook during the Second World War. Not many people know that Australian diggers fought alongside Sea Dyak headhunters in Borneo, behind enemy lines, or that Australia's undercover Z Special Unit played a significant role in winning the Pacific war.

After the firefight we had ten Japanese soldiers, including the sneering officer, huddled in a small group. A strip search yielded several concealed knives. Bujang and the rest of the Sea Dyak guerrillas peered longingly at their necks, making professional assessments. But everything was different now: Japan had officially surrendered and I could hardly let them take heads anymore.

All the time, Lena stood next to me, watching with fierce concentration. I have rarely seen such intensity on anyone's face and although I often wondered what was on her mind, it wasn't until fifty-three years later that I found out.

This is the story of my war, from my baptism of fire in one of Australia's first commando units in the jungles of New Guinea, to my career as a guerrilla with Z Special Unit in Borneo.

I'm eighty-one years old now, love vodka and pretty ladies, and believe that life is for living. Writing a book has been a completely new experience for me, so forgive me if it's sometimes a little unorthodox; that doesn't worry me because the events I describe actually took place. I've probably always been a bit unorthodox myself, anyway, and I'd rather be unorthodox than boring. There are few things worse than a bore.

CONTENTS

PART ONE

New Guinea
1941–1943

1

From Melbourne to Wau

People said that if you went to war, you did it for God, King and Country. What a load of crap. When I joined the army everyone was joining up and the general feeling was that you had to be in it. And I wanted to enlist as much as anybody. It was the sense of adventure. I would have volunteered to fly to the Moon if that had been going at the time. Anyway, the war had started whether we liked it or not, and I thought it was better to take on the enemy in another country than wait until they reached my own backyard.

My own backyard had been happy and relatively trouble-free. I was born in Melbourne on the 30th of October 1922. My parents were not wealthy, but careful management meant that we never went wanting. During the Depression people knocked on our door regularly to ask for any kind of work in return for a meal and no one was ever refused.

My father worked in Melbourne as a banker. My mother, as a young lady during the First World War, played piano for servicemen at a seamen's mission – chaperoned, of course – and her talents were in great demand. Later she arranged piano lessons for me, but I gradually dropped out as I played more sport. I'm sorry now, because I'd love to be able to belt out some trad jazz. My mother was very modern by the standards of the day and protective of her brood. Along with my brother Denis, who was three years older than me, I was fortunate in having a good education, which stood us in good stead.

I realise now that my parents must really have stretched themselves financially. Their sacrifice was not wasted; I enjoyed school and passed my Honours Leaving Certificate at fourteen. I intended to study medicine, but, being too young to enrol at the university, I decided to follow my father into a bank job – at least until I was old enough to commence my studies. The hours were not too long and left me time to improve my tennis, golf and swimming. I managed to win a few competitions and fancied I had some sort of sporting future. All that changed on the 3rd of September 1939, when Prime Minister Robert Menzies famously announced that it was his 'melancholy duty' to declare Australia at war due to Britain's declaration of war on Germany, a consequence of Hitler's invasion of Poland. Australians rushed to join the armed services and that took care of a large slice of the unemployment problem. At sixteen I was too young to join up. My brother Denis was living in Launceston and enlisted fairly early in the piece. He ended up in the all-Tasmanian 2/40 Battalion.

Of course, Germany wasn't the only problem. Japan had already invaded Korea and China and was a more direct threat to Australia. Britain and Australia sent armed forces to various parts of southeast Asia, but everyone seemed to have a poor opinion of Japanese fighting capabilities. They were to be proved wrong.

The Japanese didn't bother to declare war. They just bombed the hell out of Pearl Harbor and advanced south quickly without much opposition. When Singapore fell in February 1942, most of the 8th Australian Division became prisoners of war. This included my brother, who was serving in Timor with his infantry battalion. We heard nothing more of him for years. My parents were devastated and I felt so sorry for them. It was a worrying time for most Australians because the threat of invasion was real. Most people's way of life changed dramatically overnight, never to be the same again.

At this stage, I was already in the army, having enlisted on the 4th of October 1941, just before my nineteenth birthday. The ill-fitting uniforms, outdated weaponry and rifle drills with broom handles didn't worry me at the time, but the disorganisation was amazing. I was promoted to corporal and sent away to various army schools to learn anti-gas warfare, tank and anti-tank warfare, weapons familiarisation and intelligence operations. None of it proved useful in my later escapades.

During this time I heard about new specialised units being formed. This development was supposed to be secret and the word "commando" was quite new to us. The value of having small formations of highly-trained mobile, independently operating troops first became apparent when the Brits were forced out of Europe at Dunkirk. The idea was to allow a numerically superior force to pass by, re-form at their rear and then systematically create mayhem with hit-and-run raids and sabotage. The first British commandos, or Independent Companies, proved highly successful with many daring raids that supported Churchill's vow to keep Europe afire.

In 1941 the first British team arrived to pass on their skills to specially selected Australian volunteers, who would then train local recruits. The following year, while on an army intelligence course, I made enquiries and my application to join was accepted on condition that I passed the training.

When I arrived at the commando training centre in September 1942 I found an atmosphere of total commitment. Every man was a fighting machine and I spent the next six weeks in intensive training to become one myself. The site was hidden deep on Wilson's Promontory, the isolated southernmost tip of the Australian mainland. We generally referred to the base as Foster, after the nearest town. It was ideal for the purpose, surrounded by dense bush, rugged hills and valleys and daunting cliffs along the coast.

All potential commandos had to sign their consent to all kinds of hazardous operations, including suicide missions. We came under the extreme provisions of the Official Secrets Act, but of course we just signed everything.

The successful completion of the course meant a posting to an Independent Company, as the commando units were called here too. Each was self-contained, consisting of about 273 fighting soldiers. The training was extremely rigorous and it was survival of the fittest; unsuitable applicants were quietly discarded.

The instructors taught guerrilla warfare as an art, using all types of weapons. I was introduced to the Bren gun and Thompson submachine gun, which were little known in Australia.

We ran up and down mountains, along soft sand and forced our way through thick bush. We learnt unarmed combat and the art of silent killing, and were trained in all types of weaponry. Captain White, who had the rather unimaginative nickname Blanc, told us, 'If the war up north continues the way it is, I can promise you some of the bloodiest fighting ever seen in history.' It sounded a bit heavy at the time, but it turned out he was spot on.

There were lighter moments. Wilson's Promontory abounded with deer and I'd never tasted venison before, but became quite partial to its flavour while we were out on live-off-the-land exercises.

Soon I was like the people I'd met on my arrival: fit, focused and with a definite purpose in mind. I anticipated a posting to an Independent Company, but when my six weeks were up I was told that instructors were required for a new jungle warfare school opening at Canungra in Queensland. The top six trainees of my cadre, including me, had been selected to go. This was all very flattering, but it was not the reason I'd joined up.

There was no choice, however. By November 1942 I was facing my first batch of trainees at Canungra, barely two months after having begun my own training. The weather was warmer and more pleasant than on Wilson's Promontory, but something was lacking. Jungle warfare training was nowhere near as tough as commando training and, compared to Wilson's Promontory, Canungra was a piece of cake.

There was an obstacle course, there were forced marches through the bush and provision was made for physical training and instruction in unarmed combat. There were lecture rooms and even a parade ground for drilling. That was a horrible thought; I hadn't done any drilling for ages.

Most of the trainees didn't want to be there and some were extremely aggressive about it. They reckoned they hadn't volunteered for this and resented taking orders from people two to three years their junior. But once we demonstrated our capabilities we had no further trouble. The first intake of trainees left and a second arrived. And so on. The pattern continued and didn't give me much satisfaction.

Meanwhile, the 2/3 Australian Independent Company had returned from New Caledonia to re-form nearby at Wongelpong. Their new Commanding Officer, George Warfe, was a battle-hardened infantry veteran with a track record in the Middle East and a reputation as a fearless close-combat soldier. A demanding but highly respected leader, he was knocking the Company into formidable shape. He came to Canungra from time to time, so I grabbed the first chance to approach him about joining his commandos.

Meeting George Warfe was quite an experience. He was like a coiled spring, full of power and energy and looked straight through you with his cold brown eyes. I explained I didn't see much future in teaching jungle warfare to people who were plainly not interested.

He simply said, 'I'll check you out.'

A couple of days later he asked to see me. 'I could arrange for you to join up,' he said, 'but unfortunately I can't take on anyone with any rank.'

Suddenly I had the solution. 'What if I revert to private?'

'Why would you do that?' he said. 'Most blokes are trying to work their way up the ladder.'

'Yes, but what if I do revert to private?'

'Well, I could arrange a transfer then,' he said.

'Okay, I'll do it now.'

'Do that and we'll organise something later on.' His piercing gaze seemed to soften for a moment.

So I had myself demoted to private. I signed forms confirming that it was at my own request and so forth. Apparently no one had heard of this being done before. In January 1943 I transferred to the 2/3 Australian Independent Company, ready to leave for parts unknown.

Almost straightaway we went to Townsville and embarked on the *SS Taroona*, which used to do the passenger run between Melbourne and Tasmania. It made the trip to New Guinea in disguise, painted grey and with one funnel removed.

Our first glimpse of Port Moresby was late one afternoon, basking in the tropical heat. In the distance we saw the ominous Owen Stanleys, shrouded in mist, where so many Australians had already fought heroically.

The Japanese bombed Port Moresby every night I was there. Fortunately our camp was just out of the town so we weren't directly affected. American trucks were everywhere, and it amused me that the drivers leapt from their vehicles into roadside ditches whenever there was an air raid, leaving their headlights on. I couldn't blame them for wanting to take cover, but those headlights illuminating the sky in all directions made the bombers' job so much easier.

By this stage we had been issued with our combat gear. I had a Thompson submachine gun, a .38 calibre Smith & Wesson revolver, a knuckleduster knife, a jungle knife, several hand grenades, an emergency first aid kit and rations. As the Tommy gun was calibre .45 we had to carry two types of ammunition. Most of us got around this by doing a deal with the Americans, swapping our .38s for their .45 Colt automatic pistols. The guns had to be kept in pristine condition at all times. The slightest bit of grit or mud in the working parts could cause them to fail. Keeping them clean in the jungle was to prove one of our biggest challenges.

We stayed in Port Moresby for only a few days. We were meant to be the advance guard for an American offensive, but the Japanese changed all that with a sudden all-out attack on Wau. This had to be stopped at all costs, because if they took control of the airstrip they could have seriously endangered Port Moresby. So up we went to Wau.

It was a small township in the Bulolo Valley, an area rich in alluvial gold deposits. The airstrip had been built in the early 1930s to fly in mining machinery, one part at a time. Nestled 4000 feet above sea level and surrounded by jungle-covered mountains reaching a further 2000 feet, the airstrip was about 1100 yards long with the upper end 300 feet higher than the lower. Only one plane could fit on the ground at a time. Provided the wind was reasonable, an incoming plane could land on the lower end, taxi uphill, turn around, unload and then take off downhill. Visibility was often extremely poor due to cloud and mist and heavy tropical rain. There were also severe up and down thermal draughts.

There was no road to Wau; the Americans flew us there in slow, unarmed Dakota transport planes. Each could carry only about sixteen of us and the weather was shocking and buffeted us in all directions. Kittyhawk fighters escorted us for protection, but the mountains were covered so thickly with mist that I only caught a couple of glimpses of them through breaks in the cloud, buzzing forward and back like angry wasps.

The Japanese were already on the southern fringe of the airstrip and we were told to expect a fighting reception. Sure enough, Wau greeted us with the explosion of mortars and the crackle of machinegun fire. It felt very strange to land uphill. The Dakota slowed right down, but never actually stopped. As soon as the doors clanged open the American aircrew began screaming at us.

'Let's go, let's go! Goddamn, let's go!'

Of course, they weren't actually going anywhere. We jumped from the moving plane and raced to the end of the airstrip, hoping the Japanese bombs and bullets wouldn't catch up with us. As soon as we got there we returned fire. There was no time to think or wonder what we'd got ourselves into. Our survival instincts kicked in and our training served us well.

The Dakota turned around and took off down the strip. Another one landed immediately. But full marks to these American aircrews. They were sitting ducks while they disembarked us on the ground and worked skilfully and bravely under enormous pressure.

We spent that first night in the open, near what had once been tennis courts. It was pitch dark and nobody seemed to know what was going on. George Warfe went from man to man, checking our positions and seeing we were all right. He acted like he couldn't have cared less about the enemy fire, and his nonchalance was a great help to those of us who had never been shot at before. There was no sleep; the firing continued all night. We were issued with passwords and told to look sharp for enemy infiltrators. A Japanese attack was expected either during the night or early in the morning. And snipers had already killed two of us.

It was an intense introduction to armed combat and the stand-off continued for a couple of days before the Japanese were forced back and Wau was ours. They had sent some 2600 of their finest from their base at Mubo, and a hell of a lot of them didn't make it back. It must have broken their hearts to have been so close and then have us upset their plans. Not that we gave a stuff about that.

2

Fighting in New Guinea

Three tracks led from Wau to Mubo: the Black Cat, the Buisaval and between them the Jap Track, so called because at first only they knew about it. Surveyed by the Germans in 1926, it had fallen into disuse and was reclaimed by the jungle until the Japanese obtained an old map from German missionaries. They had used this forgotten route to bypass the Wau defenders so our company soon had patrols on all three tracks simultaneously. There was extensive fighting and we suffered many casualties as we gradually forced the Japanese back.

George Warfe attached me to the I section – Intelligence – which meant gathering information in the field. And 'in the field' meant anywhere. We lived on whatever food and water we could carry and frequently went without for a couple of days. Emergency rations, often in short supply, consisted mainly of concentrated food, cubes of soup, apricot, raisins or cheese. Regular issue biscuit was always called dog biscuit, because it was hard enough to keep a dog busy. Sticking to the high spurs of the terrain as far as possible, we could see the streams down in the valleys, but fetching water usually meant a day's hike there and back. My immediate concern, however, was running out of ammunition. We were soaking wet all the time, either from perspiration or rain, and often covered in mud. As I say, keeping weapons clean and dry was a constant battle in itself.

Wau was so high up we could watch the planes dog-fighting: twin-tailed American Lightnings against the Japanese Zeros. The Americans shot down many Japanese fighters, which were trying to destroy the transport and supply planes before they could land.

Night came like a blind being pulled down. At about five everything just went black. Out on patrol we would lay a few booby traps, then, taking turns to guard, try to doze until dawn while we became more and more uncomfortable in the jungle rain. The booby traps were always removed as soon as possible, usually the next day. They included tripwires attached to hand grenades, and also AP (antipersonnel) switches that fired a .303 bullet through the foot of anyone who stepped on them.

One day on patrol we came across a fellow commando lying dead in a shallow stream, face down in the water. He was a few years my senior and his kindly encouragement had been a huge boost to me when I first landed at Wau. I won't mention his name because I don't think his family was told what happened to him, but he was like a big brother to me. Now here he was, clothes stripped from his body and both buttocks carved off. It was the first evidence I'd seen that the Japanese were resorting to cannibalism. At that moment I was filled with an intense hatred and disgust for people who could do such things to fellow human beings.

In the rainforest the sun never really came through and, just to make life even more difficult, around nightfall the rain usually bucketed down. If you were in close contact with the enemy, you'd hear their dogs howling as the soldiers chanted, perhaps building up the nerve to attack. Then a bugle would blast and they'd come screaming down the track, led by an officer waving his sword. It was unnerving the first time you heard it in the twilight, but you got used to it. All you could do was kill as many of them as possible. Later on the dogs stopped howling. Maybe they ate them.

George Warfe proved a real buccaneer. He wore a Colt .45 automatic pistol on each hip and carried a .303 calibre rifle with bayonet, which he used very effectively. He was a natural leader and that steely stare of his bored right through you and said, *Been there, done it all and don't fuck me around.* Although he didn't suffer fools, he was always fair and never asked for anything he wasn't prepared to do himself. But then he was fearless and would, in fact, do anything. I never heard George raise his voice; he just quietly said what he wanted and you did it. In war histories he's often described as 'the legendary George Warfe'. We called him George or Warfey, but not to his face. He addressed us by first names or nicknames. He always called me Wally.

The whole unit admired and respected him greatly, and in a unit such as ours that was really something. Generally, I've found most people in positions of authority too filled with their own sense of self-importance to win any real respect. This certainly applied to Brigadier 'Mudguts' Moten, who commanded the Wau military area. An old-school soldier, he had little time for the new concept of Independent Companies and had been critical of our activities and reprimanded some of the people involved. Looking back, it seems to me that Moten expected our commando company to do far more than was possible. Maybe he thought we were expendable or wanted to make a scapegoat out of George. Anyway, George was more interested in his own men and weathered the storm.

One day George sent for me. 'Wally, the Brigadier wants to look at the action and talk to some of the blokes shooting the bullets. Take him up towards Black Cat Track. If you can give him a bit of a fright it wouldn't hurt, but for Christ's sake don't get him killed.'

I was introduced to Brigadier Moten, who wore an immaculately pressed uniform. I threw him a smart salute, something I hadn't done for quite a while.

We set off. I pointed out various positions and landmarks and explained what was happening at each one. He said he knew many of them by name and he seemed quite interested in what I was saying. The gunfire rang louder and finally I noticed some of our commandos concealed beside the track, firing to their front. Above their heads the jungle growth was being shredded by Japanese gunfire.

'Down, sir!' I shouted, pushing Mudguts flat into the mud. I fired a quick burst from my Tommy gun. Pointing out our forward positions near the track, I suggested that it wasn't safe to go any further. He agreed, so we back-pedalled to his headquarters. His own staff looked at his dishevelled appearance with surprise.

'This young soldier has just shown me the front line where the bullets are being fired and I now have a better appreciation of the situation,' he said jovially, adding, 'Thank you, soldier.' I threw him another salute, thinking, Kiss my arse, and departed. In training they said you salute the uniform, not the person, so I didn't feel too bad. When George learnt what had happened he had a good laugh.

Being the fighting soldier that he was, George decided to take up a patrol himself and give a bit of respite to some of his hard-pressed, exhausted troops. He chose twelve men, including me, and took us straight up the Jap Track. After two days we lost all radio contact. We ran out of food but kept going, managing to ambush and kill many Japanese. One afternoon, hungry as buggery and wondering what the hell to do, we came to a spur overlooking a large party of Japanese preparing a meal. I expected the order to attack, but George sent the whisper around, 'Let them finish cooking their food. Then we'll shoot the bastards and eat it ourselves.'

It was almost an hour before dinner was ready. Then we opened fire, killed them all and had ourselves a hot meal. Normally you wouldn't have touched the crap, but it was the best food we'd had for days.

The following morning we spotted a patrol of our own blokes. Ever the actor, George fired a shot in the air. As they ducked for cover he shouted, 'Over here!' They helped themselves to the Japanese leftovers. It turned out they had been sent to find us and together we traced our way back down the Jap Track, tired and hungry. We had been gone a week and were buggered. But we were satisfied with what we had accomplished and, on top of that, we'd done it without casualties.

This was the end of my involvement in the Wau campaign, but the Powers That Be had plenty more in store. It was decided that if the Japanese suffered a surprise hit at Salamaua, the site of their main immediate base, it would create serious problems for them. Our commando company was to move to Bulwa, further up the Bulolo Valley, and then on to the Japanese supply line between Salamaua and Mubo. We had to carry everything ourselves: food, water, ammunition and reserve supplies. Thankfully we now had local porters to help us, the gentle and deservedly famous 'Fuzzy Wuzzy Angels'.

Our task was to establish a base at Missim, the site of an old mission station ('Missim' being pidgin for 'mission'). It was only about eighteen miles as the crow flew, but we weren't crows and had to do it the hard way. This meant three or four days of sheer hell. Not only did the track twist and wind through thick rainforest, it went over Double Mountain, the worst New Guinea track Australian soldiers ever took on. Also known as 'Susu', (pidgin for 'a woman's breasts'), Double Mountain is the highest peak of the Kuper Range. It was a heartbreaking nightmare, 10 000 feet high and mud all the way. The track was often either a sheer height or drop. We had to sling our weapons to free both hands and pull ourselves up or to keep ourselves from falling when we went down. The sun never penetrated the heavy mist and everything was damp and rotten.

On the Kokoda Trail, which was tough enough by all accounts, eight natives were allotted to carry each stretcher case. But Double Mountain required sixteen natives with a ten day turnaround: four days to bring supplies forward and six to carry a stretcher case back. Because of the shocking difficulties negotiating the track, the wounded were frequently dropped from their stretchers. Poor bastards.

As we slogged our way forward we were under constant attack from the smaller locals. Mosquitoes delivered various types of malaria, against which we had no preventatives. Then there were the ticks, lurking particularly in the kunai grass, which would burrow through skin and leave the unwanted gift of scrub typhus. If you didn't see them first, you'd feel their irritating itch. There's no point in plucking a tick out; the head breaks away and sometimes continues to burrow on its own. Instead we stuck a pin or needle in the tick's backside to make it retreat and drop off. Nudging it with a lighted cigarette also did the trick and this became our usual method. Unfortunately we had to wait for a safe haven before this procedure could be carried out.

Because it was so wet there were leeches everywhere. I never saw them on the ground or on leaves; they tended to announce their presence on your body with a telltale itch. It was revolting to find them stuck there, bloated with your blood. As with the ticks it was a two-person exercise to get rid of the disgusting things, but only when circumstances permitted.

Towards the top of Double Mountain it became extremely cold, particularly at night. We heard later that snow sometimes fell there. The perspiration and rain or mist on your body felt like it was turning to ice. You just huddled up miserably and waited for dawn, when it was time to get going again.

At about five in the afternoon, as the rain and darkness came on, there were nearly always earth tremors. Sometimes you'd see a whole ridge shake like a jelly. It was all completely unreal.

At least we didn't encounter the enemy on Double Mountain. Maybe they didn't know about it, or perhaps they just thought it was too hard. Maybe they thought no bastard would be stupid enough to try.

3

Walpole's Track to Goodview Junction

Missim was the base from which we raided and hit the Japanese. At first there were problems getting enough food and ammunition in to sustain long-range sorties. Finally some biscuit bombers eased the situation with airdrops, but the arrival of a large part of the company was delayed as a result.

The biscuit bombers flew as low as possible over a designated position when they dropped supplies. Some items had rough parachute arrangements to lessen the impact, but many were broken or crushed. Later, airdrops became slightly more sophisticated with containers called 'storepedos', which had proper parachutes attached.

At length the whole company was based at Missim. We made repeated raids on the Japanese supply lines with great success. Later, captured Japanese documents showed how greatly they overestimated our numbers. Concealed in the forested ridges above Salamaua, we observed their movements from our OPs (observation posts). Their airstrip, sea anchorages and troop movements were all in plain view.

On the 23rd of April 1943, Major General Stan Savige took command over operations in the area. Savige had a reputation as a hands-on leader and was popular with the troops. He had been George's brigade commander in the Middle East and George was pleased no end, knowing that he'd have a better understanding with the new boss. Brigadier

Moten had refused him permission to attack Bobdubi Ridge, an important strategic position overlooking Salamaua, but now General Savige gave the okay with two conditions attached. George was not to incur heavy casualties and he was allowed only one platoon. The reason was simple: reinforcements were not available. George deviously managed to boost his numbers without disobeying orders by inviting along commandos – including me and some Engineer, Signals and Transport commandos – who were not attached to a platoon. Of course, George also invited himself.

Bobdubi Ridge was about two miles long. We divided into small teams and hit it simultaneously from different directions. The idea was to make the Japanese think they were encircled by a large force. The fighting seesawed for a while. We'd push them from their positions, but then they'd return with reinforcements from Salamaua and drive us back.

I had an anxious moment near Centre Coconut when I suddenly came face to face with a Japanese soldier pointing his rifle at me. My Tommy gun jammed and wouldn't fire. Shit. A million thoughts crashed through my mind in a second. I started to sidestep away when, to my amazement, the Japanese also began to turn and run. Grabbing the chance, I quickly pulled my Colt .45 and got rid of him.

After about ten days only a small pocket of Japanese held out on North Bobdubi so George ordered a nocturnal terror attack. We screamed our heads off, threw verbal abuse, whistled, threw flares and grenades and fired bullets. In the morning (the 11th of May) we found that the last of them had fled and left quite a few of their dead behind. The ridge was ours, at the price of three commandos killed and five wounded. The Japanese suffered over 150 casualties. General Savige was pleased, but reiterated that heavy casualties were to be avoided even if it meant retiring to more easily defensible positions.

The victory brought us within range of the Japanese artillery in Salamaua and also made us available for their planes to have a go at. One of their naval guns occasionally shelled us from Kela. It made a peculiar plopping noise, but fortunately caused little damage. We christened it 'Kela Kitty'.

From the ridge we watched a huge build-up of Japanese reinforcements, some landed by submarine. Reconnaissance planes flew over us and there was nothing we could do about it. The Japanese also attacked us with light artillery known as mountain guns. When they fired there was a sharp bang, followed by smoke, a whizzing sound as the shell sailed through the air and finally an explosion as it hit. We got used to it after a while as we realised that we had time to find cover at the first bang. Obviously the purpose was to force us out, and it was equally obvious that we had no chance of withstanding such overwhelming numbers. George moved us to the Namling area, where we would be able to hold firm and still continue our raids.

It was a good thing we moved. On the 15th of May the Japanese launched a heavy three-pronged assault on Bobdubi Ridge, preceded by air attacks bombing and strafing our former positions. We watched all this quite happily from a safe distance. But the best was yet to come. A larger Japanese force – thirty-four twin engine bombers and thirty Zeros – began a massive attack obviously intended for us on their own positions between Salamaua and Kela. Amazed and delighted, we cheered them on and laughed wildly. Luckily our planes were not there to distract them from bombing the hell out of their own people. There were no Allied casualties; there was not even any equipment damaged.

Later, captured documents showed that the Japanese commanders had considered it essential to recapture Bobdubi Ridge. Our guerrilla tactics had frightened them badly and led to the gross overestimation of our numbers. They had over 400 men there and reckoned our single platoon to be a force of 300 to 400.

The Allies' next move was an offensive intended to draw as many Japanese reserves as possible from Lae, prior to the attack on Lae and Nadzab. An American regiment was to land at Nassau Bay, and George's old Infantry Brigade, the 17th, was to capture Mubo. Our job was to help by cutting enemy supply lines on the Komiatum Track between Mubo and Salamaua. Accompanying us on this venture was Damien Parer, the famous Australian documentary maker.

George had a special assignment for me. 'Wally,' he said, 'I want you to find a way to the Komiatum Track so we can get there unobserved, set up ambush positions and prevent the Japanese travelling in either direction. The tracks we've used before are useless – the Japs know about them and are probably watching them. Make it south of Stephen's Track.

Avoid being seen. I want no contact with the enemy. When we go, we want it to be a complete surprise.'

I was to tell nobody what I was up to. Ever devious, George said to tell anyone who asked that I was just 'doing something for George'. I wondered how many other people he had said this to. 'I know they call me George,' he added. He gave me three days and let me pick two other commandos to take with me.

It promised to be one tough and tedious job; essentially it meant cutting a new track through virgin jungle. I chose two men and we collected our weapons – Tommy guns, pistols, AP switches, a few grenades and jungle knives. These knives were shorter than a machete, but had a heavy, wide blade for hacking your way through whatever was hackable. I still have mine and I've often used it to cut firewood for barbecues. It always brings back memories for me. We also took emergency rations, including high-calorie chocolate. There was no way we were going to light cooking fires and we had to travel lightly for mobility's sake. I also had some paper in waterproof oilcloth and a couple of pencils. George okayed the preparations, wished us luck and reminded me that I was to report to him alone.

The next morning we began bush-bashing our way, trying to keep to the high spurs instead of going up and down all the time. This was quite difficult. Half the time you couldn't see the sky and that made it hard to keep a sense of direction, particularly as the spurs shot off at odd angles. We had to be careful not to get lost. Another hazard was the noise our jungle knives made as we hacked through the foliage. Any sound travels a long distance in the jungle and it was a real effort to work as quietly and quickly as possible.

By nightfall we were wrecked. We had no idea how far we had come. As soon as we set the AP switches we dropped into an exhausted sleep. No one did guard duty. If the Japanese were going to pounce overnight, then good luck to them. They deserved it if they could find us out here.

Rising at dawn, it was bush-bash, bush-bash, bush-bash – then *bingo!* Japanese voices. Signalling to the others to wait, I crept forward. Sure enough, Komiatum Track was just below. We had a perfect vantage point, completely concealed by jungle. A party of some twenty-five Japanese were eating, smoking and laughing their heads off. We had found one of their staging stops. We were tempted to drop a couple of grenades, but that would only have defeated our purpose.

Finally they moved off towards Mubo. We waited a while, then two of us went down to the track to snoop around while the third man kept watch. Feeling cheeky, we sat down and rolled ourselves cigarettes. The peace was suddenly broken by more Japanese voices. We retreated to our secret track, checking quickly that we weren't leaving any evidence of our visit.

It was another party of Japanese en route to Mubo, about twenty of them casually chatting away. They made no effort to be quiet or conceal themselves. They were big men for Japanese, all around six feet tall, and I learnt afterwards that they were SNLP, Special Naval Landing Party. They reached the staging spot and sat down to prepare a meal. All this food was making us hungry. They were sitting ducks, but again we had to let them go. After they left we began our return trip, much easier going now that we had cut a track of sorts to follow. But it was getting dark and that meant another night in the jungle. It passed much like the night before, except that we were more than pleased with ourselves at having accomplished the mission in under three days.

We reached base early the next morning, cold, tired and hungry. George must have been pleased with my report: he smiled and gave me a taciturn 'Well done,' which meant volumes, coming from him.

As I showed him the sketches I'd made of our new vantage point I said, 'The only name you could give this place would be Goodview Junction.' He smiled again and on all future maps our new route appeared as Walpole's Track to Goodview Junction. A lot was to take place there.

'Wally,' George said, 'you can take a couple of days off, but first there's someone I want you to meet. He's a war correspondent and I want you to tell him a bit about your recent trip.'

This was Axel Olsen from the Melbourne *Argus* newspaper. His article, headed 'Stirring Exploits of Young Australian Soldiers', appeared in July 1943. The part based on what I told him about the trip to Goodview Junction mentioned no place names and was somewhat factually askew, perhaps because of wartime censorship. My father kept this and other newspaper cuttings. Of course I didn't see them for a long time, and it's only in more recent years that I've realised what a horrible shock it must have been for my parents to read about me like that in their morning paper. And at that stage they had no idea what had happened to Denis since Singapore had fallen to the Japanese almost eighteen months earlier.

I didn't get the couple of days off. George had another job for me. The Americans had landed at Nassau Bay and more were coming to Tambu Bay, about five miles south of the Japanese stronghold at Salamaua. Someone had to liaise with them and that someone was me. It meant crossing the Komiatum Track and dodging the Japanese to get there.

'You'll have to go on your own,' George said. 'We're too short at the moment to send anyone with you, but I'm sure you can handle that. I'll give you a letter of introduction to their commanding officer. Tell him what we're doing and see what you can learn from them.'

Shit!, I thought as I said, 'When do I go?'

'Tomorrow should be all right. Draw whatever stores you need and I'll okay it. If you spend a couple of days there, you should be back in six to seven days. Just see what you can find out.'

I nodded, but he hadn't finished. 'If anyone asks, just say you're doing something for George. They can see me if they need to know more.'

I've heard all that before, I thought.

'Now,' he went on, 'how are you going to get there?'

'I'll go straight down Walpole's Track and across the Komiatum Track at Goodview Junction. They won't know I'm there.'

'Well, for Christ's sake don't come back that way.' He grinned. 'We might have launched our attack down there by then. All hell's going to break loose when we do.'

After collecting much the same gear as before, I made my way to Walpole's Track. It was a lot easier the second time. The first night I spent hidden under a big tree and getting drenched by the teeming rain. It pelted down all morning, too, every step of the way to Goodview Junction. This meant I could move more quickly, because it helped deaden any noise I made. But it also helped deaden any noise from the Japanese, so I had to be extra careful.

At last I heard voices. Goodview Junction was not far off now. Sneaking down to have a look at Komiatum Track, I counted thirty-one

Japanese soldiers. Struggling to keep dry under makeshift shelters, they were talking, eating, smoking and laughing away. It was obvious they weren't setting up camp.

Waiting for them to pack up and go, once again I thought how easy it would be to roll a grenade down there and be far away before any survivors worked out what had happened. But I knew George would probably cut my throat if I did that.

It was over an hour before they had the decency to move on towards Mubo. I waited another fifteen minutes and no more of them appeared. So I whipped across the Komiatum Track and into the jungle beyond.

I was in new territory now, with only a vague idea where to find the Americans. All I could do was head in their general direction. There were several rough tracks, so I kept in the jungle to the side of one that appeared to be going the right way.

There were no signs of Japanese. I had some water and a quick bite of rations, but wasn't game to smoke; smell reaches a long way in the jungle too.

All the time the rain was bucketing down. I moved off again, as stealthily as possible, when around a bend in the track two Japanese appeared right in front of me. The rain had muffled their approach. They were off their guard and deep in conversation. I was surprised, but not as much as they were – it was all over their faces.

The number of thoughts that can flash through your mind in a split second is amazing. I considered racing off into the jungle. I was confident I could outrun them, but my presence would be made known. Shots would be fired and more of them would come looking for me. So if there was going to be noise, better me making it than them.

There was no choice. In that split second I flipped my Tommy gun from automatic to single shot to minimise the noise and got rid of them while they were still stunned with surprise. I made sure they were dead and gone wherever dead Japs went to, then hurried into the jungle.

I hid behind a big tree, hoping like hell the heavy rain had drowned out my two shots. I had no idea whether there were others nearby. After watching the track for half an hour, I felt confident enough to keep going. I figured they had been walking in a rather carefree manner and probably considered themselves quite safe.

Everything was still. Creeping over to the bodies, I relieved them of their few documents. I thought perhaps later someone might translate them and gain some information. Then I dragged the bodies as far into the jungle as I could and threw them about ten feet down into the moss-filled base of a huge rotten tree. Their weapons went in after them. I did my best to erase all signs of what had happened. The rain was going to help with that, too.

Pretty sure I hadn't been spotted, I continued pushing through the jungle alongside the track. It hadn't stopped raining and I was wet as a shag. I moved more slowly and carefully than ever now, wary of running slap-bang into more Japanese. There might be more of them next time, and they might be smarter.

If the Americans were anywhere near Tambu Bay, I had to be somewhere to their south. Glimpses of Mount Tambu helped me keep my line of direction. The rain eased off and then stopped altogether. Everything – including me – started to swelter. I went deeper into the jungle for cover, took off my soaking wet shirt, hung it over a tree and cleaned my Tommy gun and pistol.

When I moved on again, I came to a three-way junction and looked at Mount Tambu again before I chose one of the tracks. Darkness was coming on quickly, so I went further into the jungle for the night. I put out some AP switches, ate and huddled down. At least this time it wasn't raining.

When you try to sleep, or rather doze, in conditions like these, a part of your mind somehow stays on the alert. I started awake to hear the chatter of Japanese voices and I checked my luminous watch dial. It was 12.15 am.

The voices seemed to be coming from the three-way junction and I could just make out a flickering light. I had a chuckle to myself. Although I couldn't understand Japanese, one of them sounded like he was swearing and I hoped they were having a bad time. It had been quite thoughtless of them to wake me up, but I wasn't about to risk moving in the dark to check them out. How could they find me anyway? Half an hour later the voices stopped and the light disappeared. I huddled up again and dozed off.

Dawn came. I had a quiet stretch, some rations and salt tablets.

I listened for a while, but there was no noise except the creaking of rotten branches working their way off diseased and dead trees. Keeping my cover, I crept back to investigate the junction. A substantial party of Japanese had marched towards Goodview Junction by way of the third track which led to God knew where. More fodder for George's attack, I hoped. The drying mud was marked everywhere by their distinctive two-toed boots, which separated the big toe from the rest. A couple of used flares lay discarded beside the track. They had obviously used them to see their way and that explained the light I had seen in the night.

Keeping to the jungle, I followed my chosen track and an hour or so later heard more noise and voices. As I edged towards thicker foliage, the noises got louder. Then I heard a 'Goddamn'. Americans!

Finally I saw one of their sentries. He wasn't particularly on the ball and sat there staring at the ground, thoroughly bored. A second appeared, then two others, no more alert than the first man. That didn't mean they weren't trigger-happy, though, so I was careful to keep absolutely still. If I called out they were likely to panic and open fire. And there were probably others I couldn't see. I didn't know what to do, so I stayed put.

After watching for a while it occurred to me that there was a route between two of the sentries. I was pretty sure there was no one else between them and thought it might be safer to go that way, pass the sentries, say g'day to any Americans I saw and trust they had time to see that I didn't look or sound Japanese.

It took a long time. I had to creep through the jungle unseen, watch the pair I could see and look out for others I couldn't see yet. As I moved I began to notice bare patches in the jungle and that was very strange. The American encampment was not far off and as I approached it became obvious they were very comfortably set up by our standards. I passed several of them before I came to a group. I listened for a while before I decided to emerge from the bush and join their conversation.

Here I was, the only one armed to the teeth and obviously more than a bit scruffy and dirty. Silent, gobsmacked moments passed before one of them recovered sufficiently to speak.

'Who the hell are you?'

'Name's Brian. I'm an Australian, here to liaise with you people.'

'Goddamn, man!' he said. 'I'll get the Major.'

The Major was all 'Goddamn's as well when he appeared.

'Goddamn good to see you,' he said. 'I'm Major Blight, but call me Al.' I told him my name. 'Well, good to see you, Brian. You must be one of those Aussie commandos I've been expecting. Where are the others?'

'There aren't any others, Al. Just me.'

'Goddamn, you came all that way on your own? Did you see any Japs?'

'Yes, quite a few.'

He didn't think to ask how I passed his sentries and got inside his perimeter. Heads would have rolled if that had happened at our base. But then it never could have happened under George.

'So, Brian, what do you commando boys do?'

'We kill as many Japs as possible and try not to get killed doing it. I didn't speak to your sentries in case they mistook me for a Jap.'

He laughed out loud. 'They'd have known you weren't a goddamn Japanese!' It still didn't register with him that I had crossed his perimeter without anyone having seen me. 'Anyway,' he added, 'we haven't seen too many Japs around these parts.'

Soon afterwards I found out why.

4

The American Way

Properly cooked beef, vegetables, fresh bread and butter, ice cream, fruit salad – the American food was a dream come true after eight days of emergency rations. Their mess had things we'd never heard of, like demountable portable kitchens and kerosene-fired refrigerators. Unfortunately I couldn't eat much, my stomach having shrunk from frequently going two or three days without food.

Al asked me what the Aussies had been doing and was amazed at what we'd achieved and the conditions we had endured. His lot had suffered no casualties at enemy hands, but had no idea what damage they'd done to the Japanese.

He showed me their short barrel Howitzer field artillery pieces. 'What we're doing is progressing from ridge to ridge. We find one we think the enemy is occupying, blast sweet Jesus out of it and send a patrol up to take charge.'

That explained the bare patches I'd passed in the jungle earlier. No wonder they hadn't seen many Japanese. No one on Earth would have stayed on those ridges when Al started pounding them to powder.

These tactics really surprised me. George would have just sent a two- or three-man patrol to attend to the ridge. 'We'll be advancing again tomorrow, Brian,' Al announced proudly. 'You can see for yourself what we do.'

'Thanks, Al.'

Al barely believed that we could operate so differently. Our way was far more productive, however, if you could call killing 'productive'. But it was not for me to say so. He also kept asking why I was on my own. I explained that we were a small unit and the rest were just too occupied against the enemy to be spared. Someone had to go and I was picked – simple. He still seemed puzzled.

'It must be getting towards chow time again,' he said. 'I've arranged a bed for you, too.' Bed? How long had it been since I'd even seen a bed?

We headed back to the centre of the encampment, where he took me into a tent. It had floorboards and a stretcher with a couple of blankets. I almost laughed. It seemed so luxurious after long nights sleeping in the jungle with the rain pouring down. There were even lights, powered by small portable generators. Radios were playing and everyone was in good spirits.

Chow meant another meal that was first class by the standards I was used to, but again I was unable to eat much. I had an excellent night's sleep in my new five-star accommodation with bed, blankets and a comfortably full shrunken stomach. My main worry was the sentries. I hoped they'd be a little more alert during the night. The place was wide open to Japanese attack with lax sentries, plenty of noise and light and no one giving it much thought except maybe me.

I woke up to a fine morning. Al took me to the place where the Howitzers were lined up. Shells were stacked neatly and gunnery crews were standing by.

'You see that ridge up there, Brian?' He pointed vaguely to a whole heap of ridges. I'd been up and down hundreds of them by now, and if you'd seen one you'd seen the lot.

'Do you mean the one with the two tall trees?' I asked, being polite.

'No, the one to the left with the big dead tree in the middle.'

'Sure.'

'Well, some of our lookouts are pretty sure they saw Japs up there and we thought if we took that ridge – well, it's a step in the direction we want to go, anyway. So we'll open fire and see what happens.'

The gunners muffled their ears, the officer in charge gave the order to fire and away they blazed. It reminded me a little of what the Japanese were doing to us at Bobdubi Ridge except that the sound was quite different and they were far more accurate. They were very accurate. Soon the thickly forested ridge was as bare as a golf bunker, a patch of desert surrounded by jungle. But they kept on firing and blowing up clouds of dust wherever a shell struck. Blind Freddy could have seen no one was up there.

'A couple more, just to make sure,' Al announced. I nodded. I wasn't game to say a thing, because I was sure that if I did I'd be sorry later. But it was so absurd, there was absolutely nothing there. 'Okay.' He motioned a ceasefire. 'Now we wait a while and then send some guys up to claim it.'

I nodded again. Twenty heavily armed men went to the ridge, with the gun crew still on alert in case they were needed. Needed for what, I didn't know. The patrol chatted among themselves as if they were going to a picnic – 'goddamn' this and that. You could have heard them from a long way off; as I've said, noise travels far in the jungle.

When they finally reached what was left of the ridge they cheered and waved to us. Everyone around me, including Al, cheered madly as well. It wouldn't have surprised me had they fired a five-gun salute. If there'd been any Japanese around they would have had a good laugh.

'So, Brian,' Al said, 'what do you think, huh?'

It wasn't my place to criticise, so I chose my words carefully. 'Well, you had no casualties and that's a good thing. You've achieved what you set out to do and, um, morale is very high.'

He seemed pleased and proud at my response. The truth was that I thought his entire operation stank. Not only was it an utter waste of time; it could even have caused our unit problems at a later date, because their incompetence left our flank vulnerable to Japanese attack. I knew George would go ballistic when I reported back to him. At any rate, by now I had enough information on the Americans' activities. It was sunny again the following morning and I told Al that I'd be heading back.

'Which way are you going?' He was being polite; he had no way of knowing any of the tracks or landmarks. I answered honestly that I didn't know.

'I'll just play it by ear till I get near the Komiatum Track,' I said. My problem was that I didn't know whether George had begun his attack. For all I knew the place was swarming with Japanese. But I didn't tell Al this.

'Anyone waiting for you there?' he asked.

'Not unless they're Japanese – so I hope not!'

'Well, goodbye, Brian, and good luck.'

I wished them luck too and we all hoped to meet again, but under better circumstances.

I left them to their Howitzers and returned to the jungle. After retracing my steps for a couple of hours I hid behind a tree that gave me a good view of the track and had a snack of emergency rations, some salt tablets and a gargle of water. I had cleaned and checked my weapons earlier.

I had a good serious talk to myself. If George had mounted his attack, Goodview Junction and the Komiatum Track would be teeming with antagonistic Australian commandos and Japanese soldiers. All I could do was cross the Track somewhere, go bush and find my way back through virgin jungle. To get to that point I decided to stick to the jungle within sight of the track I was following. It promised to be a slow journey, but it was the safest way and above all I wanted to avoid trouble.

Reaching the junction where the Japanese had previously dropped their flares, I had a quick recce. There had been a fair amount of traffic and I wondered where this track led to, but I was not going to distract myself by trying to find out.

I kept going. As I'd started early and had no interruptions, I thought I could make it to the Komiatum Track before nightfall. This I did without anything untoward happening. The rain started up again just before dusk. I picked a spot in the undergrowth with a view of the track in both directions. I didn't hear or see anything and by now I was pretty tired. Deciding that I was still too exposed, I backtracked quite a way until I found a spot under a tree that was better hidden. Not knowing what was on the other side of the Komiatum Track, I didn't want to be floundering about there in the pitch dark. It was too easy to become disoriented and then get lost and you never knew who or what was lurking about.

I set the AP switches, ate some emergency rations and stayed the night.

It had stopped raining by morning. After a quick stretch to loosen up, a mouthful of high-calorie chocolate and a couple of salt tablets, I checked my weapons and got going.

At the Komiatum Track I could see a fairly straight stretch about twenty-five yards either way, until the track disappeared around bends. I knew the area behind me was clear of Japanese, so I studied the jungle across the track as carefully and thoroughly as I could. The foliage was pretty thick and there were no tracks leading off the Komiatum Track into it. I felt if I could get over there without being seen I'd be right. I checked out the bend at the Salamaua end of the track, where most Japanese traffic would come from. Beyond, the track curled and twisted with a series of bends, so there was no point checking past the first one.

Returning to where I had initially settled down to get a feel of things, I decided there was not much more I could do. Steeling myself, I moved out of the jungle. The ground was fairly open some distance before the track, and once I was there I was more or less committed.

Luck suddenly deserted me. Around the Salamaua bend came a party of Japanese with three dogs. My brain was racing. They hadn't seen me yet, but they would before I could retreat into the undergrowth. And even if I made it across the track they were going to see me and know where I'd come from and the direction I was taking.

They were clustered tight as a bunch of grapes and enjoying themselves with a great old chat. You could've sworn they were just taking the dogs for a walk. There were too many for me to handle on my own, yet I had the advantage of surprise. I emptied the whole magazine of my Tommy gun into them, then ripped a grenade from my belt, pulled the pin and tossed that among them as well. I threw a second grenade in for luck.

I didn't stick around for the talking to become screams and yelps. Taking off as fast as possible away from them alongside the track in the Mubo direction, I hadn't gone far when I saw an arm waving behind some bushes. An Australian voice shouted, 'Mate, over here! Quickly – and get down now!'

As soon as I hit the ground there was firing over my head. Scuttling like a crab towards the waving arm, I reached a small makeshift trench with three Australians in it. Jumping in, I put another magazine in my Tommy gun and was about to start shooting when I realised that they had stopped. I looked around and saw them all grinning at me.

'Relax, mate, there's nothing to fire at,' one said. Later he introduced himself as Don Rose. 'Between you and us, we got most of the Japs and all three dogs. The rest pissed off back around the bend. What are you doing appearing out of nowhere like that? Christ, I've never seen anyone move so fast!'

I gave them a vague explanation of why I happened to be there. They knew about George and his commandos; in fact they were with George's old 17th Infantry Brigade and were on a long-range reconnaissance patrol from the Mubo direction.

'Here we are trying to avoid contact with any Japs,' Don said, 'Then all of a sudden you appear from nowhere and blast the bloody lot of them!'

I felt quietly pleased that even though they'd been watching the area, they were not aware of my presence until I opened fire. They were all Middle East veterans and, like me, Don was from Melbourne. We became friends after the war and when people asked how we'd met we always laughed and said, 'Do you really want to know?'

We agreed the Japanese could have no idea of our numbers or exactly where we were, but conversely it was anyone's guess how many Japanese would come around the bend next time.

Staying there would be pointless. None of us was looking for trouble and we'd all accomplished what we'd set out to do.

I explained I had to get into the jungle on the other side of the track unseen. Don and his friends kindly stayed there long enough to enable me to do it. We said our goodbyes and good lucks. As I pushed into the jungle across the track there were no shots, so I assumed the Japanese had not shown their heads. I wondered whether they were skulking further up the track, or how they'd react when they finally came back around the bend and found no one waiting for them. Anyway, it was obvious that George hadn't launched his attack and I knew it would be better for me to get back before he did.

Despite the interruptions to my travelling, it was still reasonably early. Although moving quietly and carefully was always the priority, this was my fourth trip in roughly the same vicinity and my experience meant that I could move faster. Also, I now knew plenty of landmarks I could use for orientation. After a couple of hours I was fortunate to come across a patrol of our own commandos. Luckily none of us was trigger-happy; we'd all seen too much combat for that. I said I was on a job for George and asked them where he was. It was a great relief to hear that there were no Japanese on the main track and that I could use it instead of bush-bashing. I now knew I'd make it back before nightfall.

George wasted no time when I finally arrived and reported to him. 'You're all right. Good. How did you get on?'

He saw no humour in my account of the American operation. He was furious and asked me many questions. I assured him that Al – Major Blight – would confirm my descriptions of their procedure because he was so proud of it.

'We thought it was something like this,' he said when I'd finished. 'We'll fix it. You did well.'

Although American, Major Blight came under Australian command. George made his report to General Savige, who recommended to General Blamey that the Americans receive both new leadership and new rules of engagement. This transpired and although I had no further contact with them, I know the Americans subsequently did a lot better in the push towards Salamaua. Naturally I knew nothing about this at the time. George had no reason to tell me; he just wanted my report. But at least he took notice of it.

I felt sorry for poor Al and the rest of the Americans. They were lovely people and very hospitable, but their contribution in the fight against the Japanese was utterly useless.

George took great interest in my various altercations and the Japanese traffic along the Komiatum Track. The much-vaunted attack was imminent and he kept checking and rechecking the details of my observations. 'Are you sure?' he asked me, over and over.

It wasn't my place to suggest it, but I was sure George would involve me in the attack on the Komiatum Track, particularly at Goodview. After all, who knew more about the target area? But, as he often did, George surprised me.

'Wally,' he said, 'tomorrow I want you to go up to the Salamaua OP for a couple of weeks. Have a holiday. You deserve it.'

I couldn't understand why he'd leave me out. But when George said something like that, it was a waste of time trying to guess whatever devious reasoning was running through his mind. Up at the Salamaua OP, when I could finally stop and think, I realised that he had been quite right to exclude me. I would have been a distraction for the other commandos, who might have wanted to ask me too many questions about the area. The plan of attack had been laid out, based on my information, so logically I shouldn't have been needed more than anyone else. George later confirmed these suspicions.

He led the attacking force down Walpole's Track on the 8th of July 1943 and, as he'd predicted, all hell broke loose for two or three days. The forward scout opened proceedings by dropping a grenade down on the Japanese at Goodview Junction, just as I had dreamt of doing on both my visits.

With minimal casualties on our side, the Junction was secured. The Japanese sent a lot of reinforcements and many of them were killed. Four of our commandos, including George, were awarded decorations. George won the Military Cross, the citation noting that his 'determined leadership and great personal courage was a dominant factor in this operation'.

Salamaua OP was in country very high up and several hours hike away. I was tired of being in a hurry so I took my time getting there. There was a lookout platform, well concealed, over 150 feet above ground level among the thick branches and foliage of a huge tree. It was on the Salamaua side of an almost perpendicular razorback ridge, hidden in typically dense rainforest.

The lookout was a particularly dicey climb. The first section was a rough ladder to the first fork in the tree. From there up you used foot-holes that the natives had cut, together with kundu vines strung on either side. To negotiate this obstacle course in daylight was an achievement in itself, but doing it on a moonless night in the rain was damn near impossible.

The OP was manned by six soldiers, including a signaller, who radioed reports of our observations in Morse code. Watch was kept twenty-four hours a day in four-hour shifts. Through field glasses and telescope we could see the whole coastline from Salamaua to Lae, much of the KomiatumTrack to Mubo and of course Salamaua itself, which was on an isthmus. We also could also see most of the Japanese land, sea and air movements in the area.

This was a very different way of life from the one I had grown accustomed to. There were regular meals and a makeshift roof over my head so I stayed dry at night, except when it was my turn up the tree. It was the first time I'd had dry clothes for ages. On a couple of warm days I was even able to work on my suntan for a short while.

Fine nights afforded us spectacular views from the tree, with flashes from anti-aircraft guns, bombs exploding, tracer bullets from aircraft and the sweeping of searchlights. One day on my shift I was watching what seemed to be the Japanese headquarters and mess in Salamaua. A group of Japanese, obviously drunk, staggered out the door to urinate against the side of the building. Through the telescope they looked almost close enough to touch. Look at the dirty bastards, I thought self-righteously. Too lazy to use their own latrines.

At the OP I finally had time to take stock of our situation. We'd been hit pretty hard by battle casualties, scrub typhus, malaria and lack of vitamins, food and water. We had no mosquito lotion or anti-malarial drugs. The mosquito nets were useless and everyone had thrown them away. The rain made them heavier to carry and our priority was carrying ammunition, or water and food if we could get it. The thought of a Japanese sticking his bayonet in your guts while you were untangling yourself from the net was not attractive either.

The constant wet had given me two extra problems. Our woollen socks shrank dramatically and the heel of mine chafed so badly under the ball of my foot that I eventually decided to go without socks altogether. The other was that my pistol belt chafed my perpetually wet trousers against my waist, resulting in very painful ringworm. It wouldn't heal while the skin was wet, which was all the time. At the OP I managed to burn it off with undiluted iodine. The skin is still scarred quite badly, but that's okay – I don't show it to too many people.

I was only two and a half days at Salamaua OP. By now our commando company had been reduced by about sixty per cent and George needed every spare man. When the company was at full strength there had only been 280 of us anyway and the authorities had been expecting us to do the work of an infantry battalion, which was over three times our size.

My replacement arrived from an infantry battalion with some Fuzzy Wuzzy porters carrying supplies. The porters were unarmed and always happier if they had an armed escort. I accompanied them back, although we weren't expecting trouble. Not carrying anything heavy, we were making good time on the two or three-hour journey when suddenly there was a great screaming and shouting. I immediately thought, *Japs*. But this noise was different; it was gleeful.

A porter grasped my arm to show me what was happening. Further down the track a six-foot length of dirty, thick, writhing muscle protruded from a hole in the ground. Four natives were dragging it backwards as it thrashed about madly in protest. They shrieked with excitement – pythons were a real delicacy for them. As more of the struggling monster appeared, extra natives joined in to grab the increasingly exposed body. I wondered what would happen when a very angry head appeared, but they'd already thought of that. Two men were poised with raised machetes, ready to hack it off. Suddenly they must have judged that the python was almost out, because they dived forward and chopped the head off the body, which still thrashed wildly. When it finally stopped moving I stepped out the length and reckoned it about twenty-five feet long and thicker than a man's thigh. The natives hacked it into three-foot lengths. I declined their offer of a piece, thinking how lucky we were that no Japanese had heard the tumult. Once order had been restored, we made it back to Namling without further incident.

George was in a facetious mood when I arrived. 'Wally! Salamaua OP must have done you some good. You've put on weight! Now, there's something I want you to do. We'll talk about it in the morning.'

5

Assault on Salamaua

Ambush Knoll, a high point above Namling and Orodubi, was a crucial strategic position. It had been in the hands of the enemy until the 15th of July, when some of my fellow commandos forced them out. The Japanese desperately wanted it back and over the next few days attacked twenty times with more men than we had, but were beaten back every time and suffered heavy casualties. Even so, they had the knoll surrounded and our men were completely cut off from the base at Namling. Exhausted from lack of sleep and non-stop fighting, they were fast running out of ammunition, food and water.

George asked me to find a way to get supplies through to Ambush Knoll undetected. After considerable scouting, I became convinced that although three sides of the knoll were cut off, there was no sign of the Japanese on the side facing Namling. This part was extremely steep and rugged, covered with dense jungle and without any tracks. It was like Double Mountain in miniature. The Japanese had clearly decided it was impossible to negotiate.

Every available commando in Namling was ordered to carry the desperately needed supplies to Ambush Knoll. Apart from lugging heavy loads of ammunition, water and food, we each had the normal burden of our personal armaments and supplies in case we were unlucky enough to have to fight our way.

Damien Parer had recently joined our company to make a documentary, but he volunteered to carry a load and joined us without his camera.

When we set out the night was pitch dark and hammered by rain. Visibility was zero and of course we had no lights. It was one hell of a climb, but no one begrudged doing it for our own people in trouble. While the heavy rain helped to muffle any noise, it made going up the slope far more treacherous. We reached the top just after dawn. The appreciation of our mates was more than enough reward for our efforts. The Japanese never discovered how we were supplying Ambush Knoll and we continued to bypass them in this way for some time.

Gradually their attacks dropped off, as if they had become resigned to the fact that the knoll was ours. Finally George relieved the commandos on top with a platoon of his old Middle East 2/6 Battalion from Wells OP. Exhausted, the commandos retired to Namling and the infantry platoon was reinforced with the rest of its company. Anyone attacking Ambush Knoll now had to contend with a large force of seasoned Australian infantry.

At this point the role of our company changed. We were no longer to carry out guerrilla attacks on the Japanese. Two nearby forces, the 58/59 (militia) battalion and the 17th Infantry Brigade, linked up and we were now special attack shock troops. The idea was for small teams of commandos to break through Japanese defences in situations where a large infantry force wasn't able to do so.

This was all very flattering, but we weren't given any special gear to help us. We kept the same armaments we had used for months. Also, we were living on iron rations, when we could get them. Most of the soldiers in the area were eating a lot better than us.

An OP reported that an allied air raid had bombed the hell out of Salamaua and, among other things, had knocked down the church. Obviously it was unintentional, but it had caused great consternation among the Japanese and a whole heap of trucks and troops were frantically buzzing around the ruins. I couldn't imagine any of the Japanese I'd come across going to church, so it was no surprise to learn they'd been using it to store war supplies.

Damien Parer had been very active during his stay with us and endeared himself to the whole company with his courage and daring. Not only did he brave crossfire to capture the most graphic and moving film, he laboured tirelessly to help carry our supplies. His documentary *Assault on Salamaua* was a real work of art, winning awards and boosting morale when it screened back home in Australia. It is still shown regularly at the Australian War Memorial. George wrote to Prime Minister John Curtin, highly commending Damien's courage and saying how much the company appreciated his efforts.

The Japanese at Salamaua must have been getting a bit worried. We had far more aircraft now, and they were constantly bombing and strafing. The Japanese had no idea how many of us were wandering around, except that we'd killed and wounded an awful lot of them. General Nakano, their local commander, had been instructed by the Emperor that Lae and Salamaua were to be defended to the death. Brainwashed with tales of our cruelty, the Japanese troops thought it better to die in combat or by their own hand than be taken prisoner and suffer untold tortures and atrocities. Of course it was all rubbish, but apparently they swallowed it.

We had to be extremely careful, because it was common for them to booby-trap their own dead or badly wounded. Most of our supplies were now dropped by air from biscuit bombers. This was a difficult job requiring a high degree of accuracy, because we were generally on razorback ridges quite close to the enemy. Some supplies were attached to parachutes and inevitably caught on the trees. Others were just pushed out in free-fall to hit the ground like non-exploding bombs. Tough luck if you were underneath. Occasional mistakes accidentally supplied the Japanese, but fortunately only on a small scale. Fancy feeding the bastards!

Next, our company was ordered to relieve the 58/59 Infantry Battalion on Bobdubi Ridge. So here we were, back again after all this time. Bill Braithwaite became my patrol leader. He was a couple of years my senior and we'd been firm friends since my arrival in New Guinea. Like George he was a Middle East veteran, although I don't think they had known each other there. Both were fearless and very accomplished bayonet fighters. Woe betide any Jap who got within chasing distance of Bill or George.

One day out on patrol, we found ourselves pinned down by a Japanese sniper, firing from a well-concealed position up a tree.

'I'll draw his fire,' Bill said. 'When you can tell where it's coming from, see if you can get him.' Without further ado he just stood up and shouted, 'Have a go at me, you bastard!'

The sniper didn't muck about. His next shot took off the lower part of Bill's jaw. It also gave the sniper's position away and I shot him out of the tree.

Bill's jaw was a shocking mess. After packing it with two field dressings I waited until he had regained some composure. Then, at his instigation, we fashioned a sign. Bill showed me what to write with hand signals: *'Wouldn't it fuck you – I can't talk'*.

He draped this around his neck and began the long walk back for medical attention. What courage he had. The next time I saw him was at Heidelberg Military Hospital in Melbourne, but more about that later.

Around this time, calamity struck the company. George was promoted to Lieutenant Colonel and left to take command of the 58/59 Infantry Battalion.

He had been an inspiration to every one of us. He was a real leader and every single man respected and admired him. Captain Bob Hancock, who took over, was an extremely competent officer, but George was an impossible act to follow. No one came even close. It was a sad day when he came around to say his goodbyes.

The 58/59 had experienced many unnecessary mishaps in the field and was subject to severe criticism by the higher command. It was a militia battalion, made up of conscripts. The officers were unfit and utterly incompetent, and the soldiers hadn't received proper training for warfare under these shocking conditions. Of course, if anyone could have knocked them into shape it was George. And they had a big shock coming.

Along with some other commandos I was temporarily transferred to help George kickstart his new command. He figured attaching some of our Tommy gunners to their forward patrols might instil some confidence and demonstrate what they had to do. My job was to explain, to those George considered the brighter prospects, how to carry out a successful reconnaissance in unknown or enemy occupied territory.

'You should be able to do this, Wally,' he told me. 'You were an instructor when I first met you.'

Of course I said yes. But I didn't know what the hell to say to the men. Nobody had taught me how to do it. There was no formula and every situation was different. All I had done was to work out, as logically and realistically as I could, how to carry out a particular assignment without being seen or getting killed.

George announced to his charges that I was experienced and successful and that it would be to their benefit to learn something from me. Although I suppose I had been successful – if only because I was still alive – it was still flattering to hear him say this.

All I could do was explain everything I did on those trips to Goodview Junction, the American base and Ambush Knoll. And it seemed to go over well. They listened with interest and asked me many intelligent questions. Maybe they didn't believe me. I'm sure they hadn't realised that this sort of thing went on. I wondered what their mates would think when they saw our Tommy gunners in action. I sincerely hoped I'd been of some help, if only because most of them looked so miserable and unsure of themselves.

Later George asked me if I'd like to stay with his new battalion. I declined, because there was no way I could see myself taking orders from the poor sort of officer I'd seen there.

'Can't blame you for that,' George laughed. 'Now, Wally, before you go, I want to tell you something. I've recommended you for a commission. The paperwork's already in motion.'

'Thank you very much, sir.'

'You deserve it. Good luck to you.'

'Good luck to you too, sir.'

He shook hands with me. There was no salute. I was never to meet anyone else in the military who measured up to George in any capacity.

Meanwhile, the company was kept busy fighting its way beyond Bobdubi Ridge to the Komiatum Track. We knew if we could reach it we could isolate the Japanese fighting our 17th Infantry Brigade and starve them of reinforcements and supplies. But the place was lousy with Japanese and they were launching counterattack after counterattack.

We were right down level with the Francisco River. The whole terrain was flat as a pancake but almost impenetrable with jungle. The thick tangle shut out the sun and cast everything in deep shadow. The poor visibility was worsened by the profusion of what we called wait-a-while: strong lawyer vines that clung to the foliage with razor sharp thorns.

Anyone unlucky enough to walk into some wait-a-while was caught fast and could only extricate himself with difficulty. This vine was to be avoided at all costs, yet it was impossible to see before it was too late.

Captain Hancock wanted to open up the jungle as well as beat back the Japanese and requested air support, but we didn't get it.

Three-man patrols were the norm for reconnaissance. They were small enough to advance unnoticed into enemy territory, and if someone was wounded one man could stay with him while the other went back to bring a rescue party.

I went out with two other commandos towards the Komiatum Track on what we called a 'feeler patrol'. No one could tell us how far to go or how to get there; the jungle was too dense to see any distance and it was all unknown territory. We just went to see what we could find out.

Progress was extremely slow. There were obstacles everywhere, the air was stifling and everything was dank and rotten. It was probably the thickest jungle I'd ever forced my way through. Japanese were in the vicinity, but exactly where we couldn't say. At least there was no rain. That would have completed the misery.

I was wondering at our having come so far without seeing any Japanese when suddenly we were fired upon from a very short distance. They were obviously entrenched in a concealed position. All we saw was flashing as their weapons fired and the foliage was shredded by their bullets. Their firepower made it obvious that we were outnumbered. Our feeler patrol had certainly struck a feeler.

Then we ran into big trouble. My companion Alan Tait was badly hit and obviously a stretcher case. As we returned fire, the other man (whose name I forget) and I decided that I'd be the one to go back for help. Leaving my hand grenades behind to help him keep the Japs occupied, I took my Tommy gun and pistol in case I ran into problems on the way.

The Japanese were settled in nice and cosy, just waiting for people like us to come along. I figured that if the positions were reversed we'd probably have had a small patrol hidden elsewhere, so that if they tried to withdraw or fetch help they would have been caught like meat in a sandwich.

The jungle was too thick to see whether there were any of the bastards waiting for me. But I had to get back quickly or my two comrades were going to have no chance. Of course, if I didn't make it back that was going to be pretty bad for me, too.

The best thing to do was go carefully until I had passed where the secondary enemy ambush might be, then run to base as fast as the jungle allowed, trusting that my fellow commandos were not so trigger-happy that they'd open fire just because they heard a noise.

It worked and I got back in one piece. They had heard me, which was no surprise, and a reception party was anxious to know what had happened. There was no hesitation. A fellow commando was in trouble. Soon a patrol was ready to go with an improvised stretcher and it was up to me to guide them back to our wounded comrade.

We moved as quickly and cautiously as possible, frequently hearing Japanese voices and movements. When we reached the ambush site you could see the relief in the two men's faces. The Japanese were now either side of them. Alan was in a lot of pain, but he didn't complain or make a sound. Everything was deathly silent. No words were spoken as we loaded Alan onto the makeshift stretcher and set off home to base.

I could only presume that the enemy didn't hear us, because no shots were fired. The limited visibility helped, but then the Japanese were often unpredictable. You'd have thought they would want to see why our commandos had stopped firing and confirm whatever damage they had caused. But they didn't and this lack of interest probably saved two Australian lives.

The return trip was much more slow and difficult with a man on a stretcher. Once again we frequently heard the enemy talking and moving on either side, only yards away through the undergrowth. They certainly weren't as worried as we were about making noise.

It was a great relief to get back without incident and Alan Tait did recover later.

Some of our fighting patrols learnt that the Japanese had made a controlled withdrawal to more heavily reinforced fortified positions. Brigadier Hammer, who commanded the units in our group under the auspices of General Savige, issued orders that we were to 'advance with greatest speed'. We thought this made sense: take Salamaua and we all might have a bit of a holiday. Well, a rest and some food, anyway.

It didn't become known until long after the war that General Savige had also issued orders to Brigadier Hammer that he was not to influence the enemy to evacuate Salamaua before the major operation to capture Lae and Nadzab. Until then our purpose was to keep luring Japanese reinforcements to Salamaua to weaken their defences in Lae. For our already depleted and overworked company, this meant more casualties and more lives lost.

Anyway, we continued on, but experienced a temporary shortage of rations. That is, we hoped it was only temporary. We successfully ambushed several large Japanese fighting patrols, still fiercely determined to force us away from Salamaua. At last our company, or what was left of us, was ordered to move back to Bobdubi Ridge to secure the ridge's defences. To have lost such a dominating position to a Japanese offensive would have undone much of what had been achieved. Although that was unlikely, it was far better to be sure than sorry.

A few days later, on the 4th of September 1943, the 9th Australian Division landed to begin the long-promised strike on Lae and Nadzab. We had a bird's eye view from Bobdubi Ridge, and what a mighty display it was. The next day the sky was filled with over 300 Allied aircraft, apparently the largest concentration of airpower ever used against the Japanese. We felt like we were watching ants being killed with a sledgehammer.

A regiment of American paratroopers dropped down to secure various targets while fighters scurried in the air high and low to protect them. The 7th Australian Division landed on the secured airfields, while bombing and strafing went on continuously. The Japanese were caught napping and the landing was completely unopposed. No one was home in the Lae-Nadzab area – well, at least there were nowhere near as many of them as there had been. Over the past few months we had succeeded in inducing them to send their troops to Salamaua, where they'd become preoccupied with trying to blow our heads off.

We know now that the Japanese were determined to hold Salamaua. Our hierarchy had banked on this. It was good planning and probably a bit of luck as well. At the time we had started to wonder whether Lae-

Nadzab was ever going to happen. Once it finally had, we saw that we'd made it possible and that the effort had been worthwhile. The Japanese in Salamaua were watching. They must have wet their rotten pants to see that sort of firepower coming after them.

Overall, the Japanese were still fighting fiercely, however. They had over seventy barges at Salamaua, each capable of carrying above eighty troops. Over the following week six thousand Japanese troops went by barge to Lae and another six hundred-odd by submarine to Rabaul. We heard these embarkations nightly up on Bobdubi Ridge and we wished every success to the Allied patrol boats trying to sink them.

Some fanatics stayed behind to fight us before we reached Salamaua. We attacked Japanese positions on Rough Hill, which they defended with vigour. Darkness fell and we settled in for a dreary watch. The next morning we found they had disappeared overnight. Cautiously patrolling forward, we finally entered Salamaua the following day, the 11th of September 1943. Salamaua was ours, with not a single Japanese in sight.

Everything felt so different and strange. After being on acute mental alert twenty-four hours a day for months, we suddenly realised there was no one out there bent on killing us. The hell of combat at close quarters, fighting desperately against superior numbers, contending with starvation and disease – it was all over. We were the victors and proud of it.

We paid a heavy price, however. Of the 290 men who landed at Wau in January, only 34 of us were still with the company. A small flow of reinforcements had kept us viable, but the casualties in our commando unit had been higher than in any other: 65 killed and 119 wounded in action, with a further 226 evacuated for medical reasons.

The 2/3 Australian Independent Company was officially credited with killing 969 Japanese (and 3 of their trained attack dogs) in close combat fighting. The actual figure was much higher and their number of wounded or evacuated sick, which I imagine was huge, remains unknown. Of course, the real estate between Wau and Salamaua was of inestimable value to the Allied war effort.

6

From Salamaua to Melbourne

Salamaua was a hell of a filthy mess. Allied bombings had cratered the roads, shattered buildings and spread debris everywhere. And the Japanese were not especially hygienic – urinating against their own walls was typical of the way they lived there. Yet there was no reason for them not to keep clean; Salamaua was right on the sea and had no shortage of water.

An interconnecting network of trenches had been dug all over the place. The hills were pockmarked with holes and tunnels, where some of the Japanese had been shacked up for safety's sake. These places were filthy as well.

Almost immediately Allied ships appeared, and landing barges began to ferry troops, gear and supplies ashore. The place was a hive of Allied activity with people looking busy and important now that the fighting had finished.

We didn't get much chance to have a good look around. Our company's campaign had been tougher than that of any other unit and we were given top priority for return to Australia. Without delay we were boarded onto landing barges, which ferried us down the coast to Tambu Bay on the first leg of our journey home.

The ocean was another world to us. The warm sun, the fresh offshore breeze – everything seemed so clean. The sea air smelt good after months of the dank jungle with its peculiar smell of decay, to say nothing of the distinctive equally rotten odour of the Japanese. It seemed years since I had visited Major Al at Tambu Bay, where there was a thriving base now that buzzed with Australian and American forces. There was no shortage of food and we had shelter over our heads at night. Conditions were heavenly compared to what we'd been used to. And the closer we got to home, the more heavenly they became.

None of the Americans I asked at Tambu Bay knew anything about Al. Perhaps he had gone on to Salamaua, or perhaps he had gone home. Anyway, I didn't hear of him again. Poor bastard.

We took things quietly. There was nothing to do and in the services you got used to waiting. When troops were moving into action, there was no delay getting them there because that was where they were needed. But departing troops had to wait until transport was available, and that was fair enough. We cleaned ourselves up as well as we could and enjoyed the first relaxation we'd had for a long time.

Ten days later an American amphibious Infantry Landing Craft took us down the coast to Milne Bay, another small step on the way home. I took the opportunity to see the sites where fellow Australians had, not long before, engaged in serious battle with the Japanese. Once you got away from the main drag, if you could call such a small area that, it was the same dreary jungle I knew only too well.

A week later we left Milne Bay for Cairns on the *SS Sydney Hall Young*. It wasn't quite the *QE2*, but after the jungle it seemed a luxury. The three days at sea were wonderful, with fresh air, food and even a bit of lounging about in the sun.

Finally we reached Cairns. It's hard to explain the feeling in your guts when you suddenly realise you're back home in Australia. You realise how much you love it and how proud you are to be an Australian.

Bundled onto a train, we wound our way through lush rainforests and green fields to the Atherton Tablelands. Our camp was in a city of tents, next door to two other commando units. Medical advice was that a few alcoholic drinks would do us good after what we'd been through. We all had our own interpretations of what 'a few' meant, but generally we agreed with the course of treatment.

Already skinny from disease and malnutrition, we looked even worse with the yellow stain on our skin from the Atebrin anti-malarial tablets we'd been given. The plan had been to have us home on leave before Christmas and the authorities mustn't have wanted to release such a pack of oddly coloured scarecrows into the community, because we were kept pretty well fed. We were given milk, eggs, beef, poultry, lamb, pork, fruit, freshly picked corn and other vegetables – much of this produce grown or raised locally. At the time, food was still being rationed throughout the country, but I don't think anyone would have begrudged us this small luxury. We were going back soon enough to our mundane life of trying to dispose of more Japanese. Unfortunately our appetites were far larger than our stomachs, which had been shrivelled by those lean months in New Guinea.

So here we were with a roof over our heads – well, a tent was as good as a roof – and we had fresh blankets and clothes. There were even hot water showers and we actually started to feel clean.

At last, fitted out with new gear, we were sent on our twenty-eight days leave, exclusive of travelling time. This meant those going to South and Western Australia would be away a lot longer than those taking their leave in Queensland. Of course, I was going to Melbourne.

The train took us back to Cairns, where we joined an old rattler to Brisbane. The narrow gauge Queensland railway tracks seemed to accentuate the shaking, but no one worried about that. All that mattered was we were going home. On the journey the train often pulled over to a siding to make way for packed troop trains going north to the war. If any of these trains came within hailing distance, there were always shouts from our train.

'You'll be sorry!'

'Chockos!'

'What took you so bloody long?'

We didn't know who they were or even if they were chockos (militia), but that didn't matter.

Brisbane was four days travel from Cairns, with several stops along the way. Meals at particular railway stations were arranged for us in advance and we appreciated them mightily. Even average food made our mouths water. The main thing was that all the meals were hot and some included meat and vegetables. Then, of course, there was bread and butter – what a delicacy! We felt as if we'd opened a Christmas present.

At Brisbane we changed trains and spent over a week reaching Melbourne. Most railway stations had large signs shouting messages like

Save – Invest in War Bonds, or *Remember – Idle Talk Can Cost Lives*. There was a short stop in Sydney and then one at Albury, where we changed trains yet again. Now we were in Victoria on broad gauge tracks and the travelling was smoother. I was on the home stretch to Melbourne.

After trying to nap in the tropical rain with armed Japanese and mosquitoes buzzing about, sleeping on the train wasn't too bad. The rhythmic clack of the wheels going over the joins in the rails and the gentle sway of the carriage had a hypnotic effect. If you listened closely enough, you'd almost have sworn the chugging of the train was sending you a message.

You had to take care when you opened a window, though. If the wind was blowing the wrong way, the carriage filled with foul-smelling smoke from the funnel of the steam engine. When we slowed down to go through a station without stopping, there were always good-natured remarks shouted to whoever was on the platform and the passengers waiting there would always smile and wave back.

Finally, with a series of loud, shrill whistles and whoops from the engine, we arrived in Melbourne. We got out and stretched our legs and bodies, relieved that the tedious journey was over.

First move was to Camp Pell, the staging camp at Royal Park near the zoo: an appropriate place for a staging camp. Here we spruced up and drew our pay. Food ration coupons and twenty-eight-day leave passes were issued, together with as many French letters (we never called them 'condoms') as we wanted to take. After a meticulous inspection we were let loose, back home at last.

PART TWO

Australia

1943–1945

7

Back Home

Civilian life felt totally alien to me now. But it was me who had changed and it was up to me to adjust. Outside the gates of Camp Pell was a park bench and I sat down in the sun to look around at nothing in particular. This is the life, I said to myself.

I had phoned my parents the night before and they were ecstatic, almost speechless, at hearing my voice. I told them I'd be home the next day and although they wanted to collect me, I insisted on making my own way. Not knowing what time I'd be released, I knew it would be frustrating and upsetting for them to have to wait for possibly hours outside. As I travelled into the city it felt like everyone was looking at me. Of course they weren't, but whenever I caught someone's eye I'd get a smile and I'd smile in return. I'd almost forgotten how to be polite because I'd had no real need to be for almost a year.

I found myself watching people. I studied the way they dressed and what they looked like. It all seemed to be so exciting. There were girls everywhere, lovely looking girls. I'd been away from them for a long time. Far too long.

I must have looked a bit of a hick, because complete strangers would smile at me and ask if I was on leave, or going home, or whether I lived in Melbourne – even if I was all right. What wonderful, caring people. I hadn't been used to this sort of thing for so long.

In the city it was business as usual, with people scurrying all over the place, but so many uniforms about! I found the tram to South Yarra and people in uniform were not required to pay a fare. It rolled down the big boulevard of St Kilda Road, past the green lawns that stretched to the Botanical Gardens and the Shrine of Remembrance. Soon I was going to be home.

Well, what a welcome! My mother and father, their friends and relatives – all were milling around me as soon as I was in the door and there was an explosion of excited voices.

'Look at him!'

'Doesn't he look good!'

'Are you all right?'

'How are you?'

There were hugs all round and one lady even gave me an enthusiastic pinch on the left cheek of my bum. When I jumped she said, 'Oops! I just wanted to see if you were real.'

The others were crowding me so much I didn't get a chance to find out who she was. They kept saying how good I looked, although I knew I looked awful. I didn't feel too bad, but my skin was yellow from the Atebrin and I was still half-starved.

There were so many questions I couldn't answer them all. Finally I managed to single out my mother and father. We hugged and they were as pleased to see me as I was to see them, but their eyes filled with tears and I could see the look of desperation as they tried to smile. I felt really sorry for them, because apart from the worries I'd created for them, there was still no news of my brother.

These people all knew a little of what I'd been up to, because my father had meticulously collected any newspaper articles about 'the famous' 2/3 Independent Company and kept them in a file. So they had a fair idea of what life was like in New Guinea, and that made it hard for me to play things down when the questions came.

Good food and grog was laid out for me, mouth-watering stuff that I hadn't seen for ages. Some of them must have chipped in and helped with their ration coupons. They would have hoarded the grog for a while – good liquor was not easy to come by. Everyone urged me to eat and drink, but of course my stomach wouldn't let me really go for it.

After a while they wanted me to elaborate on some of the stories they'd read in the papers, but I felt that if I told them what had really

happened, they probably wouldn't believe it. None of these lovely people
had ever witnessed the kind of violence I had. They probably didn't even
know it existed. No, I thought, don't tell them. Not at this stage, anyway.
I'd either upset them or they'd start pitying me – and that was the last
thing I needed.

So I distracted them by repeating some of the newspaper stuff and
talking about the mud, the Fuzzy Wuzzies, Double Mountain, watching
from the OP, the big python – things like that. I got away with it, but I
knew that was only temporary. They were intelligent people and would
soon realise that I hadn't mentioned fighting the Japanese at all. The
newspapers trumpeted our 969 official Japanese kills; it was obvious I had
other, darker stories to tell. I'd just have to prepare myself for more
probing questions in the future.

We kept eating, drinking and talking and everyone, including me,
enjoyed it. But all the time I was thinking how much better this was than
starving in the filthy mud and rain while total strangers tried to kill you.

Out of the blue a lady said to my mother, 'How old is Brian?'

I'm as old as God, I thought. The conversation seemed to stop, as
my mother proudly said in a slightly sorrowful or whimsical tone, 'Oh,
Brian's only twenty.'

'Is that right? Only twenty?' the lady said, to a chorus of *oohs*, *ahhs*, and
oh dears. They all looked at me as I tried to keep talking and pretend I
hadn't heard them. I don't know why I did this, because she was dead
right – I was only twenty. But I didn't feel like twenty anymore.

At the evening's end they all crowded round me again before they left,
with the same sorts of comments: how good it was to see me, how well I
looked and they invited me to their places for dinner and so on. I waited
for another pinch on the bum, but alas it didn't happen.

At last, my mother, father and I were on our own. We'd been waiting
for this moment. Gathering me in a hug, they started to cry and laugh and
just say whatever was on their minds. We had always been a very close
family, but it's only now that I fully realise the trauma and heartbreak my
parents went through back then. The whole family life they had built up
had disintegrated. My brother was missing, his fate unknown, and all they
knew of my activities was what they saw in the newspapers. The details
were sketchy, but they must have been shattering to read.

'You two stay here,' my mother said. 'I'll go and clean up.'

'No, we'll all clean up,' my father replied. 'But first we'll have a drink.'

I hadn't been a drinker or smoker before the war. I'd always just been mad keen on playing sport. I probably would have started drinking anyway, as an extension of my natural outgoing personality, but the smoking was a direct result of the long periods of waiting in the army. I'm not talking about waiting in a jungle ambush. You'd never smoke in that situation; the smell carries too far. But if you were waiting for transport, for someone to make a decision, for an inspection to be made or a patrol to set off, there was absolutely nothing else to do and it gave you the shits. A lot of my friends smoked just to pass the time, so I started too and of course it became a habit. I ended up a heavy smoker and a heavy drinker – doing everything to excess, that was me – and it was a long, long time before I gave the smokes up.

My parents had developed a new habit too. As soon as they could they turned on the radio for the news, explaining that they did this regularly in the hope of hearing where I'd been. Naturally they were also aching for news about Denis.

After clearing the table we sat down for another talk. I didn't mention the bum-pinching incident – I was worried that they might not understand – but in hindsight I'm sure they would've roared laughing. My mother said a few of the ladies wanted me to meet their daughters and nieces and I supposed that was something to look forward to. Maybe. At least I hoped it was.

That night I slept fitfully, wondering if the bed was a bit too comfortable and whether I'd be better off on the floor. Then I thought no, that was wrong. I had to get used to the comfort. In the morning I decided that this new attitude had to stay. Looking at the bed, I told myself, That was good. Very good.

It might seem strange that it was so difficult to go back to civilian life after being at war. There was hot water to shave with, a lovely hot shower, clean clothes, and no need to hurry. It was all 'What would you like for breakfast?' and 'The paper's there to look at'. I felt somehow out of place – although I have to admit the luxury wasn't hard to take.

I spent most of the day with my mother. We went out for a walk, had lunch and a great old talk. All this food was going to take some time to get used to, though. My father had invited me to meet him at the Botanical Hotel at five. I arrived a bit early, bought myself a drink and waited. Some people, mostly well-to-do business types, watched me out of the corner of their eyes and gave each other a bit of a nudge. I was the only one there in uniform. I didn't have other clothes anyway – but, then, I didn't *want* to wear anything else.

My father came in and his eyes lit up. I asked him what he'd like to drink. Then most of the people who had eyed me off greeted my father and seemed to look at him, expecting him to introduce me. I saw how proud he was to do this and I could tell he'd been talking about me, based on what he had gleaned from the newspapers, the radio and the letters I'd written home. He wouldn't have learnt much from my letters, because I always dodged, as gracefully as I could, writing anything that might have caused him and my mother worry. And on top of that they were censored.

People repeatedly offered to buy me a drink, but I declined politely because I had no intention of getting plastered so early in my leave. They meant well and obviously wanted to be welcoming and friendly, but my father and I decided we'd start to make tracks early.

I soon found that most people asked more or less the same questions. I understood, because I'd have been curious myself. But the truth was that it was often hard to answer honestly without appearing boastful, and there was also no way I could answer some of the questions honestly in front of my parents. So I came up with fairly standard answers. The questions were similar to those that Al and the other Americans had bombarded me with in New Guinea:

Q: How are you? A: Fine, thank you.

Q: What was it like in the jungle? A: Not the best really. It was pretty rough.

Q: Did you eat well? A: Actually, we didn't see a great deal of food. (This one seemed to bamboozle them.)

Q: Did you see any Japs? A: Oh, yes.

Q: Many of them? A: Yes, quite a few.

Q: What were they like? A: They were animals. (They would always look sideways at this one.)

Q: Did you kill any of them? A: Oh, yes.

Q: Many? A: Quite a few.

Q: What did that feel like? A: It felt good. Very good. (They didn't like that much, either.)

Q: You were a commando, weren't you? A: Yes.

Q: What exactly does a commando do? A: He kills as many Japs as possible, without getting killed himself.

Q: Were you good at it? A: Well, I'm still around.

The questions would start to wane after that. People generally wouldn't seem to know what else to ask, although sometimes you'd get things like:

Q: How do you think the war's going? A: I think we've started to turn the Japs back, but there's still a long way to go.

Q: Are you glad to be home? A: Very glad. You realise more than ever what a marvellous place Australia is.

My father's friends finished the usual round of questions and the conversation turned to food and petrol rationing and all the planning that entailed. Grog was hard to come by, unless you knew a hotel-keeper who would do you a favour and sell you some extra. Generally the hotels tried to ration their available stock fairly evenly among their regular clientele. Then there was the black market, where you could get almost anything if you had the money. And they talked about people attaching charcoal burners to their cars, which helped make the petrol ration travel a lot further.

The hotels closed at six. At five to, the serious drinkers would line up a couple of extra beers and they had about a quarter of an hour to demolish them.

On this leave I found that my father and I had a different relationship. We were more like mates than just father and son. I thought this was good and I'm sure he did too.

When we got home my mother said over dinner, 'You must have made a bit of an impression. You've got three invitations already.'

'Sounds pretty good. What for?'

They were from three of my mother's friends who had met me at the welcome home, but I didn't particularly remember which ones. Kath from Armadale wanted me to go to a party on Saturday night. She had two daughters, attractive and well-spoken, according to my mother. Joan, a tall, dark-haired lady with a good suntan, asked if I'd go for a picnic and a swim down at Brighton with her and her daughter. She had some spare petrol and would pick me up at eleven on Sunday morning. Lastly there was Frances, a well-dressed and slightly plump lady from Malvern. My mother said she was very nice, but that she hadn't met her children. I was invited to have dinner and see a film with them on Wednesday. My mother had accepted all three on my behalf.

I still couldn't get used to all the food. I wanted to eat it, but it was beyond me. My parents and I spoke about my brother, about old times and our hopes for the future. That night I lay in my comfortable bed with my mind racing. Things were certainly moving; I hadn't had a quiet moment yet and that was good. I thought of all the questions I was being asked and the difficulty of answering them.

Then I had a brainwave. I decided to get in first and take charge of the conversation. If I asked people about themselves, how they were and what they'd been doing, it might take some of the heat off me.

For breakfast I made sure I only had two slices of toast and a cup of black coffee. My mother protested I needed more than that, but God alone knew what quantities were going to be served up during the day!

I listened to the radio news and read the morning paper. Axel Olsen was still very active writing articles. The war in New Guinea had moved northwest around the coast from where we had been. I tried to imagine what our soldiers were going through. It was difficult enough for me, so what images were in the minds of people who hadn't been there?

The next day I set off to have a browse around the city. I can't think why, except that it felt like a good idea at the time. It was a peaceful day – or anyway, it was to me. The tram passed the beautifully green lawns surrounding the Botanical Gardens, featuring the wide strip known as 'the tan', where people could exercise their horses without the worry of vehicular traffic.

My mind was ticking over all the time. I hadn't fully relaxed ever since going into the jungle and I was still worrying about what to tell people. Suddenly I had another bright idea for a conversation piece. I could ask them about events in the news. That way I could carry on a conversation for some time, and no one would think I had been away for very long. I decided to try this tactic out on my father's friends at the Botanical.

I spent the day wandering about the city, watching the bustle. The clothing shops had shortages and were not very busy. Some had a little pre-war stock and the difference in quality was readily noticeable. Austerity measures meant that trousers no longer had cuffs, suits were all single-breasted with no waistcoats, and shirts no longer had double cuffs. The materials were lightweight and shoddy.

Naturally you needed coupons to buy clothes, but some cafes and restaurants had certain foods that were not rationed. Beer rationing meant that hotels either had signs up indicating when beer would be served, or else the time was known to the regulars. A serious drinker who knew all the times could go from hotel to hotel without having to wait for his next drink. Someone at the Botanical had told me about places set up by groups like the Salvation Army and the YMCA to look after service people on leave. You could get a cup of tea or coffee or maybe something to eat, and they might even find you something to do if you were at a loose end.

I wasn't looking for any of these places, but as I walked along Swanston Street I saw next to the Capitol Theatre a large sign indicating that the Dugout was downstairs, all service people welcome.

It was beautifully set up and staffed by lovely young female volunteers. Apparently it was the place to be if you were a young lady, although dating was forbidden. There was music playing and everyone was bright, cheerful and full of fun. I had a good look around, ate a couple of sandwiches and chatted to one of the young ladies. Then I'd had enough of the city for one day and went home.

My mother was surprised but pleased to see me. We talked for a while and she played a few songs for me on the piano. She could play anything at all, either from the sheet music or just by ear. She kept herself up to date with the popular tunes of the day. She sat down and belted out 'Oh You Beautiful Doll, You Great Big Beautiful Doll', 'In The Mood' and 'I'm Gonna Buy A Paper Doll That I Can Call My Own'.

'Sing!' she shouted above her playing, so I did and we had a laugh together.

Later at the Botanical Hotel I met my father and, over a couple of drinks, tried out my new conversation piece.

'Did you see such-and-such in the paper this morning?' I asked, or 'I heard on the radio today...' And so on. Most of them didn't seem to know what I was talking about, but they looked at me with a renewed interest, as if they were thinking, Well, he sure knows what he's talking about. And it certainly stopped them cross-examining me. Either they didn't get a chance to ask their questions, or they simply forgot about them.

On the way home my father looked at me curiously, as if to say, What was that all about? But he didn't say anything and we finally got home to the delicious smell of home cooking.

8

Lovely Ladies

It wasn't long before my mother began to get telephone calls from several irate women. Strangely, they never asked to speak to me.

'Your son kept my daughter out all night,' they would complain.

'Yes,' my mother would say, unfazed by their indignation. 'Isn't it shocking what young girls get up to nowadays?'

I couldn't understand why none of these angry mothers ever mentioned their complaints to me the next time I called on their daughters. I couldn't imagine what they expected my mother to do about it, but that was the way things were at the time. Even so, in my experience 1940s Australia was a lot more liberal than many people today realise. The shortage of eligible bachelors definitely had something to do with it. Not knowing how the war was going to turn out was probably a factor, too. It seemed that everywhere young ladies were on the prowl for a man and ready to have a bit of fun into the bargain. Their mothers were happy to turn a blind eye if it meant their daughter would make a catch. For a young bloke like me, it was like being in heaven.

Anyway, on Saturday evening I was off to my first party in eighteen months. I decided not to arrive too early at Kath's place. She had a nice flat in Armadale, where she lived with her two daughters, Patricia and Phyllis. Their father was apparently away 'on some war business'. They used this phrase frequently, but no one could tell me what it meant. Once after a few drinks I'd asked if it meant firing bullets and the answer was, 'Good Lord, no, nothing like that.'

The party was well underway when I arrived. A gramophone was playing 'Don't Get Around Much Anymore'. Kath greeted me with a hug and a kiss and introduced me to Patricia and Phyllis. Something told me it was Kath who had pinched me on the bum on my first night home. Giving both daughters a peck on the cheek, I told them how lovely they looked and how nice it was to meet them.

They smiled and looked as if they were examining me but didn't know what to think. A lot of people did that. It was a bit disconcerting at first, but in the long run I didn't mind. Later I found that all the newspaper cuttings had been passed around for everyone to read. Maybe that had something to do with it.

The two Ps were slightly older than I was, as were most people at the party, but I felt like an old man among them. Phyllis took me over to a cocktail cabinet for a drink while Patricia wound the gramophone and put on another record.

I settled for a scotch and water (beer being hard to come by) and Phyllis took me around and introduced me to some of their friends. There were a couple of uniformed men complaining about how rough things were at home. Their colour patches indicated they hadn't been out of Australia.

Some of the girls were very attractive, just as the two Ps were, but they all seemed to be going steady with one or other of the men present. I must admit seduction was high on my list of priorities. Being an opportunist, if the chance had arisen I was going to seize it. In fact, the most readily available lady seemed to be Kath herself, but I thought I'd better keep clear of that one.

I could find little to talk about. The conversations were like mine had been before I went to war – they all seemed so petty and mundane. All these people knew of the war was that it caused shortages and inconvenience at home, the poor bastards. Even my conversation piece wasn't working here.

Later I learnt that most commandos experienced similar communication problems on leave. So a lot of them spent their leave in each other's company and some even looked forward to going back to their unit. But I had no intention of doing that. I was determined to persevere and try to enjoy myself to the hilt while I could.

Next morning was the beach picnic. At eleven the doorbell rang and two gorgeous ladies walked in. Joan was tall, dark-haired and suntanned, and Janet was a younger mirror image of her mother. They were both in shorts, full of energy and all smiles. This was more like it.

'Where's Brian?' Joan said. Grabbing me, she planted a kiss fair and square on my lips.

'Brian, this is my daughter Janet.'

Without missing a beat, Janet said hello and planted a nice wet kiss on my mouth. No half measures here. I thought I was pretty fast, but this pair left me for dead!

'Let's go,' said Joan, leading the way to her 1938 Pontiac. We packed the boot with all the tasty things my mother had prepared. 'We'll all fit in the front seat,' Joan said. 'You get in the middle, Brian.'

The two of them kept their lively chatter up all the way to Brighton Beach, laughing and occasionally nudging me in the ribs. When we got there we took the collapsible canvas stools, rugs and towels to a nice secluded spot. It was a perfect summer day.

Turning our backs on each other, we put our bathers on. I didn't have any, but I'd brought a second pair of shorts.

'Last in's lousy!' laughed Joan. We had a bit of a swim and tossed a beach ball around for a while. Afterwards we sat down in the sun to drink a lovely cold beer. Joan's husband, an accountant, was away 'on war business' with the army paymaster's office. Joan occasionally did volunteer work in hospitals for the Red Cross and Janet, who had been training as a nurse, lent a hand at the Dugout. She was about a year older than me. It seemed I was always the baby in any gathering.

I asked Janet where her boyfriend was. Joan laughed and said, 'Oh, don't ask that! Janet was engaged to this creep and she's only recently broken it off.'

'I'm sorry,' I said. 'I should've minded my own business.'

'No, don't apologise,' Janet replied. 'It's all history.' Apparently that was why she'd put her nursing training on hold.

Joan poured us another beer. 'Tell us some stories, Brian. You're the first commando we've ever met.'

They looked at me so openly, earnestly and expectantly that I knew I had to say something. All thoughts of seduction momentarily vanished as I tried to work out what to tell them.

I started with a couple of my standard stories, but Joan interrupted and said, 'Brian, I heard those at your mother's place and I've already told them to Janet. Please, you must have some more interesting stories.'

Some intelligent person was always going to pick me up on this, sooner or later. I thought for a while, then reluctantly told them about the long patrol I'd been on with George out of Wau. I described how we hadn't eaten for a couple of days when we ambushed the Japanese patrol and took their food. I told them how shocking it tasted, but how it eased our terrible hunger. They were both open-mouthed. Immediately I wished I hadn't told them.

'Shit,' Janet said.

'Janet, please!' Her mother glared.

'Brian, I'm so sorry,' Janet said.

'There's nothing to be sorry about.'

Joan said, 'You poor thing.'

'No,' I said. 'Don't feel that way. It wasn't like that. There were worse things.' I only said that to make them feel better, but soon realised I'd really put my foot in it, because they kept asking me questions for the rest of the day and evening.

All the invigorating sea air had us famished. The food was delicious and we did a first class demolition job on it, without giving even a thought to rationing. My pre-jungle appetite seemed to be returning at last.

Joan decided to have a nap in the sun, so Janet and I went for a walk along the sand and around the rocks. We drifted together and our arms went around each other. Janet whispered, 'Come home with us and have a meal. If it's late you can stay the night. Mum said it's okay.'

Back at the picnic spot, Joan was yawning and packing up the remains of our lunch. We all had another swim and a beer and then set off in the Pontiac.

The sun was setting by the time we arrived at their place in Hawthorn. Soon I was comfortably seated, freshly showered, sipping a fine drink from a delicate crystal glass and casually nibbling at a very tasty savoury. I remembered mugs of muddy water that tasted of water purifier and army dog biscuits smeared with bully beef. But I had to get these jungle thoughts out of my mind.

I also had to put more thought into dodging people's questions. My two lovely hostesses continued to ask about the story I had told them, hinting that I should tell them more. Somehow I managed to sidestep gracefully and, without being rude, I hope, suggested maybe another time.

We weren't very hungry, so Joan served us up a cold salad to peck at. 'It's getting late,' she said, after we had helped wash up. 'You'd better stay the night, Brian. There's plenty of room.' Janet gave me a sly nod.

'Thank you very much,' I said and rang home to say where I was.

Janet took me to a nicely furnished spare bedroom and handed me a new toothbrush and a towel. She wrapped her arms around me, gave me a passionate kiss and whispered, 'That's my bedroom across the hall. Come over later when everything's quiet. I'll be waiting for you.' I just nodded. What was there to say?

I gave Joan a goodnight peck on the cheek and got a nice hug and a kiss on the lips in return. I must be a bit slow, I thought to myself and made a mental note to smarten myself up.

I cleaned my teeth, had a wash and lay down. After a short time, everything went quiet and there were no lights apart from the moon shining through the window.

Janet's door was slightly ajar. I'd only opened it about halfway when I was grabbed and dragged over to the bed. 'You came,' she whispered. Obviously, I thought, but I wasn't silly enough to be facetious and say so. I was too damned pleased to be there.

She closed the door quietly. Then she hurled herself back on the bed and we attacked, almost desperately, ripping off each other's clothes. Janet was a real killer. What passion, enjoyment and exercise we had! It seemed as though it would never end, but at last, completely worn out, we curled up together and slept. During the night, we woke several times. I didn't count, I was too busy, but when we did, we'd wear ourselves out once again, only to fall into another exhausted sleep.

Dawn was breaking and I could hear the chirping of birds. Janet wrapped her arms and legs around me and breathed in my ear. 'Darling, it might be better if you go back to your own bed now.' Then she said, eagerly, 'Let's do some more organising tomorrow.'

I nodded. 'Of course,' I said.

Slinking back to my own borrowed bed, I could only think over and over, This beats the shit out of being in the rotten jungle.

This time I was woken by a smiling Joan. 'Wakey, wakey, Brian. Did you sleep well? What would you like for breakfast?' She smiled at me mischievously. Christ, I thought, she's a good sort, too. 'The bathroom's free. I put a razor in there for you. Janet looks flaked out, so I thought I'd let her sleep. I think she rather likes you, you know, Brian.'

'Well, I'm very pleased about that,' I said.

My conversation piece had worked well at the Botanical Hotel and my father told me how impressed the regulars were that I seemed so knowledgeable for someone so young. I told him what I'd been doing. 'I must tell that one to your mother.' He smiled. 'She'll get a good laugh out of that.'

One of my acquaintances at the hotel, a nice chap named Ben, offered me some spare food and petrol ration coupons. My family had no car, but the petrol coupons were a godsend and I put them to excellent use.

Janet phoned me later that day. 'I just wanted to say hello,' she said. 'How are you?'

'Not too bad, considering,' I replied.

'I'm exhausted. I'm going to bed early tonight. On my own. Can I see you soon?'

I promised to phone her the next day. 'Tell your mother I have some petrol coupons for her.'

'That's lovely, Brian. I know she'll really appreciate that.'

We said very fond goodbyes to each other.

Over dinner my mother reminded me that the following Saturday was my birthday. I was going to be twenty-one. 'I don't want to do anything startling,' I told her. 'I know it's difficult with the war on and, really, it's just another day anyway.'

Ben's ration coupons came in handy when we bought grog for the party. John, the licensee of the Botanical, was more than happy to sell a returned digger some alcohol to help celebrate his twenty-first birthday. The petrol coupons went to any invited guests who needed them. I'd insisted that no one bring presents. 'They're no good to me anyway,' I said. 'I'll be going away again soon. Leave all that until after the war.'

We decided that I'd invite Joan and Janet and my mother would ask several people. Janet said she'd love to come, but wanted to see me before Saturday. But the next night I had to see Frances, her two daughters and son. Thinking quickly, I told her that I had family matters to attend to and that I'd phone her on Thursday and see if we could arrange something then. Reluctantly, she agreed.

Frances had a well-kept place in Malvern. I arrived around five o'clock, and she opened the door as I approached, ushering me in with a quick hug and kiss. Inside, the whole gathering turned to stare at me.

I found out afterwards that the buffet dinner was being held mainly because there was new blood on the scene – me. It was all quite flattering, but no one was very interested, except maybe Frances herself. I even sensed a bit of antagonism towards me. They were a self-centred lot and I found that amusing, but I felt sorry for Frances and the effort she had made. They didn't deserve her.

Frances's husband was a federal parliamentary secretary at work in Canberra.

Taking me over to the bar, she fixed me a drink and introduced me around. Her daughter Irene had a boyfriend away in the army, but not overseas, and her son Noel was in military uniform. The rest of the party comprised Frances's other daughter Dorothy and three young couples. It didn't look like there'd be too much excitement. Deciding to get in first, I asked them all what they'd been up to. Sometimes the girls seemed about to ask me a question, but the look on their boyfriends' faces always shut them up.

Frances pulled me aside and gave me another drink. 'Poor Brian. You're not making first base, are you? I think they're a little afraid of you. Maybe it's my fault. I told them about you before you arrived.'

I smiled and squeezed her arm. 'Thanks. You're the best sort here, anyway.'

She laughed. I offered her some food ration coupons, but she thanked me and told me they were okay. After dinner the three couples left and I went with Frances and her family to see the movie. I bought a box of chocolates for them on the way. Movietone news footage of the war was followed by Ronald Colman in *Lost Horizon*. We munched the chocolates and I thoroughly enjoyed myself.

Back at Frances's place for a nightcap, I politely declined the offer to stay over. Frances smiled. 'Brian, we loved having you. You're the only one who bothered to thank us. I hope you'll come again.'

At this point I began wondering how I could delete the word 'jungle' from my conversation. It cropped up all the time and I thought maybe I should avoid mentioning it. But it was impossible – the jungle was so firmly entrenched in my mind, body and soul. I decided that if people didn't like it, then up them.

The next morning there was good news in the paper. Damien Parer's documentary *Assault on Salamaua* was about to open at various theatres. This was a perfect opportunity. Now if anyone asked me questions about the war I could tell them they'd get a firsthand idea of what our commando operations were like from the film. I couldn't wait to try this out on someone at the Botanical Hotel that afternoon. I was keen to see the film myself and arranged to go with my parents the following week. But we didn't get there.

After helping my mother with the shopping I went to see Janet and got an extremely enthusiastic welcome. Joan poured drinks and thanked me for the petrol ration coupons. We ate a lovely lunch and I told them about *Assault on Salamaua*.

Joan always saw a friend for afternoon tea on Fridays. 'I'll see you tomorrow for your birthday if you're not here when I get back,' she said as she was going and gave me a big hug and kiss.

The front door had barely closed when Janet pounced. 'Let's go to bed now,' she breathed. 'I've missed you so much.' I needed no further encouragement.

She examined me minutely and caressed a few scars. 'What are these?' she said. I explained that some were shrapnel nicks or wounds and some were the result of tropical ulcers. Nothing very serious.

'You must think I'm terrible, Brian, doing this, but I couldn't help myself.'

'Of course not. The thought never entered my mind,' I answered truthfully.

Hours passed. The sun was going down as we showered together, then slumped into comfortable chairs to relax and enjoy a drink.

'I like you, Brian,' Janet said suddenly.

'That's good,' I said. 'I feel the same way about you. And I've still got a fair bit of leave to go.'

'We'll do some planning,' she said and I thought, Who am I to complain about that?

When Joan got back home she kicked her shoes off and said, 'Janet, please pour me a drink. I'm exhausted.' That made three of us. We agreed to go to the beach on Sunday again, the morning after my birthday. After two fond goodbyes and a few words whispered by Janet, I headed for home.

I slept soundly and woke to a beautiful sunny day. My twenty-first birthday. I didn't feel any different, but it was nice to still be alive and in one piece. A lot of people I'd known weren't fortunate enough to reach this ripe old age.

My mother and father wished me a very exuberant happy birthday. 'Today is Spoil Brian Day,' my mother said. She also said how sad it was that Denis wasn't there. And that was true; he was never out of our thoughts.

The party consisted of Janet, Joan, and six of my parents' friends. Some of these brought along their sons and daughters. I thought they were a bit staid at first, but they loosened up after a few drinks. There was no shortage of conversation and Damien Parer's documentary proved ideal for fending off questions about New Guinea.

My mother belted away on the piano: 'The Charleston', 'The Black and White Rag', 'Moonglow'. We sang, danced, drank and laughed. There was another pianist, so I got my mother up for a dance, but the substitute was not in the same class and my mother had to go back to work.

There wasn't much chance for an intimate talk with Janet, but she reminded me about our beach date the following morning. We had a surreptitious hug and a nuzzle, if you could call it that. What a gorgeous girl she was!

The next day at the beach passed pleasantly enough. My mother made us snacks from the party leftovers and my father wrapped some bottles in wet towels to help keep them cold. Joan invited me to stay over again but I declined, pleading that I'd arranged to spend the evening with my parents. I really hadn't spent a great deal of time with them yet.

9

Malaria Bangs

The next morning my mother couldn't wake me. Curled up, completely out of it and shaking uncontrollably, I must have been a truly horrible sight. It was my first real attack of BT malaria. There had been no warning. My poor parents hadn't any idea what was wrong with me and were beside themselves. Soon a military ambulance was rushing me to Heidelberg Military Hospital.

Malaria affects people in different ways. Initially it knocked me out cold and I shivered for quite a long time. Then it went into reverse. While I was still insensible and thrashing around, my temperature skyrocketed and perspiration streamed off me. I gulped like a landed fish. Eventually the fever broke and some kind person dried my body and made me drink liquids. Finally I opened my eyes, wondering where I was and what had happened. The whole ordeal was utterly exhausting.

And so, only thirteen days into my leave, I was hospitalised for what looked like being a long stretch. They said I was a very bad case. It was days before I even started to feel like Brian again and then, *bang*, it was off the planet again with no notice whatsoever.

My parents visited me in hospital before the second bang hit and I assured them there was nothing to worry about. Afterwards I asked the hospital staff, with whom I'd become quite friendly, not to notify my parents unless my life was threatened. They already had enough problems and I was glad they never found out about the second bang.

Heidelberg Military Hospital was a huge complex – practically a self-contained city. It had the best medical care available and even its own shops, radio station and entertainment theatre.

My malaria bangs – I called them that because they always hit me suddenly – developed a vague pattern over the next five or six months. After an attack I'd be hit again about two to two-and-a-half weeks later, then about three weeks after that one, then back to two-and-a-half weeks. It took me a week to ten days to recover my senses each time.

In between bangs I kept busy helping to broadcast the hospital radio program. This was great fun. I also helped organise shows in the theatre. One night, short of entertainers, I was conned into going on stage myself. I sang 'I'm Gonna Buy A Paper Doll' as loudly as possible, with the live band blaring out behind me. Much to my surprise, I was clapped and cheered with shouts of 'Encore, encore!' But I wasn't going to try my luck again, although even I was quite pleasantly surprised at the way it sounded.

My old friend Bill Braithwaite was in the hospital too, so I tracked him down.

'Wally,' he croaked. 'Good to see you.' It was good to see him, too. The doctors had done a remarkable job on his jaw.

We went out on day leave for a drink, which he managed through a straw, his mouth still healing after the operations. He was one tough man. Later we both joined Z Special Unit, but didn't work together. After the war he remained in the army to become Commanding Officer of the Special Air Service Regiment. I've met several people who knew him in the SAS, and not one of them had any idea his jaw had been shot off.

I was also lucky enough to have two heavy affairs of the heart at Heidelberg. Both ladies were in the army. I had my own comfortable – and lockable – nook at the radio station, which I put to good use.

One of these lovely ladies, Mary, worked full time at the radio station. She was full of laughter, petite and beautifully rounded in all the right places. I called her 'Little One'. Angela became 'Diet', because she was a fully qualified specialist dietitian. She was a natural blonde, with the same voluptuous body the movie star Betty Grable appeared to have – I say that because I only know firsthand what Angela had. We had fantastic carryings-on in my private nook. Diet and Little One were never together with me, of course, but when I went down with a bang they'd both visit me in their time off. They were absolutely lovely in every possible way.

Apart from the bangs, I was far more cosy at Heidelberg than I'd expected to be. I was in regular contact with my parents. Janet also visited, but there was no opportunity for any hanky panky. She said she missed me greatly, but there was nothing I could do about that. 'I'll wait for you, Brian,' she said. I smiled my agreement, but as a realist I knew that life had to go on.

During my stay in hospital, news came that the 17th Infantry Brigade and my Independent Company were to take a March of Honour through the streets of Melbourne. The date was set for Thursday the 18th of November 1943. I was recovering from another bang at the time, when Dr Mike Gordon, the Medical Superintendent supervising my case, said to me brightly, 'You'll be going to the march next Thursday, Brian.'

'Sure,' I replied. 'Who's going to carry me?'

Without missing a beat he said, 'We will. You wouldn't want to miss it, would you?'

I played along. 'No, of course not,' I said. 'I'd be devastated.'

But despite the jocular manner, Dr Mike wasn't kidding. When Thursday morning arrived they spruced me up with a shave and a wash, gave me fresh sheets and fixed a sign to the bedhead behind my pillow:

Brian – a commando with 2/3 Australian Independent Company.

A couple of bottles were placed in the bed in case I had to pee. 'Sandra's going to look after you,' Dr Mike said. 'She's got some lunch for both of you and she's all yours for the day.'

I didn't know quite what to say. 'Thanks, doctor, it's very kind of you. I greatly appreciate it – sir,' I added, because he'd been so kind.

I hadn't expected anything like this. I was wheeled outside to find six military ambulances and another five beds the same as mine. Their signs indicated they were all 17th Infantry Brigade.

The lady driver and her offsider slid me, bed and all, into the ambulance. Sandra, my lovely young nurse, hopped in after me – into the ambulance, that is, not the bed. Soon we were moving in a convoy, with sirens blaring now and then. Finally Sandra told me we had pulled up outside Melbourne Town Hall. The doors opened and I was wheeled to a space set aside at the front. My lovely guardian supervised my every move.

Dressed in their finery, all the dignitaries had assembled to see the march go past. 'Hello, Brian! Good to see you, Brian,' they said, reading my name from the sign.

The march was down Swanston Street, through the city centre and past the Town Hall, where the official party was to take the salute. Sandra could see far more than I could and said the streets were packed in every direction with a seething mass of people. Thousands of voices made a rolling noise like heavy waves pounding the seashore. Soon this noise turned into screams, shouts and cheers. A band started up. The roar increased as the marchers came into view – and what a sight they were!

They looked exactly what they were: proud Australians. These were the fighting soldiers, commandos and infantry who physically fought the enemy and fired the bullets. They had proven themselves under impossible conditions. I was proud to be one of them, but here I was propped up in a hospital bed, watching.

The noise got louder as the march progressed. Loudspeakers blared explanations of what particular units had achieved. Suddenly, mention was made of our commandos and the 'legendary' George Warfe. Then I saw them, led by George, who was smiling and waving at the crowd. Sandra grabbed my arm. 'Brian! There's your mob,' she said. 'Can you see them?'

'Yes, thank you, darling,' I said, taking her arm. It wasn't proper army behaviour, but who cared on a day like this? I certainly didn't.

They all looked great and the crowd cheered wildly. Finally the marchers had passed by and the sound of the crowd dropped back to a loud murmur. The excitement had gone and the people didn't seem to know what to do with themselves. Some of them wandered over in our direction to chat. A few of them had brought alcohol and were kind enough to offer me a drink, which I gratefully accepted.

'Brian, do you think it's all right for you to drink?' Sandra asked.

'Of course,' I said. 'Don't you remember the bottles in the bed?'

I knew that wasn't what she meant, but it seemed to put the lid on any objection. I had a few drinks with the crowd, answered a few questions. It was all very enjoyable. Then, out of the blue, I heard, 'Wally! What the fuck are you doing here?'

There he was, large as life – George Warfe, in a very happy mood. Obviously he'd had a few, and who could blame him?

'Just having a look,' I said, extremely pleased to see him.

Then I introduced him to Sandra. 'You always were a lucky bastard, Wally,' he said. He pulled out a large flask and offered me a drink, explaining that he'd heard the announcer say there was a commando in one of the beds outside the Town Hall.

'I thought that I'd have a look, but I didn't expect to see you,' he said. 'You should be going to OCTU soon. I despatched all the documentation and gave you the strongest possible recommendation.'

We chatted away for a short while longer until George said he had to go. 'Best of luck, Wally,' he said. 'We'll all miss you badly in the unit. Sandra, you look after him.'

'Oh yes, sir,' lovely Sandra stammered. 'Of course.'

'Thanks for coming to see me, sir,' I said, 'and the best of luck to you, too.'

'He's quite a man,' Sandra said after he had gone.

'He's a great man, in my book,' I said. 'The greatest.'

Sandra couldn't stop talking about what she'd seen and heard and everyone listened to her with great interest. I thought of trying to get her back to my private nook at the radio station, but she was promised to someone who was away with the army. I was tired, too; it had been a long busy day for a sick young commando. I went to sleep.

About a week later, after I'd been back at my broadcasting duties for a few days, Dr Mike told me I was to be sent to a convalescent depot at Ballarat. He warned me that I'd still get malarial relapses, but there was a camp hospital and an army general hospital there to look after me in that event.

I thanked him for looking after me. Then it was time for very fond goodbyes to both Little One and Diet. I knew I'd miss them both greatly. Sandra had a bit of a weep. 'Brian, I hope you'll be all right,' she said.

'I only need to remember how you looked after me and I'll feel better,' I said. She wrapped her arms around me and for that moment I felt just a bit jealous of whoever it was she was promised to.

Soon after phoning my parents with the news of my transfer, I was on my way to Ballarat in an army ambulance, riding up front with the lady driver.

10

Banged Up in Ballarat

I had never been to Ballarat before and found it quite a large place with a bleak wind blowing through it. Maybe someone thought all that fresh air would assist the convalescing.

I was told to report any signs of a bang coming on and had to have my temperature taken every morning. And I needed a leave pass to stay out overnight. The convalescent depot was on the outskirts of town. It had good recreation facilities but, like any military establishment, was nothing exciting. In the town I found a place similar to the Dugout in Melbourne called the Servicemen's Club, also staffed by lovely young volunteer hostesses.

The hotels seemed pretty dead, except for Craig's, a friendly place with a nice elderly barmaid called Nancy, who had extremely watery eyes. She would always tell her clientele how she loved her 'boys', the servicemen. She knew we didn't have much money and generally refused payment for every third drink.

Over the next five months, six bad malaria bangs saw me hospitalised in either the camp hospital attached to the convalescent depot or the army general hospital, which was separate. I was looked after extremely well, but the bangs were very wearing on me physically.

All the action in Ballarat seemed confined to the Servicemen's Club and Craig's Hotel. Most of the young men had gone away to the war and a lot of ladies were on the prowl for eligible males. Soon I found myself pleasantly overwhelmed with invitations to parties, dinners and other functions. The invitations invariably snowballed. I'd go to one and be asked to another. I was even invited to play tennis and golf a couple of times. It was neverending and no one was ever backward in coming forward.

It all started at the Servicemen's Club with a lovely young hostess, Margaret, who invited me to a party at her place one Saturday night.

'I'd love to, MT,' I said. Her friends all called her by her initials. 'Perhaps I'd better get a leave pass.'

'Oh yes. You might want to stay the night.'

There was no trouble getting leave passes. The Depot CO, Lieutenant Colonel Ken Baker, apparently went to a lot of these parties himself. After one bang, when I was ruled too sick to be issued with a leave pass, my would-be hostess Marion phoned and asked him to let me go because they 'needed' me. Lieutenant Colonel Baker told me about it himself when he granted me the pass.

MT had her own self-contained apartment attached to her parents' house, a lovely place in a beautiful garden setting. I never did get to meet her parents – not that it mattered. MT greeted me at the door with a big hug and kiss. 'You're all mine tonight, Brian,' she said. 'Come in and I'll introduce you.'

'This is Brian, my commando,' she said clearly and possessively, as if to say, If you don't like it, then piss off. I smiled at this and said hello to everyone.

'Basin Street Blues', one of my favourite numbers, was playing softly on the gramophone. The gathering was predominantly ladies and MT introduced me to more of them. They were all friendly and eager to talk. Most of them were obviously unattached. In many instances, when MT moved me on to meet someone else, I felt eyes following me. Occasionally, I had a surreptitious look back and the lady I'd just left gave me another smile. Naturally I smiled back, wondering what I'd got myself into. You wouldn't even dream of being in such a fantastic situation!

The men were a fairly motley and dismal lot. No wonder the ladies were all on the prowl. One exception, however, was a big bloke with 9th Division colour patches. His name was Steve Barlow and he'd been at the convalescent depot for some time. Clearly he had charm and charisma; he had his own group of admirers around him, all laughing.

Steve was older than I was and seemed to attract a more mature – or should I say a slightly older – type of lady. A Victorian like me, he had been a publican before the war. His nickname was 'Stook', an abbreviation of 'Stuka'. He had been one of the Rats of Tobruk and a mate of his told me that when the German Stuka dive bombers came over to bomb the Australians at Tobruk, big Stook would stand out in the open, firing his Bren gun at them from his shoulder. I could imagine him doing it, too. We became friends in Ballarat and then again once the war had finished.

MT laid out a luscious buffet meal in the dining area of her apartment. I offered to help her, but she insisted I mingle with the crowd instead. In the few minutes she was away I was given two invitations: the first from Kirsti, who asked me to a dinner party. She seemed full of fun and I accepted straightaway. Then Rhonda, who had been making eye contact with me, asked me to a Sunday afternoon party. There were two more invitations later that evening, from Annie and Isobel. Anticipating this, I decided not to get too carried away because I was sure I wanted to spend more time with MT.

I explained to Annie and Isobel, separately of course, that I would have to check with the depot before I could confirm. They were disappointed, but I asked for their phone numbers and offered to call them as soon as I knew the score. That seemed to reassure them, but they made me promise that I'd ring.

MT's food was lovely and I complimented her on it. Pleased no end, she wrapped her arms around me and said, 'Brian, I have all sorts of talents.'

'I bet you have,' I said.

Someone put 'I'm Beginning To See The Light' on the gramophone. People began to shuffle and dance. Others came over to quiz me, because I was the new arrival in town.

They were the same old questions. What does a commando do? Tell us about New Guinea, and so on. But I was an old hand at this now and my strategy went like clockwork. 'Of course,' I added, 'you'll all be able to see *Assault on Salamaua* at the theatre and that'll answer most of your questions, because it's basically about our commando unit.'

Now the gramophone was belting out 'Sweet Georgia Brown'. That sounded pretty good to me and I had a dance with MT. We were all enjoying ourselves. The buffet had taken a hammering, but MT had plenty of food in reserve. People didn't seem to be as worried about rationing here.

The party started to wind down by early morning. The crowd thanked MT as they left, but she said to me, 'Don't you dare leave, Brian.'

'If you say so,' I said.

My four propositioners also farewelled me, each one giving me a hug and whispering, 'See you soon, Brian.'

As the stragglers left they eyed me as if they were thinking, Why isn't he going as well? Maybe it was just my imagination. Anyway, I simply gave them my best smile, said nothing and nursed my drink.

Finally we were alone. I looked at MT and said, 'What do we do now – clean up?'

'Of course not, silly. Time's too valuable. I've got a lady coming in the morning to do all that.' She wrapped her arms around me. 'Let's go to bed. I've been waiting all night.'

As she dragged me into her bedroom I didn't protest. Apparently there wasn't even time for us to clean our teeth. The bedroom was very feminine, with every available surface covered in furry toy animals, dolls and ornaments. MT heaved the bedclothes upwards and sent bunnies and dolls flying everywhere. We hit the sheets and were at each other, while dozens of tiny glass-bead eyes watched from the floor.

Later that night I went to the bathroom. When I got back I couldn't help but gaze in admiration at MT stretched out on her bed. She didn't have Janet's suntan or Diet's Betty Grable body, but she was beautiful. We woke to daylight and the sound of dishes rattling in the area where the party had been. 'That'll be Bonny, cleaning up the mess,' said MT. 'I'd better get up and see her. But not yet.' She giggled and we grabbed each other again.

Finally she went out to see Bonny and came back with a toothbrush for me. 'That's yours, Brian, but I'll keep it here for you. Can we do it all again soon, please?'

We showered and had something to eat after Bonny had looked me over and said hello. By now it was getting on in the afternoon and I was due back at the convalescent depot. I promised I'd phone and we kissed goodbye.

A couple of days later I was felled with a big bang and lugged off to the general hospital, because they'd decided that I was too crook for the camp hospital. Of course, I knew nothing of this for some time.

A kind Red Cross lady, Merle, phoned MT, Kirsti, Rhonda, Annie and Isobel for me. I also asked her to contact my parents and give them a very light appraisal of my problem.

MT visited me and we planned to do something together over Christmas, which was fast approaching. But just as my health began to improve another bang hit me and I was out of it for ages again. It looked like Christmas would be long gone before I was out of hospital.

When I was finally allowed to leave, I'd lost weight and felt weak. Back at the convalescent depot they told me I had to take things quietly for some time, but what the hell.

First on my list was MT. When I phoned she still seemed more than interested in our association, so I made arrangements to see her. Then I rang the four other ladies and also Marion, who had phoned Lieutenant Colonel Baker because she wanted me to go to her party. In hospital I'd met another young lady with the AMWAS (Australian Medical Women's Auxiliary Services). Her name was Dulcie, but she was far too lovely to have a name like Dulcie, so I asked for her second name. 'Beryl,' she said, so I decided to call her Dulcie Beryl. It better suited someone with her beauty and she liked it, so there was no problem. Then there was Pat, the police superintendent's daughter.

I was soon extremely busy. Making sure these arrangements didn't conflict and keeping everyone happy was almost a full-time job. Often I had to make an afternoon meeting, followed by an evening date somewhere else. It was just as well that I was unable to work and leave was freely available. Whenever a bang put me out of action, Merle helped by ringing them all for me. And she had great fun doing it.

Life continued in this way for the next couple of months. Then in March 1944, a catastrophe struck. The army medical board downgraded my medical category from A1 to B2. This meant that I was no longer fit for active service. I was devastated, although realistically I should've expected it. They told me I'd just have to face up to things. Not only was I not going back to my Independent Company, I was now ineligible for OCTU (officer training) irrespective of George's recommendations.

Over the next couple of days I came to two decisions. First, there was no future whatsoever for me in the army (how wrong I was!). And second, if I stayed in Ballarat I'd either drink myself or fuck myself to death, or both. I didn't want to become a civilian while the war was still on, even though I knew I could probably get a discharge on medical grounds. And I didn't want to become an army 'base wallah', doing some mundane office job as one of those six or seven soldiers supporting each man who did the fighting. Of course, being in Australia was better than the bloody jungle, but the war had to be fought and I strongly felt I wanted to be back there. The fighting soldiers took great pride in their achievements and I wanted to be at the front lines with them.

My only chance was the navy or the air force – if I could talk my way round my medical history. The navy didn't appeal to me, and if I joined the air force it had to be as a pilot. How fussy could a sick person get?

So the next day I went to the RAAF recruiting office in Ballarat. I met MT at Craig's afterwards but kept the application form hidden. She said I wasn't my usual bright self, but I managed to avoid an explanation. Silently breathing a sigh of relief, I realised I had to smarten myself up in the future, because I didn't want to tell MT or any of the others what I was up to. Not knowing what the future held, I thought it was pointless upsetting our relationship unnecessarily. I was itching to get back home and complete the RAAF documents. Soon MT had to leave me to meet some friends in town, so we arranged to spend the weekend at her place. Gleefully, I took a tram back to the convalescent depot.

The application form included only one troublesome question: 'Have you ever had malaria?' Thinking it pretty stupid to tell an outright lie, I wrote 'yes', but conveniently forgot to provide the required explanation in the space next to it. If they queried me I planned to talk my way out of it. Sure enough, when I lodged my application the following day the clerk noticed my omission.

'Sorry,' I said, reaching for a pen, 'I must have missed it.'

He was somewhat impatient. 'Well, you haven't got malaria now, have you?'

'No,' I answered, in all honesty.

'Very well. You'll hear from the RAAF in due course.' He scribbled something in the space and I heard no more about it.

Making the application lifted a huge load off my mind. It was a relief to have done something constructive about my predicament. At Craig's, Nancy and others asked what I was looking so smug about, but I didn't tell. I raised my glass and said, 'To life. Life's for living. Good luck.' No one had any idea what I was talking about. They probably thought I'd gone nuts, but at least they smiled.

I spent the next weekend having a marvellous time with MT. Then, about a week later, Lieutenant Colonel Baker told me I was going back to Heidelberg Military Hospital, where some new treatments might be of help to me. He added that he knew I'd made a few local commitments. 'How long would it take you to say all your goodbyes and clean your slate?'

I asked if a week would be okay.

'Right,' he said. 'Let's say we'll send you back in seven days.'

'Is there any likelihood I'll be coming back?'

'I very much doubt it.'

It was very kind and decent of him to give me seven days. MT headed the list of people I wanted to contact before I left, with Dulcie Beryl second.

'Well, the weekend's all mine,' MT said when I rang with the news. 'Come to my place.' No arguments there. Then I arranged to meet Dulcie Beryl one night during the week.

Unfortunately I had more goodbyes to say than days available. Even with separate afternoon and evening arrangements, there just wasn't time to see all the other ladies. So I rang Marion, Annie, Kirsti, Rhonda, Isobel and Pat to tell them about my orders to return to Melbourne. 'They haven't given me enough time to see you,' I told them, 'but I just had to ring and say goodbye and thank you for the wonderful times we had together.'

Their reactions varied, of course, but they all said they'd miss me. They also seemed to have the impression that I'd probably be back and I forgot to correct them. They were lovely people and I'd miss them all. I also made sure I said goodbye to Nancy at Craig's Hotel and Merle, my Red Cross friend.

Dulcie Beryl's parents lived in Melbourne. She said she would see me when she came down and that I could spend the weekend with her. I nodded, but I had my doubts about it.

At MT's place we had our usual fabulous weekend in and out of bed, enjoying good food and grog and lying in the sun. When it came to an end, she told me very emotionally, 'I'll miss you, Brian. But I know that we'll be together again. I just feel it.'

Apart from Dulcie Beryl, I never saw any of them again. When Lieutenant Colonel Baker said goodbye he asked with a smile whether I had cleaned my slate. I told him I had and thanked him for looking after me. That was the kind of place the convalescent depot was.

I've never been back to Ballarat, but I think about it a great deal and have many fond memories. It was a wonderful town when I was there.

11

Cancelled Flight

Heidelberg Military Hospital hadn't changed at all in four months. Dr Mike Gordon, Sandra, Little One and Diet all greeted me warmly and asked me about Ballarat and I smiled and said that it had been fine.

Dr Mike looked me over. 'Your medical condition is about the same, but you look slightly better,' he told me. Little One said that the boss wanted me back at the radio station.

I phoned my parents to tell them I was back in Melbourne. They were pleased to hear from me, but extremely worried that there was still no news of my brother. There was nothing they could do and that made it far worse.

I also rang lovely Janet. She was surprised to hear from me and noticeably cooler. The reason soon came out: she had a new 'friend'. This was no surprise. I hardly expected her to stay at home twiddling her thumbs for four months, and of course I hadn't even had the decency to keep in touch with her while I was away. I was going to miss her, but life moved on and the recent past became history.

A couple of days later a big bang put me out of action for ten days or more. Dr Mike tried some new medication. He reckoned the attacks would reduce in severity from now on and I hoped to hell he was right. But otherwise life at the Heidelberg Military Hospital returned to the old routine. Back at the radio station there were liaisons once again with Little One and Diet in the private nook. I also found myself another lovely young lady to keep me company. Pam was a nursing friend of Sandra's and just beautiful. Dulcie Beryl visited me a couple of times when she was in Melbourne. She was more serious than the other girls, who seemed totally happy-go-lucky. My next bang arrived and although I completely lost it, according to Dr Mike it wasn't quite as bad as the time before. He was very pleased with the result, but cynically I suspected that the bangs were merely diminishing with time, rather than because of the treatment.

A much milder bang followed. A couple of weeks later Dr Mike told me I was being posted to G Branch at Victoria Barracks, Melbourne, although I wasn't a hundred per cent fit. That's for sure, I thought. After all I was still medically graded B2. Another attack would see me straight back in hospital. Dr Mike gave me ample supplies of the new medication, and showed me how to increase my dose without side effects if I felt a bang coming on. If it didn't work I was to go to hospital immediately.

He said goodbye and I thanked him for looking after me. I had a fond farewell with Sandra and separate, very fond, farewells with Little One, Diet and Pam.

On the 9th of June 1944 I reported to Victoria Barracks and was sent on to the Albert Park Barracks nearby, where I was billeted and told to report for duty the next day. Albert Park Barracks was a sprawling conglomeration of mainly prefabricated huts, a mixture of offices and accommodation. I was allocated a small partitioned section in one hut, with a camp bed and a clothes locker. It was not as comfortable as the hospital, but excellent accommodation compared with anything offered by commando life in the field.

I reported back the next day. Everyone was smartly dressed, looked very important and called their superiors 'sir' – which for me meant almost everyone. There was little restriction as long as I reported for work on time and stayed until the end of the day. I was issued with a pass and came and went as I pleased.

There were very few returned soldiers at the barracks, apart from WW1 veterans, and I was surprised to find myself frequently asked my opinion from a soldier's perspective. Anyway, here I was, one of the six or seven soldiers working behind the scenes for every fighting soldier in the field. This was what it had come to.

Shortly afterwards, there was good news from the RAAF. My medical and interview had been arranged. I took several days leave to attend them and on the 27th of June the RAAF advised that my application had been successful. They had classified me medically A1 and accepted me as aircrew, pilot only. I was delighted to have my escape from the barracks confirmed in under three weeks.

The main hurdle in going from one service to another was waiting for the administrative bumf. You couldn't just transfer; you had to actually be discharged from one service and then had to enlist in the other. The army and air force didn't seem to liaise much on such matters – my army medical records were not shown to the RAAF and it was just as well.

By now I'd noticed that a couple of extra slugs of Dr Mike's new medication seemed to stop a bang coming on, so I decided to hoard as much of the stuff as I could. I didn't get much reaction from my parents to my news. I don't think they wanted their sons in any of the services, although I knew they were proud that we were. They merely said, 'If that makes you happy, good.'

A fortnight later, still waiting at the barracks for my discharge, I had a visit from someone important. I knew he was important because he obtained a private office to see me. He was a captain, very fit, and about six feet six tall. He wore parachute wings and the colour patch of an AIF Infantry Battalion returned from the Middle East.

He shook hands and smiled. 'Hello, Brian. I'm Tony Gluth. Sit down, please. You were hard to find,' he said. 'What are you doing here?'

I told him my sad story.

'I can take you out of here now, if you like.'

I asked him how. 'Unfortunately,' he said, 'I'm not permitted to say too much before you're with our organisation. Have you heard of SOA?'

'No.'

'Special Operations Australia,' he said. 'We wage clandestine war in Japanese-occupied territory. I can't tell you more unless you join us. You must also sign an acknowledgement that binds you in accordance with the Official Secrets Act.'

'I did that when I joined the commandos.'

'Well, you'd have to do it again before I could tell you more.'

'But what about my B2 medical category?'

'Oh, come on, Brian. That's no problem. You ought to know that. After all, you're B2 in the army and A1 in the RAAF, aren't you? If you want to do something, there's always a way.'

'Yes, but why me?'

'George Warfe told me to get you. He reckons you're ideal for our type of operation.'

I smiled. 'How is George?'

'He's fine. Well, what do you think?'

'If you'd asked me two weeks ago, I'd have jumped at it, but I'm in the RAAF now. Pilots wear clean clothes and shower regularly. They shoot planes down or do some strafing and then go home for a nice meal, a few drinks and maybe see a bird or two. I'm sorry, but I think that's for me.'

'Well, here's a phone number if you change your mind. You can ring this number twenty-four hours a day. If I'm not there leave a message for me and I'll arrange for you to be with us in twenty-four hours. No bullshit. Now let's go and have a drink.'

Gluth had known George in the Middle East and was keen to find out what I'd done with him. I talked a bit about New Guinea over a few pleasant drinks. Tony was glad to hear about it. 'It doesn't surprise me,' he said. 'George was always a real tiger.'

When it was time to go our separate ways, he shook my hand. 'I hope I hear from you, Brian. Good luck.'

The bumf finally ran its course by the 21st of July, when I was sent orders to report to Camp Pell for my discharge. My enlistment in the RAAF commenced the following day. A couple of days later I was issued with a uniform, a whole lot of gear and I was hustled off to the Air Force base at Point Cook outside Melbourne.

No one else in my intake of aircrew trainees had prior military experience. When the instructors realised this, I was spared rookie training and attached to an intake that had already done it, but I was still the only returned soldier in the group.

There wasn't much to do at Point Cook except train, but it was what I was there to do. I looked forward to becoming a pilot, but on the 25th of August, only thirty-four days into my RAAF career, all aircrew training was suspended until further notice.

We were asked to change our mustering status to general duties or ground crew. I was paraded before the Commanding Officer, who wasn't too bad a bloke. He would have liked me to switch to ground crew, but knew I was for aircrew only and had no power to change my status. 'I know how disappointed you must be,' he said. 'What do you want to do?'

Tony Gluth's offer sprang to mind. I told him about SOA approaching me just before I joined the RAAF, and said I'd like to find out if they still wanted me.

He pushed the phone across his desk. 'Give them a ring.'

When Tony Gluth came on the line he didn't waste any time. 'Are you sure you want to join us?'

'Positive,' I said.

'I'll have you here in a couple of days.' Where 'here' was I couldn't even guess. 'Are you with the CO now?'

'Yes.'

'Would you let me speak to him?'

I passed the phone over and the two of them had quite a conversation. The CO finally put down the phone and said, 'We were talking about a few people we both knew in the Middle East. They'll be sending a signal ordering you back. You'll just have to wait.'

This time, however, there was no bumf at all. The very next day I was sent to RAAF headquarters in Melbourne for discharge. The day after that, the 28th of August, I reported to the army at Royal Park in full RAAF uniform to re-enlist in the AIF.

12

Welcome to Z Special Unit

In early 1942, when the Japanese were advancing relentlessly towards Australia, General Blamey proposed an initiative similar to that of the British Special Operations Executive, which had caused the Germans big trouble in occupied Europe. MacArthur, the overall South-West Pacific Area Commander-in-Chief, approved and Special Operations Australia was formed.

The idea was to insert specially selected people into Japanese occupied territories, their brief to create extreme mayhem, working with the local population as much as possible. Operatives were to subvert local co-operation with the Japanese, arm and train locals in guerrilla warfare and obtain their assistance with sabotage, ambush and kidnappings.

Circumstances in the Pacific were very different from those in Europe. Distances were far greater, for starters. In Europe if you spoke the right language you could pass for a local, but in the Pacific theatre a white face created instant suspicion, no matter how fluent you were. And if anything went wrong behind enemy lines, there was little hope of rescue.

For security reasons SOA was given the cover name of IASD or ISD (Inter-allied Services Department). This was later changed to SRD (Services Reconnaissance Department). A special holding unit was set up to administer Australian SRD personnel. This was called Z Special Unit, and it is by this name that SOA or SRD is better known.

On the 29th of August, the day after my re-enlistment, I went to see Tony Gluth at Harbury, a beautiful old mansion in South Yarra. It was one of Z Special Unit's secret bases. He appeared shortly and led me into a large day room that had been converted to an office.

We had a laugh about the roundabout way I had finally arrived. 'You people must have an awful lot of clout,' I said.

He answered very seriously, 'Brian, Special Operations Australia has a tremendous amount of clout.'

He explained that Z Special Unit was a bit like the Air Force in that air crew did the fighting while ground crew looked after them. Z Special Unit had operatives to do the fieldwork and non-operatives to keep them there.

'You'll be an operative, Brian. I'm operative as well, but I'm also in planning. I'll fill you in more later, but for now tell me about yourself. I know a fair bit about you, but I'd like to hear in your own words just how experienced you are.'

I outlined my commando training at Foster, my instructing career at Canungra, and my reversion to private to join the 2/3 Australian Independent Company. He interrupted at that point. 'Shit, you reverted to private?'

I went on with my story. I told him how my recommendation for a commission fell apart when I was categorised medically B2. Then I told him about some of the escapades George had sent me on in New Guinea, and why I declined to join the 58/59 Battalion with him. I told him I had a great dislike for the Japanese, and why. Finally I said, 'I must have done something right because I'm still in one piece.'

'Yes,' he said. 'George said you'd had more experience than most of us.' I felt very flattered and shut up. 'Well, you won't have any trouble fitting in with our type of operations. But first there's the paperwork.'

Then it was sign this, sign that, sign the Official Secrets Act again. 'I have to attach a brief summary of our conversation and what you've told me about yourself for other people to read. Is that okay?'

'Of course,' I said.

'Good. Welcome to Z Special Unit. You'll find we talk very little about it; in fact I wear my old unit's colour patches and you should do the same. You'll also find we don't talk about our operations – past or future. If you don't know what someone else is doing, you can't give any information away. Now I realise you know all about jungle warfare, but there are other things you need to learn. All sorts of things.'

He passed me a slip of paper. 'This telephone number will be answered twenty-four hours a day. If anyone pulls you up don't bother with lengthy explanations, just tell them to ring this number and any problem will be sorted out quickly.'

I kept nodding my head and saying 'yes', or 'right', acquiescing in everything he said.

'There's a couple of people I'd like you to meet from our planning section,' he continued. 'Stay here. I won't show you around the building. What you don't see you don't know about. It's better that way.'

A few minutes later he was back with a Major Dick Cardew and a Major Bingham. They greeted me affably and said they'd heard a bit about me. Later I learned Cardew was a Z Special Unit operative and Bingham was an Englishman who had been with the British SOE in German-occupied Holland.

All they wanted was just to look me over. I laughed and said this to Tony. He laughed back, saying, 'Does that worry you?'

We chatted a bit longer before Tony decided we'd done enough for one day. He asked me to come back the next morning at ten. 'By then we'll have worked out what to do with you.'

I left Harbury with an open-ended pass, so I didn't have to report anywhere else at any time. The Botanical Hotel was just down the road. I felt like a drink or two, but I wasn't in the mood to evade questions from my father's mates about what I'd been up to. So I found another pub on my way back to the barracks.

The next day Tony Gluth asked me if I'd ever heard of Fraser Island. It had become a Z Special Unit base, host to a variety of specialist training courses.

'You'll learn a few new tricks there, I assure you,' he said. 'But there's something I want to warn you about. You'll find quite a strange mixture of people there, untrained and inexperienced by your standards, but I don't want that to put you off. You'll meet service people who have volunteered for hazardous operations without having been overseas or seen any fighting. A lot of these are from the Australian Armoured Division. They're highly skilled in their own way, but untried in jungle combat. You'll also meet commandos like yourself.'

I mentioned Dr Mike's special medication for my malaria. Unknown to anyone else, I had continued to have a few minor attacks, but they were becoming less powerful. I asked Tony about getting a further supply without creating a fuss. 'No problem,' he said. 'I'll arrange it.' And he did.

Everything was ready for me: relevant passes, food and travel vouchers, transport bookings. I was to fly to Brisbane the following morning, take a train north to Maryborough and then a boat across to Fraser Island.

Tony handed me a folder with all the travel documents and asked whether I had any questions.

'No, but thank you very much for the help that you've given me. I think I'll just play it by ear and find out as I go along.'

'That sounds like a good idea,' he said. 'Now, how about a drink?'

I told him about my association with the Botanical, so we went to the Fawkner instead and had a very interesting chat about our mutual friend George Warfe, New Guinea, the Middle East and so on. Tony had done two or three operations with Z Special Unit. 'But I won't tell you about that, Brian,' he said with a smile.

At length we parted, wishing each other the best of luck. It was still early, so I stopped off at another hotel. I had a good look through my travel documents and they were certainly detailed, marked high priority everywhere. I'd never seen anything like it.

If I needed any more proof of Z Special Unit's clout, I got it the next morning at the aerodrome, where I was to board a military plane for the flight to Brisbane, via Sydney. I checked in and was waiting with other passengers when up raced a full-blown colonel, resplendent in red staff trimmings, his aide scurrying close behind. He announced that he needed to go to Sydney urgently but didn't have a booking.

When he was told there was no passenger space left, he declared matter-of-factly that someone would just have to be put off the plane. He was told it wasn't possible.

'We'll see about that,' he said, eyeing the passengers until he spotted me, standing there with no badges of rank. 'What about him? Surely he can wait for another plane.'

'I'm sorry, sir,' said the officer in charge. 'That man has high priority.'

'High priority!' the colonel scoffed. 'What's *his* high priority?'

He strode across to me, pointing his finger. 'What's your high priority, soldier?'

I stood politely to attention, but I didn't salute. Stuff him. Just to annoy him I said, 'Beg your pardon, sir?'

He barked out his question again, but this time the pointing finger shook slightly.

'I'm not at liberty to say, sir,' I said. 'But if you ring this number everything will be explained.' Anticipating exactly this kind of trouble, I had already made up six little cards with Tony Gluth's number on them.

'There's no name written here. Who will I be speaking with?'

'Just whoever answers the phone, sir,' I said, careful to sound extremely polite this time.

The colonel only got angrier. 'You're not trying to be smart and be insubordinate, are you, soldier?'

'No, sir. I have no reason to do that.'

'What's your name, soldier?'

'Brian Walpole, sir,' I said, now with my best *get stuffed* intonation.

He went off with the phone number and his aide in tow, muttering, 'We'll see about this. I'll fix that little so-and-so.' The other passengers smiled behind his back. When some of them asked me what it was all about, I just said they'd have to ask the colonel. Not that they could, because he didn't get on the plane. But that was his problem, not mine. I learnt one thing, though: flying beat the hell out of travelling by troop train.

It took three days to get to Maryborough, which was pretty fast, considering wartime circumstances. Tony Blair of Z Special Unit ferried me across to Fraser Island in an old beaten-up landing barge. It was a lovely place, with a wonderful climate, golden beaches and a great variety of wildlife, including dingoes. Today it's a tourist paradise, but there were no holidaymakers in 1944. It was a restricted area and the only visitors had a very different purpose.

Most of the civilians Tony Gluth had warned me about were Englishmen who had been working in the southwest Pacific ahead of the Japanese invasion, but had shot through before the Japs arrived. Perhaps I should say 'employed' instead of 'working', as I'm sure none of them had done much work themselves; the local people did it all for them. I call them 'civilians' because even though they were now in the army with some kind of rank to accompany the uniform, the ones I met had little training and acted as though they were still civilians.

On paper the plan to use their talents made a lot of sense. They knew parts of Japanese-occupied territory extremely well, spoke the local languages and had personal interests in the country the Japanese had taken over. Their local knowledge supposedly made them ideal to insert into the regions they knew best as support for the trained operatives. It's not my place to say how valuable other operatives found these people. But the two I worked with in Borneo were way out of their depth and, even worse, the local population disliked them intensely.

Tony Gluth was true to his word. I was not asked to learn anything I already knew. The physical and unarmed combat training was mostly pussycat stuff compared with commando training. But I pushed myself physically, knowing how important it was to get into top shape. I didn't quite reach the peak of fitness I'd had in my commando days, but after what had transpired that was probably an impossible goal. Dr Mike's medication kept my bangs away, but when extending myself physically I sometimes had to press my hand over my spleen, which had become enlarged by the malaria. In time it would shrink back to normal.

Still, there were many new experiences. I took great interest in learning a couple of languages and became fairly fluent in Malay. Some of the explosives were new to me, such as PHE (Plastic High Explosive), which was like plasticine and only needed to be moulded around whatever was to be blown up. It was light in weight, very powerful and safe to handle as well because it didn't explode until a detonator was inserted and activated. Even setting it on fire or firing bullets into it wouldn't make it explode.

Other weapons I hadn't encountered before included the Sten submachine gun and the Wellrod pistol. Both came with silencers and fired with just a *phut* sound. They were slightly heavier than their conventional counterparts and their obvious advantages were balanced by a slight loss in accuracy and firepower efficiency. They were also susceptible to stoppages from a bit of mud in the parts.

The Australian-made Owen submachinegun was a beauty, especially for jungle fighting. With very few working parts, stoppages were rare – even when we were working in mud and water. It was quite different from my old friend the Tommy gun. It had a slim magazine, which held a lot of 9mm bullets.

I was also greatly taken with the Browning automatic pistol. It held fourteen bullets – a lot for a pistol – and could fire on either automatic or single-shot. The 9mm ammunition was the same as for the Owen gun, which was convenient, and much lighter than the .45 calibre stuff I'd lugged around New Guinea for my Tommy Gun and Colt.

I still had my commando knuckleduster knife, now complemented by a very neat stiletto. And I decided I wanted a Bren gun too, as long as I could find someone to haul it for me. This accurate and devastating light machinegun fired a heavier bullet, .303 calibre, but was difficult to carry if you had to run.

Something else I learnt on Fraser Island was how to use folboats. These two-man canoes consisted of a black rubberised canvas skin held in shape by lightweight pliable struts, which slotted together to make the frame. There were four paddles, two of which fitted together to give each canoeist a double-bladed paddle. Otherwise two could be stored in the canoe as spares.

A folboat sat very low in the water. It moved silently and was almost invisible from a short distance, even in daylight. It was ideal for short and long-range water reconnaissance. You could get right under the enemy's nose. It dismantled into two packs, one for the skin and one for the struts, so the two canoeists could each carry one pack as well as his usual gear.

It didn't take long to gain confidence in handling these boats, even in rough water, because it was easy to flip them upright if they capsized. Twice during training I used them on three-day live-off-the-land exercises, which involved fossicking for food on small uninhabited islands or atolls.

Once I shot a swan while it was in flight and had a hell of a job finding it in the scrub. When I finally cooked it over an open fire, feeling utterly famished, it was so stringy and tough that it was barely edible. Later, on a small desolate island, I walked right up to a herd of wild goats who just stood there and looked at me, so trusting and innocent. Apologising to this poor little kid, I shot it between the eyes while the rest of the family bolted. It made a beautiful meal, but I felt a real shit. Another casualty of the war, I told myself.

Folboats were used to sink ships. We practised getting alongside targets and lowering limpet mines about six feet below the water line, using a device that looked like a broom handle. A magnet then held the mine against the hull until the timing device set it off.

After I'd learnt all I could at Fraser Island, it was off to Leyburn RAAF Base for parachute jumping. What a laugh, I thought, I've only just left the RAAF! I must admit to having been a bit nervous on the day of my first jump, but more experienced hands assured me it was a piece of cake.

'Watch the red and green lights,' my instructor said. 'And when I say go, you go.'

Suddenly the moment had arrived and I heard him scream the signal to go. Out I went, into a new world. My nerves vanished and I looked around in wonder. I could see for miles in every direction. It was just me and this eerie quiet, broken only by the hiss of passing air and the flapping of my parachute.

I had a great landing, gently hitting the ground on the run with no forward roll necessary.

Beginner's luck, probably. Over the next couple of days I made three more jumps. None was as copybook as that first effort, but I won my parachutist's wings and was whisked off to Melbourne, priority travel again. By now I was feeling pretty good, both physically and mentally, and had a chuckle about how worried that B2 medical status had had me only a short time before. It's truly amazing how you can change things if you are determined enough.

Back in Melbourne I stayed with my parents. They were pleased to see me and thought I looked well, but I wasn't able to say much about what I'd been doing. They wanted to know how I'd managed to move from the army to the RAAF and then back to the army, but I just said, 'Well I'm here and that's the main thing' and left it at that. There was still no word of Denis. They asked me about the parachute wings and I was able to say with a grin, 'That's for jumping out of a plane.'

The next morning I kept my appointment with Tony Gluth. He remarked that I looked much better, then got down to business and said I was going to Western Australia.

'This is absolutely top secret. We want to train you to operate a one-man submarine. No one knows about this and you are to mention it to no one. Good luck.'

The usual documents were ready and I was to leave the next day. Calling into the Fawkner for a quiet drink, I browsed through the folder and found that I was going to Garden Island, offshore just south of Fremantle.

Saying goodbye to my parents wasn't easy. All I could say was that I was going to Western Australia and I tried to distract them with other topics. I hated having to confuse them, but I couldn't answer their questions honestly and there was no way I was going to tell them outright lies.

13

Sleeping Beauty

Travelling to Perth for the first time made me realise just how big Australia was. My ultimate destination was Careening Bay on Garden Island, where a campsite had been newly hacked out of the virgin bush. It was another Z Special Unit place, although here they preferred to call it SRD, which meant the same thing.

The isolation was complete. It was just a cluster of huts, sheds and tents among the ti-trees and native cypress, with a long jetty that stretched out into Careening Bay. About ten of us had arrived for the one-man submarine course. Most of them I recognised from Fraser Island, but one new face stood out clearly because he was such a loudmouth. Andy Hands was an Englishman who wore an RAF uniform boasting parachute wings and the rank of Squadron Leader. He bored us senseless with continual booming reminders that he had dropped into Albania to take the surrender of a quarter of a million people, which seemed rather a lot to me. He didn't enlighten us as to whether he had any assistance in this intrepid undertaking and none of us bothered to ask. But he kept on and on about his triumph.

The ten trainees soon became six. Two men were ruled out because they had false teeth, which were unsuitable for clenching the breathing apparatus. And then Squadron Leader Hands panicked as soon as his head went under water. He came up spluttering and waving his limbs wildly. 'I'm not going on with this!' he bellowed, stalking off. We never saw him again. Claustrophobia lost us another man, too; there was no way you could pilot a one-man sub if you couldn't handle the confined feeling of working underwater.

The one-man sub was known officially as the MSC – motor submersible canoe. We preferred to call it by its codename – Sleeping Beauty, or SB – and we came to do so almost lovingly.

Made of mild steel and aluminium, the Sleeping Beauty was about 4 metres long, 70 centimetres wide and weighed about 270 kilograms. It was propelled by a car's starter motor and powered by four standard six-volt car batteries. There were two forward speeds, half speed or full speed, and reverse. Travelling at up to 4.5 knots on the surface and 3.5 below, it had a range of some 20 kilometres or more and was unaffected by weather conditions.

The pilot's neck-to-toe suit was made of a light rubberised fabric, but you needed several woollen pullovers or longjohns underneath to keep you warm. They worked well, rather surprisingly, even if water seeped into the suit. A noseclip prevented you inhaling water or outside air and watertight goggles completed the outfit.

To breathe underwater we used a slightly modified Davis Escape Apparatus, standard for conventional submarines. This was a cylinder of pure oxygen connected by hose to a demand valve in the mouthpiece. The latter sealed around the outside of your lips to shut out seawater. Exhaled breath travelled through a protosorb canister (protosorb was a chalky type of substance) where it was purified and re-breathed with a small quantity of fresh oxygen from the cylinder. The whole unit was known as an oxygen re-breather.

We were shown firsthand how to tell if you were breathing bad air. Putting on our Davis Escape Apparatus minus the protosorb canister, we were taken for a walk with a minder on either side. After a quick burst of oxygen the cylinder was turned off and soon we had only our own unpurified air to breathe.

It wasn't long before we collapsed. The minders revived us by ripping the mouthpieces away so that fresh air hit us immediately. I have to say that the hallucinatory feeling I experienced just before I came to was absolutely fantastic. Gulping my first lungful of fresh air, still drifting in an altered state, I swung a punch at my minder, convinced that he was taking something good away from me.

The Sleeping Beauty had a rear rudder just above the propeller and a hydroplane on each side to control its depth in the water. Buoyancy was controlled by two water cylinders set alongside the pilot's legs. A dashboard in the cockpit had a depth gauge, compass and a seven-day clock, all luminous. I don't know why it was a seven-day clock. Maybe they were going cheap at the time.

The pilot sat in the Sleeping Beauty with head and shoulders protruding. People said the joystick was from a Hurricane fighter plane, but whether that was true or not, we all became adept at handling these subs and they ran beautifully.

Almost in one motion you'd start the motor, put it in reverse, adjust the hydroplanes and open the valves to allow some water into the buoyancy tanks. The Sleeping Beauty would slip backwards and submerge. Then you'd turn off the motor and adjust the buoyancy until you were suspended in the water, completely weightless. Restarting the motor, you were now free to go to wherever you wanted.

Navigation was by compass if there was a bearing to your destination, or simply by sight if you were cruising on the surface. But our favourite method was porpoising.

To porpoise, the pilot would set the hydroplanes to direct his Sleeping Beauty to the surface. When submerged, the craft's reflection was always visible on the underside of the water's surface, even at night. Then, just as the prow was about to meet this reflection, you'd direct the hydroplanes to dive. But the top of your head and eyes briefly broke the surface, virtually undetectable to an observer.

We practised night and day and learnt how to negotiate antisubmarine nets. This was simply a matter of diving to the seabed, turning off the motor and lifting the bottom of the net high enough to drag your Sleeping Beauty underneath.

One night, having completed my practice, I was walking along the floodlit jetty when I noticed one of our pilots with his Sleeping Beauty on the seabed. As he started the motor, a huge stingray, perhaps ten feet across, flipped off its sand camouflage and started to follow him. Gently flapping vast wings, it kept a short distance behind, staying right on his track.

It was a fascinating sight. Several of us watched until the man brought the Sleeping Beauty in and the ray ghosted away out of the floodlights. I asked him whether he knew that a huge female stingray had been tailing him. At first he didn't believe me, but the others confirmed it and after a while he asked, 'So how did you know it was a female stingray?'

I said, 'Well, you're not queer, are you?' We all had a good laugh.

Like the folboat, the Sleeping Beauty was useful for placing limpet mines. Many times we practised on operating, fully crewed ships and warships without ever being detected. The Sleeping Beauty was as good as invisible. Its minute motor was silent and undetectable by radar, and the oxygen re-breather created no bubble trace.

The Sleeping Beauty was a marvellous little craft and we developed great affection and respect for it, although it was far more lethal than it looked. I became a qualified Sleeping Beauty pilot, as they called us, and so in the long run I suppose I did become a pilot – even if it was in the army rather than the RAAF.

14

Mavis and the Detective

All work and no play would certainly have made Brian a dull boy, but we had a generous amount of leave from Garden Island. Rockingham, on the mainland across from Careening Bay, was a nice enough beach resort, in peacetime anyway, and I went over a couple of times but there wasn't much action. The local people were curious to know what we were doing 'over there' and we told them we were working on a new type of mobile laundry and left it at that.

Perth had far greater attractions – like Mavis, a gorgeous young lady I was lucky to meet there. We hit it off straightaway and whenever we had the time she'd show me the sights of the city.

One beautiful summer's evening she took me to King's Park. We found an isolated spot where the ground rose steeply and gave us a fantastic view across the city and the gentle curves of the Swan River. It was a great place to be on such a warm, clear night with someone so beautiful.

Spreading our rug on the lush grass, we sat down to our snacks and drinks. There was no problem making good conversation, but after a while I got a particular kind of feeling that had never let me down. I hadn't had it for a long time – in fact since I'd been in the jungle. Someone was watching us.

I listened sharply, then whispered to Mavis to keep talking while I slipped away for a few minutes. I pointed to where I was going and whispered, 'Don't worry.' She nodded coolly and kept on talking.

I slid away a short distance and did a quarter circle, then started back to where she was quite merrily chatting away to herself. Nearby a shadowy figure looked down on us, or rather, just on her. But the stupid bastard couldn't see that.

He was wielding a camera with a flash attached and some other gear was lying on the ground, but it was too dark to make out what it was. I was dirty on this character for whatever he thought he was doing or had been doing up till now. Luckily my jungle training hadn't left me.

I jumped him hard, commando style. I had been taught thoroughly and had learnt well. It flashed through my mind that it would be easy to kill him, but I had no intention of doing that. Putting him in a deathlock, I kicked his legs from under him. He tried to speak but couldn't.

'Try anything funny and I'll break your bloody neck,' I whispered in his ear, giving him a solid knock in the bum with my knee for good measure.

'Please let me go,' he spluttered, almost crying. Among his gear I saw a bag and a large torch.

'It's all right,' I called to Mavis. 'Come and see what I've got. This maggot was snooping around with his camera, trying to take some pictures.'

Mavis came over, picked up the torch and shone it on a pale and rather frightened face.

'You're going to answer a few questions,' I told him. 'Try to be smart and you'll be sorry. Understand?' He nodded, so I dropped him to the ground, while Mavis kept the torch on him.

It turned out he was a private investigator named Alfred R Sleep. I suppressed a laugh, thinking how poorly he measured up to his intrepid fictional counterparts. If Perth had a Philip Marlowe or Sam Spade, he certainly wasn't in King's Park that night.

'I know that name,' Mavis said. 'The creep's always in the papers giving evidence in some divorce hearing.'

I gave him a quick nudge. He admitted he was on a case, but had made a mistake. 'You made a hell of a mistake,' I interrupted. 'What's the case?'

'That's confidential,' he said.

Another nudge revealed that a certain John S had retained him to gather evidence that his wife Annette was having it off with someone in the army. I asked whether he had any photos of this Annette and the soldier and again he said, 'That's confidential.'

My next nudge in his ribs was a bit more enthusiastic. He pulled a file from his bag and in the torchlight we saw photographs of a man and woman, with notes about their personal particulars.

'These photos don't look anything like us. Even the descriptions don't fit. What sort of a private investigator are you?'

'I made a mistake,' he mumbled.

'I'd like you to offer to give these to me,' I told him.

'Why would I do that?'

'Because I know you'd like to.' *Nudge.*

'Uh, would you like to take these papers with you? You can keep them if you like,' he said.

'Thanks very much, Alfred,' I said. 'Very decent of you.'

'But why do you want them?'

'Because I'm going to contact Annette and tell her what you and her husband are up to.'

'Oh, no. Don't do that.'

We weren't going to learn any more and I'd obviously frightened the life out of him, so I let him go after making him apologise to Mavis. It only took another couple of nudges. Mavis bit back a smile as he mumbled his regrets. Then I thought of something else.

'Why aren't you in one of the services?' I said.

'Because I'm medically unfit,' he almost whined.

'You can beat that if you really want to. Trust me, I know. Now piss off!' I said.

He snatched up his gear and, looking at me sideways, scuttled off into the darkness like a big cockroach. I put my arms around Mavis and said, 'You were marvellous, darling. So calm. You didn't appear frightened or worried at all.'

She just laughed. 'Brian, I've got a wonderful idea. Let's go back to my office and have a couple of drinks in peace and quiet.'

Mavis was the personal assistant to the head of an insurance firm with offices in the centre of town. It was a plush set-up: a grandly decorated suite with kitchenette, bathroom, toilet, refrigerated bar and large comfortable-looking divans.

'The boss does a lot of entertaining here,' she explained. 'Sometimes I help; it's part of my job.' Then she smiled. 'And, no, we're not having it on together. He's happily married. I'm sure he wouldn't mind if he knew we were here drinking his grog. He's that sort of person. In fact he'd probably like to meet you.'

We turned on the radio and danced to 'The Dark Town Strutters Ball'. My hobnailed boots must have helped raise the pile on the carpet a bit. Then we lay back on a divan, finished our drinks and attacked each other passionately. We romped away for what seemed like hours.

'You'd better come home with me, Brian,' Mavis said at last, 'but I've got to be back here to work in the morning.'

'Darling, I'm in your hands.'

And so Mavis took good care of me, but we didn't get much rest.

The next day I arranged to meet her during her lunch break. I tracked down Annette after trying a couple of numbers in Sleep's dossier. At first she was outraged, but calmed down a bit when I said I only wanted to warn her to be on her guard. I told her she looked like a very nice lady in her photo and that I liked helping nice ladies. She laughed and said she'd like to meet me. I said, 'No, but you look after yourself.'

Over lunch Mavis had a good laugh about my conversation with Annette, but she also had more serious things to say. 'Brian, I'm very fond of you, but I'm also a realist. I know nothing long term will come from our relationship. You beat about the bush and can't tell me the real reason you're in Western Australia. That's fair enough, but I've decided I'm not going to become any fonder of you than I am. I'll miss you greatly when you go.'

I took her hand and told her how lovely I thought she was and she rewarded me with her beautiful smile.

After that, there were more nighttime excursions to the office and a few daytime ones on weekends as well. But it all came to a sudden halt when the course at Careening Bay finished. Mavis was a beautiful person in every possible way and our parting was very sad. We'd had a wonderful time together and had been good for each other and I thought about her all the way back to Melbourne. But I never saw or heard from her again.

15

Before the Operation

I had a feeling that I'd be going off on a job soon. Of course, to minimise the leakage of information, we weren't told about operations in advance or where we were going. But our training had covered just about every contingency and I was now in very good nick. I had even been instructed, by way of charts and diagrams, how to remove my own appendix if I had to.

My parents were glad that I seemed to have beaten the malaria, but they knew not to ask about my upcoming mission. I did tell them about Mavis and even the encounter with Alfred R Sleep, which raised a laugh. My mother played me a few songs on her piano including 'Mississippi Mud' and 'The Organ Grinder's Blues', one of my favourites.

Janet had news for me when I rang her: she was now 'bespoken'. 'Don't worry,' I said, 'It won't worry me if you'd still like to come out with me.' But she didn't want to. She was very clucky about her 'bespoken' and that was the end of it.

Dulcie Beryl, however, had phoned my parents to ask after me while I'd been away. We saw each other several times and everything went extremely well. She invited me home to meet her family and stay the night and I did. But when I asked her, 'Whose bedroom – yours or mine?', she was quite emphatic. 'Oh no, Brian. Not at home.'

Her family thought I was a very nice person, apparently, and her father in particular was impressed.

'What do you think about us having a closer relationship?' she asked the following day.

I thought I'd better clarify at once what she had in mind. I didn't mind making the odd promise to get my own way, but I had no intention of tying myself down. Using Janet's old-fashioned phrase, I said, 'Do you mean become bespoken?'

Quick as a flash she said yes. I explained there was no way in the world I could do it, because my future was so uncertain. 'It'd be completely unfair to a beautiful person like you,' I said.

She was not at all happy with that, so I backed off. It was a pity; I liked her very much. But the next time she rang my parents they very politely told her I'd gone away 'somewhere' – and of course I had.

While I was in Melbourne I also bumped into a fellow commando from New Guinea, a specialist sniper named Noel. We'd never been particularly close, but all commandos had something in common. During the tortured Double Mountain climb we thought we'd reached the top, only to find another peak above us. There were no Japs about, but we didn't know that at the time. We were absolutely fucked, that's the only way to describe it, and Noel was so disgusted he heaved his rifle down the mountainside. Then he had to clamber down to retrieve it, which only made even more work for him.

Anyway, Noel asked me along to a party in Malvern. The hostess was a lady named Alexandria. 'Call me Alex,' she said. Her house had a small ballroom and a busy corner bar. People danced as the gramophone screamed out 'At the Jazz Band Ball'. Alex introduced me to various people, fixed me a drink and then called over a beautiful lady.

'Brian, I'd like you to meet my daughter Tuppy.'

'Hello, Tuppy,' I said. 'Would you dance with me?'

'I'd love to.' Her smile was like a breath of fresh air mixed with sunshine. We danced to 'Singing the Blues' and that was the start of something.

But I never found out why she was called Tuppy. She had a boyfriend who was away with the navy, but that didn't seem to worry her or Alex – and it certainly didn't worry me. Tuppy and I hit it off extremely well and Alex seemed to notice. Later in the evening Alex told me she also had a son, George, overseas in the navy.

'Brian, you're welcome to stay here in George's bedroom any time,' she said, 'and I've told Tuppy just that.'

I thanked her and gave her what I thought was a cavalier kiss on the cheek. She smiled in return. With Tuppy's prompting (not that I needed it) I took up Alex's kind offer on many occasions – beginning with that night.

Everyone had left and I'd retired to George's bedroom. The lights were out and suddenly I heard a quick rustle of clothes falling to the floor. Before I knew it, Tuppy was under the blankets next to me. I hadn't even heard her enter the room. She would have made a good commando.

'I'm here, Brian.' The announcement was hardly necessary. 'Move over, quickly.' I obliged and poor old George's bed got a good working over.

On another occasion I took Tuppy to the Embassy nightclub in the city. The owner was worried that my boots would ruin his dance floor so we danced on carpet instead. Tuppy was a beautiful lady with a lot of feeling and great company to be with. We had marvellous times together and the war seemed a long way away. But of course it wasn't.

In Ballarat an attractive lady named Ethel had told me that her two daughters, both in their early twenties, were sharing a flat in Melbourne. She gave me their phone number and said I should look them up. Mary, the elder of the two, was a well-known concert pianist, while Barbara was a qualified pharmacist.

When I rang their flat, Mary answered with her lovely husky voice. 'Mother told us about you. When are you coming out to see us?' she said. The immediate welcome left me speechless for a few seconds.

'When would you suggest?' I asked eventually.

'As soon as you can organise a friend to come with you.'

The lucky man was Stan, a Z Special Unit operative with whom I was quite friendly. He was slightly older than me and had already been on at least one operation, which he naturally never spoke about. As a Sydneysider he didn't know many people in Melbourne and was only too pleased to string along.

Next day we arrived at the girls' Toorak flat with bottles in our arms and smiles of anticipation on our faces. The door opened to reveal two lovely young ladies.

'Come in, come in,' they said, one holding the door open while the other gratefully relieved us of the bottles.

The four of us got along extremely well and fell into two conversational pairings: Stan with Mary and myself with Barbara. From here on we all saw a great deal of one another, sometimes all together and sometimes as separate couples.

But there wasn't much time at our disposal. Stan and I were soon leaving for some unknown destination up north. He'd obviously hit it off with Mary, because he bought her a diamond ring. They seemed very happy and we threw an engagement party for them.

Although I got on famously with Barbara, on the other hand, we never discussed becoming 'bespoken'. We simply went out and had fun and she left suggestive scented notes around for me to find. She was just lovely.

Although I was a lot fitter then than I had been in Ballarat, I was starting to feel a bit overworked from all the exercise with Tuppy and Barbara. Then at last Z Special Unit informed me I was going north. Where and why, they didn't say. Unbeknown to each other, Tuppy and Barbara took considerable trouble to give me memorable and energy-sapping farewells.

They told me they'd wait for me and that they would miss me.

'Please write, because I'll write to you,' each of them said.

'Of course I will, darling,' I told them. It was sad to leave all this behind.

And I never did see either of these lovely ladies again. By the time I returned they were both well and truly 'bespoken', and good luck to them. It didn't surprise me, and I simply hoped they'd be happy.

Saying goodbye to my parents, of course, was a different story. They wished me luck and gave me all their love. I could see the anguish in their eyes as they held back their tears and I felt so sorry for them.

PART THREE

Borneo
1945

16

Operation Colt

And so I found myself roughly halfway between New Guinea and the Philippines on Morotai Island, now one of the northernmost islands of Indonesia. Invaded by the Japanese and then recaptured by the Allies, Morotai was host to a massive base that was a stepping stone for further island-hopping campaigns. There were still some Japanese down one end of the island, but no one seemed particularly worried about them. Cut off from supplies and support, they were just left to starve.

Z Special Unit had a few parties of operatives on the island. One group was sent to parachute into enemy territory, but the Liberator they were flying in struck a tree as it approached the dropping zone and no one survived.

This came as quite a shock. I'd been talking to a couple of these men only the day before and it reminded me that life was precious and that the only certainty about it was uncertainty. Shortly afterwards, six of us got the word to go.

This time we were travelling by sea. SRD had several specially constructed vessels, officially called Country Craft but known to us as 'snake boats' because of their individual names: *Tiger Snake*, *Black Snake*, *River Snake* and *Sea Snake*.

The Melbourne-built *Tiger Snake* was designed to look like the native junks that were used throughout the southwest Pacific. She was 70 feet long and although the right sails made her look the part, a diesel motor gave her a speed of 8 knots. Her concealed armaments included a 20mm

Oerlikon quick firing gun and three 5-inch Browning machine guns.

The *Tiger Snake* had a crew of about seven. The lavatory was a box with a hole in it, mounted on the stern overhang and with a khaki canvas screen around it for modesty's sake. Ablutions were carried out on deck and we showered regularly during the frequent tropical downpours.

We six operatives became deck dwellers because of the cramped conditions. In fine weather it was absolutely balmy, both day and night but rough weather made things most unpleasant.

After sailing for several days, we joined an Allied fleet primed to invade the Japanese-held island of Labuan off northwest Borneo. Labuan looks tiny on the map, but is really quite big, although dwarfed by the vast landmass of Borneo nearby.

On the 10th of June 1945, we watched offshore as the big ships and attacking planes blew the shit out of the Japanese on Labuan. After this softening-up, landing craft packed with troops advanced on the shore. The fighting troops on the ground were Australians from the AIF 9th Division. When the beachhead was secured, the *Tiger Snake* moved landwards to discharge the six of us and our gear. On shore a marshal directed us to a campsite that was being set up beside an ancient graveyard, close to the ocean. Labuan was transformed into a huge Allied base, similar to Morotai, and this camp became Z Special Unit's Labuan home. We were the 'Special Task Detachment' of SRD, attached to the 9th Division HQ. Our function was to obtain, by whatever means necessary, any specialist intelligence or other information from Japanese territory that was needed.

Settling down by the graveyard, we were given our grog issue. We soon found there was an air force camp nearby, filled with administrative people more interested in selling their ration than drinking it themselves. On the day of their grog issue, a couple of us took a jeep and trailer to buy up their excess, and we got it for a good price.

Our food was supplemented by rather unconventional fishing. Large shoals cruised close to shore and if you tossed in a grenade they would float stunned to the surface, where you could take your pick. They were delicious and there were plenty of them, too. It wasn't very sporting, but we didn't have any fishing gear with us.

Our first assignment was a straightforward kidnapping job. We had to infiltrate the Japanese-held town of Sipitang on mainland Borneo, capture a senior Japanese Kempeitai officer and spirit him back to Labuan in one piece, where our experts would interrogate him. The codename was Operation Colt.

The mainland was five hours away by 'workboat', which was a specially built 40-foot motor launch. We had assembled our gear and boarded the boat by eleven at night on the 15th of June 1945, when suddenly the whole thing was aborted. The American navy, despite having confirmed that morning that it was okay to proceed, now said they didn't have enough time to warn their ships against interfering with us. This was somewhat disquieting, because we were all keyed up and now had to unwind.

Next morning our party leader Frank Oldham went aboard the American navy command ship *Rocky Mount* to see their chief of operations. He provided a complete description of our workboat and gave him our radio wavelength. Details of the operation, including our exact landing spot and estimated arrival and departure times, were supplied. The Americans assured Frank that they now knew what we were doing. They even gave him the recognition signals for the next forty-eight hours in case we ran into any trouble. That night, the 16th of June, at eleven, we loaded the workboat again and set off for Sipitang.

Apart from the workboat crew, there were six operatives and an interpreter. Frank Oldham was a Middle East veteran and, like me, had been a commando. Happy Croton got his nickname because he never smiled. He had been in Malaya, but before the Japanese invasion he'd gone to China with a team of Australians to teach guerrilla warfare. That hadn't worked out and they'd all come back. He had also been on a job with Z Special Unit. The other three operatives – Ross Bradbury, Brick Fowler and Chick Outhwaite – were volunteers from the armoured division, as yet untried in combat. A Malay boatman named Latif was on board to guide us to our landfall in the dead of night. We also had two Chinese, mainland dwellers, who knew the Kempeitai officer's movements and had volunteered to lead us to him.

It was a beautiful tropical night. I couldn't help thinking how marvellous it would have been to have a passionate and good-looking young Australian lady with me. For five hours we'd been chugging along as quietly as possible. It was quite wearing to be constantly on alert, peering into total darkness and listening for any potential danger.

At about four in the morning the coastline of Borneo appeared in silhouette a quarter of a mile away. The skipper whispered his approval that our navigation was spot on, adding that we should start getting ready 'to piss off', as he put it, in the very near future.

Suddenly the workboat was hit by a blinding light and we stood out like dog's balls. We couldn't have been more exposed if we'd tried.

The searchlight was quite close by and was followed by a normal challenge signal. Our signaller rapidly flashed back the correct recognition signal. At least we now knew they were American and not Japanese.

This was not completely reassuring, however, because here we were, just off an enemy coastline, trying our best to proceed undetected while being lit up like a prize on offer to anyone who wanted it. Behind the beam the dark outline of the American ship towered above us like an enormous shadow. They kept flashing the same challenge, forcing us to return the recognition signal repeatedly.

I suggested to Frank Oldham that we shoot their searchlight out, but he ruled against it, saying that if they were trigger-happy they might blow us out of the water. There was no doubt they had the firepower to do it, so it clearly wasn't a good idea. Instead we flashed 'We are an Australian patrol', but to no effect. The challenge signal kept coming.

'Oh, just tell them to fuck off,' I said, now at my wits' end. The skipper was exasperated too. He grabbed the lamp and crudely flashed '**** off', as the official report (by a Major Holland) later put it. Much to our amazement the searchlight was extinguished immediately and the silhouette of the American warship dissolved into the night. To quote Holland's report again, 'they "****ed off" light and all.'

We looked at each other and smiled. But we'd lost almost one-and-a-half hours. There was no telling whether the enemy on shore had been alerted to our presence, but every chance that a reception party was being prepared for us. The question was whether we should abort. The decision was ours and we decided to proceed – surely we couldn't be stuffed around any more.

It was now well after five in the morning. Latif sat on the prow, peering ahead into the dark and directing the helmsman with hand signals.

We hoped to the good gods that the Japanese out there were not waiting for us.

The workboat slowly scraped the sandy bottom where the ocean met the land. We disembarked and raced like lightning into the cover of thick jungle. Then the workboat reversed to wait for us at sea. Latif's directions had been perfect.

Frank Oldham had worked out our movements beforehand. I was up front, with the two Chinese guides pointing the way. We needed to make up lost time and he figured that, as the most experienced, I had the best chance of getting us there safely and fast. Following me were the three former armoured division men, and Happy and Frank brought up the rear. The interpreter, an elderly gentleman, stayed with them. After bringing us to the Kempeitai officer, the guides were to go to the rear to avoid danger.

I felt pretty sure no one was waiting for us, because if they had been they would have hit us by now. So we'd been very lucky.

Chick Outhwaite was immediately behind me. He had huge feet and someone said he was so bloody clumsy he could trip over a bloody matchstick. He was fidgeting and making more noise than all the others combined. I hissed at him to be quiet and that seemed to work for a while, but soon he started trying to cock his submachine gun, which he shouldn't have done. I stopped the patrol and quietly told him not to do it. Then Frank ordered him to uncock his weapon.

We hadn't gone far when inevitably he tripped. Bullets burst from his submachine gun and churned up the ground around my feet. How they missed me, I don't know. Obviously he hadn't uncocked at all.

Without stopping to think I swung around and hit him under the jaw with the butt of my Owen gun. He dropped like a log and the others were momentarily stunned. I told Frank I didn't want Outhwaite anywhere near me, so Frank told him to piss off down the back and shut up, and later gave him a severe dressing down.

I knew it was an accident, but afterwards I refused to go on any other operations with him. One of our guides was so upset I wouldn't have been surprised if he'd wet his pants. I suggested we wait for at least five minutes to see whether there was any reaction to our gunfire. But not even a birdcall disturbed the total silence.

We continued on in the pitch dark, steering around as many obstacles as we could, then one of the Chinese guides touched my arm to stop me. He pointed a shaking hand to a light in a distant house.

'Kempeitai there,' he said fearfully and scuttled to the rear.

I advanced slowly, straining to see anything that might have meant trouble. But there didn't appear to be any obstructions. I tossed a pebble here and there at intervals, but when there was no reaction I concluded there were no sentries.

Lights glinted through cracks in the doorway and shone from the windows. There was a faint murmur of voices, but I couldn't distinguish what was being said, or the language they were using. A couple of minutes later I motioned to Frank that I wanted to crash the front door. He nodded approval.

Taking a couple of deep breaths, I moved quietly forward, kicked the weak doorlock out of its socket and burst in with Frank and two others following. The rest stayed on guard outside.

In the house six Chinese men petrified with fear sat round a table. They were having a gambling night, playing mah-jong. There was no bloody Kempeitai officer or any other Jap in sight. What a stuff-up! Furious, I turned to have a go at our Chinese guide, but Frank stopped me – and quite right, too.

A little questioning revealed that one of the mah-jong players, who had been trying to gather his wits about him, knew where the Japanese Kempeitai officer lived and would show us where he was. He seemed to have more courage and sense than our original guide, so we went with him. We were on the fringe of the township, a cleared and settled area with nowhere near the cover we had on our approach, although at least it was physically easier to move around without it. I suppose we couldn't have had it both ways.

Dawn had broken and it was becoming lighter by the second. Our original timetable would have had us well and truly on our way back by now and the locals were coming out to see what was going on. As we spoke to them, both directly and through an interpreter, we soon had several points confirmed. First, the mah-jong player's information was solid. Second, the Kempeitai officer was hated and feared for his brutality. He had no bodyguards and the local Japanese troops generally stuck to the central part of town where their billets were. Life had been pretty quiet for them here over the past couple of years, so there was no reason it should have been any different this morning.

Soon our mah-jong playing guide pointed to a house, quite nice by local standards.

'Kempeitai lives there,' he said. I thanked him and he smiled.

As we approached the house there was tree cover on the right and a grass ditch about four feet deep on the left. Frank and another man took the trees and I led in the ditch, with Happy Croton. The others stayed hidden to cover our backs and ensure that none of the locals warned the Kempeitai officer we were there.

Moving in the ditch meant going slowly so that we could remain as inconspicuous as possible. Shortly, after some hard-earned progress, a Chinese man approached us. I tried to wave him away, but he came right to the lip of the ditch and looked down at me.

'Would you like a cup of tea?'

He spoke courteously and his English was perfect. Very discourteously, I showed him my Owen gun. 'Fuck off now, and quickly!' I hissed.

Startled by my rudeness, he scuttled away. I went back to our tediously slow progress to the Kempeitai officer's house, with Happy Croton right behind me. Then, from the corner of my eye, I saw the same Chinese man carrying a cup on a saucer. He came over, bent down and offered it carefully to me. I assumed it had tea in it. Only one cup, too. Poor old Happy was going to miss out.

I didn't waste time telling him I didn't like tea. I just straight out told him to go away, threatening him as firmly – but quietly – as I could. He was stunned, as if he couldn't understand my behaviour, then backed swiftly away with a hurt look on his face. I knew I'd been rude, but what else could I have done?

There was no point staying in the ditch now. The offer of a drink would have been a dead giveaway to anyone watching. It was best not to stuff around anymore. I signalled my intention to Frank and we moved as quickly as possible towards the Kempeitai officer's house. It was now almost eight in the morning. We reached the door simultaneously, pushed our way in – and astonished the sole occupant, a young local woman. Such an anticlimax after all that time wasted crawling along the ditch! Her name was Suzie and she was the officer's cook or housekeeper. She insisted that he forced her to do whatever it was she did and that she didn't like him.

At first she was frightened and worried by our intrusion, but when she realised that we meant no harm she told us the Kempeitai officer had left about half an hour earlier and had no idea that we were in town. She didn't expect him back until evening.

We ratted the place, gathered all the documents for our Intelligence people and collected several weapons. We told Suzie she had nothing to fear unless she tried to contact her boss. She hastened to assure us that she had no intention of doing any such thing.

Watching the house all day in pairs from temporary headquarters in a house nearby, we relieved each other every few hours. During that time we talked to a lot of the locals and picked up a lot of useful information, then late in the afternoon five of us surrounded the officer's house and left one operative, the interpreter and the two guides at our base.

At about seven, when it was getting dark, one of the locals came racing up with news that the Kempeitai officer was not far away. He offered to take us to a place where we could intercept him. We had already questioned this man and judged him to be reliable. Soon we were in ambush position along a fairly wide jungle track just outside the town, where our quarry was due to pass.

The operation went like clockwork and the Kempeitai officer walked straight into our clutches, accompanied by a Chinese collaborator. We just stood up, surrounded them and took both men prisoner. The astonished look on the Japanese officer's face was reward enough for all our troubles.

He didn't say a word after his capture and our immediate task was to keep the understandably aggrieved locals away from him. We rewarded our guides and helpers from our supplies and recorded their names so that when the Japanese were kicked out and a civil administration was set up, their efforts and loyalty would be duly recognised.

The next day – the 18th of June – we took our prisoners to the coast and boarded the workboat at one in the afternoon. This time there was no need to stifle the engine noise. Travelling at a decent pace, we were back at Labuan in only two-and-a-half hours. With the additional captive, documents and intelligence from locals, we had more than exceeded our expectations. And we'd done it without any gunplay – unless the friendly fire round my feet was counted.

We were all tired and hungry and felt as if we'd been away for months. After a makeshift shower, we had a huge meal washed down with beer. Next came sleep, and plenty of it. The following few days we took it easy, sunbaking, fishing, drinking beer and, of course, avoiding all discussion of what we'd been doing. But if the Kempeitai officer did eventually reveal anything worthwhile under interrogation, we never heard about it.

17

The Wild Men of Borneo

The holiday didn't last long. One morning the six of us were told we were going into Sarawak to wage guerrilla war for an unknown period. We were ordered to check all our gear, replace anything we were short of and be ready to depart by flying boat 'very soon'.

SRD had the use of at least two Catalina flying boats, fabulous craft that could land and take off on either land or water. They carried huge loads over vast distances without having to refuel and could stay in the air for a couple of days at a time.

My guerrilla group was codenamed Semut 3, from the Malay word for 'ant'. Malay was the most widely distributed language in Sarawak, although there were many indigenous languages. Of these, the most important one for our purposes was Sea Dyak. I had been learning both this and Malay on Fraser Island and would soon have an opportunity to test my skills.

We boarded a cat boat piloted by the intrepid Wally Mills. Revving up his two huge motors, he started the takeoff run across the calm waters, but the cat boat just would not take off. It was overloaded. Wally got around this by piloting towards some small ocean swells in the distance and bouncing on each wave or swell as it came. Every time the cat boat thumped off a wave it bounced slightly higher in the air until finally we were airborne.

Our destination was Sama, at the ulu, or headwaters, of the Rejang River. This mighty watercourse could accommodate large ships for many miles upstream, but the headwaters were only accessible by small local craft, fashioned from logs and navigated with the cumulative experience of countless generations. It was dangerous territory even without the Japanese presence. Torrents of raging water crashed over waterfalls, washing logs downstream at a furious clip, and there were crocodiles everywhere.

Wally Mills was careful to dodge the swift flow of jungle debris on our way to Sama. Cat boats had quite thin hulls and weren't built to withstand heavy knocks. As for the enemy, we just had to keep our fingers crossed we weren't about to catch a Japanese bullet or two. The cat boat came to rest finally and we breathed a sigh of relief. With the motors off we realised what a deafening noise the river had made. The crew tied the cat boat up like a regular boat and ferried us ashore.

I'd already cleaned my weapons, but my first act on arriving was to ensure that my gear was ready in case of any surprises. This included the L pill, a lethal cyanide mixture encased in a small waterproof capsule. If you fell into enemy hands you could safely hold the L pill in your mouth and if you didn't want to deal with whatever torture was coming your way, you had the option to bite the casing open and swallow the poison. Next moment you were gone, taking your information with you and upsetting your would-be torturers no end. Not that you would have cared about that.

Bill Sochon, the leader of Semut 3, was an Englishman I'd known on Fraser Island. He was bombastic, obnoxious and utterly useless. A former assistant housemaster at the London Borstal Institute, he'd been assistant supervisor of prisons in Sarawak and was put in command due to his local knowledge and experience. His military field experience, however, was zero. On Fraser Island I once went on an extended folboat exercise with him and found he didn't pull his weight – and he had plenty of it. He assumed he could pull his rank instead. He also had trouble pronouncing his Rs – 'hurry' came out 'huwwy', 'rubbish' was 'wubbish' and so on. Just having to listen to him was quite annoying. And even if we were in the jungle, his table manners were disgusting. He was impossible to respect and I knew I was going to have trouble with him. But although I had the right to be withdrawn at my own request, I didn't think it would come to that, because I figured he wouldn't have wanted to lose my services. I think he realised that his own abilities were minimal.

Sochon had another Pom with him, Pip Hume, who had worked for one of the British oil companies in Sarawak. While not obnoxious like Sochon, he was equally incompetent. Without any military experience, he was supposed to be arming and training the indigenous people to fight alongside operatives like myself. The idea was to re-form the Sarawak Rangers, a law enforcement body that had existed before the war. I suffered the services of his trainees on a future job, but more of that later.

Sochon himself welcomed us warmly. The Japanese had just vacated Kapit, the next township downstream. Headquarters were being set up there, so we went straight down. He suggested we settle in, have a meal and then plan our movements. Kapit was only to be a staging or base camp for him and a few others. Settling in didn't take long, of course, because all we had was what we were carrying and I was soon free to meet the first of my Sea Dyaks.

As a schoolkid I'd heard stories and learnt in school about those fierce headhunters and pirates, the 'Wild Men of Borneo'. Enthralled, I had often wondered who these people could possibly be. But I could never have imagined the experiences and adventures I would one day have with them.

The real 'Wild Men of Borneo' were the Sea Dyaks or Iban, an attractive, happy and independent people. Highly intelligent and quick to learn, they were also utterly fearless. If they liked you they took you to their heart and would do anything for you.

They lived in longhouses, generally built by the banks of a river about eight feet above the ground. The only way to enter was by walking or climbing up a notched tree trunk. The inside was partitioned off, with a long corridor running along the front. Most of the rooms had their own fireplace and contained rattan sleeping mats and other belongings. This usually meant a collection of smoked heads hanging on the wall. The flooring slats were spaced slightly apart and food scraps were just pushed through to the ground, where countless dogs, chickens, pigs, and goats lived pretty well on whatever fell from above.

The Sea Dyaks were marvellous hunters, of both people and animals. They cared lovingly for their parangs, wide knives almost of sword length that could take off a human head with about three or four chops. I saw them do it many times. Parangs were also used to chop wood, trees or whatever else needed cutting. They also had razor-sharp spears of various lengths. Their sumpits were blowpipes that fired darts with deadly accuracy. Sometimes the darts were poison-tipped, depending on the purpose at hand. The Sea Dyaks were excellent fishermen and boatmen and could take their prahus down the worst of rapids.

They always had two alcoholic drinks in copious supply. One was a strong rice wine, quite palatable when you became used to it. The other was arak, a clear spirit that almost lifted your head off when taken neat. Experimentation soon revealed that mixing it with wild-growing lemons made it more drinkable. Small enough to crush between a thumb and finger, these lemons were tart and easy to find in the jungle.

Whenever jungle-dwelling Sea Dyaks went into the towns – and that wasn't often – the Chinese, Malays and Indians would exploit them mercilessly. They didn't like it, but generally accepted it. Now, however, the Japanese were trying to take away everything they had. Naturally the Sea Dyaks hated them and had been waging their own war of resistance whenever the opportunity arose. But if some of the townspeople who had been exploiting them got in the way, that was just too bad.

Not long before the war, the British had outlawed headhunting in Sarawak. This did nothing to deter the Sea Dyaks, of course, who had been at it for centuries. And so, on arriving behind enemy lines, the SRD let it be known that they would pay the Sea Dyaks the princely bounty of one Straits Settlement dollar per Japanese head. This was about two shillings and sixpence in Australian currency at the time, or twenty-five cents. Occasionally there was trouble when we had to refuse them payment for Chinese or Malay heads, but overall the system worked quite well.

The Japanese made our task easier by making enemies of the local population with pointless cruelties. Bashings were commonplace and we saw so many people who had been wounded horribly by cuts from a Japanese sword or bayonet. Others were routinely tortured by having water poured down their throats. Then there was the sun treatment, which forced the victim to kneel in the boiling heat with a block of wood behind the knees and stare into the sun. Closing your eyes or looking away resulted in a severe beating. The Japanese also prostituted and enslaved according to their requirements, looted everything they wanted and left the locals to starve.

Some of the Sea Dyaks' guerrilla tactics against them were ingenious. One trick was to cut trees almost right through, hold them up with rattan vines and then topple them onto a prahu load of Japanese passing underneath. During the ensuing confusion the Sea Dyaks would attack. The same tactic also worked on jungle paths.

Once when a Japanese patrol was approaching a longhouse, the Sea Dyaks had their prettiest unmarried girls strip naked as the soldiers emerged from the jungle. The girls then waded into the river to their waists and began to play and giggle. Fascinated by the show, the Japanese failed to notice the warriors creeping from hiding spots behind them, armed with deadly parangs. Soon headless, the soldiers' bodies were rolled into the river to float home to the Japanese garrison downstream.

Another tactic was for a small warrior party, armed with sumpits, to hide near a jungle track ahead of a Japanese patrol, which was usually about eight men. After the Japanese passed by, a poisoned dart was fired into the last man's neck. When they realised they were one down, the patrol would backtrack to find him in his death throes. Repeat performances by the Sea Dyaks reduced the patrol one by one until the hysterical survivors took off for base, panicking and thoroughly demoralised.

One Sea Dyak operation nearly turned into a fiasco, but fortunately for them it ended with the massacre of a large party of Japanese. It was masterminded by three penghulus or chieftains of neighbouring longhouses in the ulu of the Rejang quite a way above Kapit. Finding that a large party of Japanese was spending the night at an old Borneo Company resthouse nearby, the penghulus invited them to a welcoming feast at one of the longhouses.

The idea was to ply them with grog and the seductive attentions of unmarried young women. When the Japanese became incapacitated, out would come the parangs. The Japanese commander, however, didn't think dinner was such a good idea, so he decided on a short visit to the longhouse after his troops had eaten their own meal.

The Sea Dyaks waited impatiently for several hours. Later that evening the Japanese finally strolled over to see them, complacently leaving their weapons behind. That sort of luck didn't come by every day. There was now no need to provide any hospitality whatsoever. Screaming their war-cries, the Sea Dyaks fell on their would-be guests and the longhouse soon had a proud new display: twenty-nine Japanese heads.

It was time to meet my new friends. At least I hoped they were going to be my friends. The Sea Dyaks spoke little or no Malay, so I was glad I'd learnt something of their language. I felt confident that I could communicate with them, helped along with a smile and a bit of sign language. In New Guinea I'd found the natives always appreciated my efforts to speak pidgin and would smile and help me out. Much to my delight, the Sea Dyaks reacted similarly. I quickly became reasonably proficient in the language and I'm sure that helped me win their respect.

Quite a number of them were hanging around the base in small groups, pointing at and discussing everything they saw. Pip Hume was showing one group how to aim a rifle. They were all dressed up in their warrior gear and holding onto their weapons tightly.

No point in stuffing around, I thought, going straight up to the nearest group. I smiled, waved and said hello in their language. They looked surprised and muttered to one another. Then, as if deciding it was all right, they returned my greeting and took an interest in me.

I offered them a couple of chocolate bars from the emergency rations, demonstrating how to remove the silver foil wrapper and suggesting, much to their surprise, that they should eat the chocolate. They were very wary, so I popped a piece in my mouth. After following suit they began beaming smiles of pleasure at the taste and nodding their approval to me and to each other.

Soon other groups came over to see what their mates were laughing and talking about. They spoke so quickly that I could only grasp the gist of their conversation, which seemed to be that both the chocolate and I were okay.

The Owen gun over my shoulder attracted a lot of interest. Occasionally a warrior stepped forward to stroke it, along with my pistol, knuckleduster knife and grenades. This didn't worry me as long as it made them happy. I kept on talking and occasionally made a hand signal if

I couldn't find the right word. Sure enough, they had a giggle and tried to help me out.

'Do you have plenty of Japanese heads?' I asked them.

'Oh, yes!' they chorused back very seriously, patting their parangs.

When I had to go I said I hoped to see them again soon. I waved and smiled and as I turned to go, I got a smile or two in return.

I wondered why they were so keen to touch my weapons. Surely they would've seen the same gear on other operatives. The next day I understood. Watching the others interact with the Sea Dyaks – especially the two Poms, Sochon and Hume – it was obvious that they treated them like servants. This was, of course, how they had treated all indigenous people before the war; the British Raj and all that crap. But here they were, still trying it on during the war and expecting the locals to like them. Wishful thinking! They were said to be masters of local knowledge, yet they couldn't see that the Sea Dyaks didn't appreciate being spoken down to. And how could they, when Sochon and Hume didn't even have a handle on the Sea Dyak language?

The Sea Dyaks were proud, self-contained and direct. If someone didn't like them, that person could just go and get stuffed as far as they were concerned. And I agreed with them. Maybe at the time it simply suited them to tolerate Sochon and Hume under the circumstances. They were certainly cunning enough to think that way.

The next morning, armed with more chocolate, I went out to see some of my new friends. At first they had all looked the same to me, but I soon recognised individuals. Spotting the group I had spoken to the day before, I greeted them in their own language.

I told them my name was Brian and got them to repeat it a couple of times. Then I asked for their names, though none registered with me. I told them that I was from Australia, that I had been fighting the Japanese for ages and had taken a lot of Japanese heads. They understood the bit about the heads, but I had to work hard to explain the rest.

Australians were a lot like Sea Dyaks, I said, and very different from the British who had been in Borneo before the war. I added that the Australians only came here to fight the Japanese and would go home as soon as the war had been won.

Explaining this much was a long and laborious task. I had them repeat words like 'Australia' over and over again until I was certain they wouldn't forget. I sketched on the ground to illustrate what I was saying and show them where I came from. Then I made it as clear as possible that the Poms came from a long way away in totally the opposite direction.

18

Two Good Friends

Our first target was the nearest Japanese garrison, downstream towards Song. It was vital for us to safeguard our headquarters from surprise attack by getting the first strike in. The Sea Dyaks paddled six of us there in prahus and it was a two-hour trip. That was the way they measured distance: by paddle-time.

We set up ambush positions on both sides of the Rejang. Nothing happened overnight, unless you counted the crocodiles barking – whether angrily or not I couldn't say – fish jumping and birds screeching. The next morning, having successfully guarded our headquarters, we travelled further downstream a fair way before we pulled the prahus in to the river bank. The Sea Dyaks hid them in the jungle and showed us a track leading to a secret position overlooking Song. Well, they called it a track, but it looked like jungle to me. But they certainly knew what they were doing and I quickly came to trust their judgement completely. They seemed to operate intuitively, always knowing just how far they could go without bumping into the enemy. Maybe that was why the Japanese and everyone else were scared shitless of them.

This jungle-track-that-wasn't led us to a spur which offered a bird's eye view of Song. There were Japanese everywhere, unaware of our scrutiny. It reminded me of the view from Salamaua OP in New Guinea. It was a well established base and it certainly looked as if they were there to stay.

Suddenly a group of local Sea Dyaks appeared from nowhere and struck up an animated, though hushed, conversation with our lot. They said the Japanese here had started killing Sea Dyaks on sight. We got plenty of information about the Japanese from them, in fact everything we'd come for. We invited them back to Kapit if they wanted to join us.

It was clear that the Japanese weren't expecting visitors. As we moved towards Song we came across a group of them, laughing. When they saw us they stopped and checked around, but I couldn't understand why. We weren't looking for trouble, so we immediately opened up on them and the screaming started. I saw several fall, but we didn't stop to say hello.

Most of our new Sea Dyak friends decided to stay in the Song area. We made it quite clear we were returning soon and that there would be several air strikes on Song. Of course, we had to explain what an air strike was and tell them that they should make themselves scarce when they heard the planes. They agreed to warn any other locals still in the area.

They also agreed to spread rumours greatly exaggerating our strength. Later I learnt that every time the story was retold our numbers grew and ultimately the Japanese believed they were up against quite a large force.

We returned to Kapit with a few extra Sea Dyaks. We'd planned to return to Song after replenishing our supplies, but two significant events changed all that.

First, I met Dave Kearney, an Australian who was second in command of our Semut party. He was a few years my senior in age, but not in experience of jungle warfare. We became good friends and I had a lot to do with him.

A former champion wrestler and athlete, Dave left school at fifteen to work as a navvy. His father had been out of work for four years and Dave had joined the army on the first day of recruiting, when he was twenty-one – anything was better than the pick and shovel, he said later – and he was on the first ship to the Middle East. Working his way up to Captain, in New Guinea he gave daily summaries to Australia's Commander in Chief, General Blamey. Later he wrote, 'By the time I came to Z, I couldn't strip a Bren, but I knew a lot about the army. I knew bullshit when I saw it too, and there was a lot of it in Z.'

Dave's involvement in Z Special Unit grew from his friendship with Jim Cairns, later Deputy Prime Minister in the Whitlam government. They had been close since they were teenagers. Cairns had even taught him how to drive. Dave stayed at the Cairns house when he came back from the Middle East and one day he met Bill Sochon there, who later secured him the position with Semut 3.

Although Dave knew very little about combat, he was smart enough to acknowledge that. He was always pleasant and easy to get along with and while I would never have agreed to go into action with Sochon, Dave was a different story. He listened, learnt, acted soundly and was always dependable in a crisis.

The second significant event occurred while I was talking to the Sea Dyaks. We were carrying on our usual good-hearted chatter when I noticed a young warrior watching me intently. He stroked my Owen gun and only spoke occasionally. His face was familiar; he had been there the day I told the Sea Dyaks my name.

Our eyes met and he gave me a cheeky smile, which I was destined to become used to. Looking at me with eyes that seemed to bore right through me, he said in his own language, 'You take me with you. I kill for you. I die for you.'

This wasn't a rare statement among Sea Dyaks and I'd heard it before, but somehow it sounded different this time. It sounded like me asking George Warfe whether I could join his commando unit.

'What's your name?' I said.

'Bujang.'

One thing I had already learnt was that Sea Dyaks liked quick decisions. Bujang looked pretty bright to me and the others seemed to defer to him, so I didn't stuff around. 'Okay, I'll take you with me,' I said, feeling sure that I could arrange it.

He gave me that cheeky smile again and nodded. 'My friend come too.'

'Who's your friend?'

Bujang grabbed the arm of the smiling warrior alongside him. 'Unting,' he said.

Placing a hand on their shoulders, I said I'd call for them before I left. It turned out to be a superb day's recruiting.

Dave Kearney was to lead our return trip to Song. Along with us went Ross Bradbury and Brick Fowler, who as our signaller was supposed to keep us in touch with the outside world. I don't know why he was called 'Brick', but he was rather solidly built. Frank Oldham and the rest had moved onto other operations and I didn't work with them again.

We didn't know how long we would stay so we took a lot of stores with us. We took a Bren gun too, which I knew how to operate, strip and maintain. It was a lovely weapon, but a bit heavy. We needed a few Sea Dyaks to help fight and to help us carry the gear. This was my chance to put Bujang and Unting forward, but the names meant nothing to Dave. I suggested that Bujang choose the carriers and another couple of armed warriors, because he could pick the best men available. These Sea Dyaks had been given some rifle training by Pip Hume.

'Okay, do it,' Dave said. And I did.

Our Sea Dyak recruits were paid for their services and were issued with food and basic clothing such as jungle-green trousers, as most of them had only loincloths. When I found Bujang and told him to select the right people and meet us in the morning, he was spellbound. He stared at me, then the cheeky smile reappeared. Grabbing my arms, he said gleefully, 'I go now. Everything is all right. I arrange and we come in the morning.'

Meanwhile, the RAAF agreed to stage several air strikes on Song shortly before our attack. These would be fairly low key, with just two or three planes, but devastating to property and morale nonetheless.

Bujang arrived with Unting and his Sea Dyak entourage just as dawn was breaking, and they were raring to go. I introduced them and there were smiles all round. Quickly we sorted out who was to carry what and then set off towards Song.

The value of having Sea Dyaks in the lead, among them preferably Bujang himself, soon became obvious. Their inbuilt jungle radar was so strong that the risk of walking into a Japanese ambush, let alone getting lost, was next to zero. Planting AP switches at night was unnecessary. There was no way an intruder could surprise or elude a Sea Dyak sentry.

Bujang took particular interest in me. For the rest of the war he did everything he could to look after me and protect me and I was grateful. He seemed to consider me his personal responsibility and I didn't mind at all. Indeed, I was lucky to have him.

19

Ambush at Song

Overlooking Song was a high, isolated spot which became our base camp. An air strike was due later that day, so we went out to locate some good ambush positions. By the time we came back the Sea Dyaks we had met on our first visit were waiting for us.

Suddenly we heard aircraft. An air raid warning blared out and as we watched, the Japanese raced into the jungle to hide. Two RAAF fighter bombers came into view and made three runs over Song, bombing and strafing and making a mess of things. It was thrilling to watch.

After speaking excitedly with the other Sea Dyaks, Bujang had something to ask me. They all reckoned the air strike was marvellous, but could we do it again? Now knowing where the Japanese went for shelter, he suggested taking his warriors into the jungle to surround them and pick them off when they emerged after the planes had gone. It was an excellent idea, and we requested another air strike for nine o'clock the next morning.

There was still time for us to get into an ambush position before dark. A Japanese patrol was going to relieve one of their outposts and they had no idea that horrible people like us were about.

Dave Kearney, Ross Bradbury and I, Bujang, Unting and two other Sea Dyaks went to try our luck. Bujang insisted on coming up front with me to show me the way. I knew what I was doing, having survived the far tougher jungle of New Guinea, but I let him lead with me and was glad I did, because his senses were much more acute than mine. It took forty minutes to find our position. I had discussed with Dave the way we had conducted ambushes in New Guinea and he left the placing to me. I drummed the procedure into everyone before we set out. Basically, it was essential that no one opened fire until the person leading the ambush did so. Then everyone had to fire immediately.

We were spread out so that when I fired, the main part of the target would be directly in front of me and two or three others. On either side we positioned a man to dispose of anyone trying to escape.

Before long we heard voices. Noise travelled at night, of course, and our patrols were always trained to proceed in silence. But the Japanese seemed to like talking and laughing in the jungle. Maybe they were naturally cheerful, or perhaps it gave them Dutch courage. Maybe they were just plain bloody stupid.

They were still talking and laughing as they drew level with me. But not for long. I opened fire and the others followed. It was a cumulative, almost simultaneous, burst of fire. Then silence. None of them managed to run and I quickly counted six bodies.

Although satisfied with the result, I felt almost indifferent. I'd seen many bigger ambushes than this one, but for the others it was their first and it really surprised them. After we'd ratted the corpses for anything that might prove useful, I said, 'Quick!' and snapped my companions back to earth. The Japanese weren't carrying any documents of interest.

It is proper and sensible to disappear as quickly as possible after any ambush, regardless of its success. But as we turned to go, Bujang and his mates closed in on the bodies, whooping with delight. *Hack, hack, hack –* it was just like chopping wood. Next thing they were laughing and holding up their trophies by the hair, ear or nose. What could I say? It was their culture and, considering the way they'd been treated, I didn't blame them at all. Besides, it would have been a brave, stupid and potentially dead man who tried to stop them. I didn't necessarily condone what they were doing, but it didn't worry me either, given what I'd seen the Japanese dish out and with my brother Denis still in their hands.

We returned to our temporary base quite pleased with ourselves, the Sea Dyaks proudly waving their trophies for the others to see. Normally they moved like ghosts in the jungle, completely silent and almost invisible, but obviously taking heads was considered a time to let your hair down, so to speak. But there was no point in fart-arsing around. I called Bujang aside and told him that if the Sea Dyaks made all that noise while they cut off Japanese heads on future patrols, they would never come out with us again. I explained that the noise would attract other Japanese and we might get ambushed ourselves. I impressed on him that the whole idea was to surprise the Japs, without giving them the opportunity to surprise us.

I took my time explaining all this, because their co-operation was vital to the outcome of future operations. 'We're very pleased to have you and the other warriors with us,' I said, putting my hand on his shoulder. 'But please tell them what I have said. Be sure they understand.'

He looked at me seriously and went to put a hand on me, but stopped, shrugged and gave me a wry smile. His rifle was in one hand; two Japanese heads were in the other. 'I go now. I do it now,' he said and he was gone.

Dave agreed completely with what I had done. We had a considerable amount of cash with us, about 10,000 Australian pounds worth of local currency. This was standard practice on an operation with so many unknown contingencies. Our money was good legal tender, not the worthless crap the Japanese circulated, and the locals knew it.

'How about making a big deal of it, Dave?' I said. 'Pay the Sea Dyaks for the heads instead of waiting for them to ask. It'll be good public relations, and you're the one who should do it.'

Again he agreed that my idea was good, so we made quite a happy little ceremony of it. Bujang and another each received two dollars, and the other pair received one dollar each. They smiled as the others looked on enviously. The word would now spread.

So Brick Fowler reported our success to HQ. We cleaned our weapons and sat down to a meal of cold hard rations, not wishing to light a fire so close to the enemy. Similar to American rations, this food came in proper tins and included tasty morsels like concentrated ham and eggs. It was like dinner at the Waldorf compared with what we'd had in New Guinea.

Bujang came over smiling and brandishing his two dollars.

I put my hand on his shoulder. 'That's very good. You deserve it.'

He said he'd spoken very strongly to the other Sea Dyaks. 'No one will make noise again. Is that all right now?'

I told him it was and he seemed quite pleased.

'Is your food all right?' I asked.

'Very good,' he said. I went to ask about posting sentries, but he explained that he'd already taken care of it. He pointed around our perimeter, and although I couldn't see his sentries I knew he was as good as his word.

It was a good breakthrough and looked like we were getting to understand each other. I thanked him and he went back to join his friends, while I went over to tell Dave and the others what I'd discussed with him. Then, over a few rice wines, we planned our movements for the following day.

The Sea Dyaks would have to take their positions surreptitiously at least a couple of hours before the air strike. By placing ourselves in an ambush position further back, if they were pursued by the Japanese they could lead them to us.

There were an awful lot of Japs in Song, far more than our little patrol could afford to take on. All we could do was niggle them and kill a few here and there. After what we had planned for the following day, a large force was probably going to come after us. We had to be packed and ready to piss off downstream as soon as our ambush set-up had outlived its usefulness.

When I found Bujang he grabbed my arm and started to show me where his sentries were, all over again. I said I wasn't interested because I had every confidence in him. I told him we needed to have a long talk.

I explained our plan in detail, several times. He kept nodding his head, so I made him repeat it back to me and he was almost word-perfect. He grinned. Then I asked if he could organise the others to be ready on time. He puffed his chest out. 'Of course!' he said, almost indignantly.

'Will you be going after Japanese heads yourself?' I asked with a smile, 'Or staying to look after me?'

Poor Bujang hung his head. 'You mind? I get some Japanese heads. It won't take long. Then I look after you.'

'Of course I don't mind. I'll see you early in the morning.'

He smiled again.

We were up and about well before daylight. It promised to be a lovely day with a clear blue sky. A good day for fighter-bombers and headhunters. After eating and packing we moved to our positions. Bujang took six warriors with him, armed only with parangs. We set up our ambush after concealing our gear in a nearby hollow.

We had to wait a considerable time for the air raid. Whatever Bujang and his friends did to pass the time, we looked at our watches constantly, anxious for the show to begin. At six minutes past nine we heard aircraft engines. Down in Song the sirens began to wail and Japanese soldiers, chatting away, hurried into the jungle to hide under their favourite trees. This time a trio of fighter-bombers caused considerable damage with three strafing and bombing runs. The sirens sounded the all-clear and the Japanese came out, had a stretch and a bit of a talk, then ambled back into Song. None of them was armed.

Suddenly Bujang and his six warriors were at them, attacking in silence this time. The first lot of Japanese who were hacked made surprised and horrified noises. Others, seeing what was happening, ran screaming towards Song for their lives. They made no attempt to help their friends. Most of them got away, but eleven didn't.

Realising that there was no one left, Bujang and the others made their way to our ambush and brought with them eleven new trophies.

I congratulated Bujang but wondered how the Japanese investigating patrol would react when, expecting enemy combat, they found nothing but eleven of their comrades minus their heads. I told him it was time to go downstream.

'I come back,' he said and raced off.

We started out, circling Song in the jungle, and in no time Bujang re-appeared with his rifle and other gear, but no heads. I didn't ask him what he'd done with them, but I suppose he had got a friend to mind them.

Having Bujang and the other Sea Dyaks with us made it a lot easier to move. We were in virgin jungle with no tracks or indications whatsoever, but they could avoid obstacles as though they didn't exist. They hadn't been through this area, but it was like they walked this way every day of the week. And we didn't have to worry about some rotten Japanese bastard hiding behind every tree and bush either, because Sea Dyaks could smell them a mile off.

After two hours we stopped in a clearing for a meal. Brick Fowler reported our successes and current movements.

'Time to be the big fellow again, Dave,' I said. 'How about paying out some more head money?' This he did, much to the enjoyment of the recipients and the envy of the others. I laughed to myself, thinking that Dave, famous as the man with the money, would soon be inundated with heads, including those of indigenous people.

I asked Bujang how all the other Sea Dyaks were getting along and he said they were happy. They enjoyed the food we gave them and wanted to know when we would be getting more heads. I smiled – what else could I do? – put my arm on his shoulder and said, 'Tell them soon.'

'Good,' he said. His eyes lit up over his cheeky grin.

We stayed about two hours, but it wasn't wasted time, because we were more organised and comfortable and now moved more quickly.

After some considerable time I was looking forward to another rest, when Bujang suddenly put up his arm to stop us and motioned us to hit the dirt. We dropped and I listened hard, but couldn't hear anything strange apart from the local wildlife.

'I go and look,' Bujang whispered.

Moments later he returned with another Sea Dyak, grinning from ear to ear and wearing all his warrior gear. Bujang introduced him as the penghulu (chief) of a nearby longhouse. We had been invited to eat and drink with them.

Conferring with Dave, I asked Bujang to thank him, but we had to decline his kind offer, although I said we might call in if we came back this way and asked if he'd seen any Japanese recently. I was going to get Bujang to ask him how far it was to the Rejang River, but on second thoughts decided that even though the penghulu was an ally, the fewer people who knew what we were doing, the better.

The penghulu told us there hadn't been any Japanese near his long-house for some time, because they mostly stayed in Song and travelled by river. We said our goodbyes politely and moved on. I asked Bujang if we could get to the Rejang River downstream of Song before nightfall without bumping into anybody. He thought we could and, sure enough, we arrived at the banks of the Rejang just as the sun was disappearing and all the shadows growing longer and closer to complete darkness.

We found a secluded spot just back from the river bank, too high for anyone to look down on us and we'd have good fresh water tonight. The flow was so fast that the river was self-cleansing. Our intention was to have a quiet night, do a couple of ambushes around the Song perimeter and then go back upstream and do the same thing again. That was our plan, but it very quickly got stuffed up.

20

'More heads, Bujang!'

'I hear noise,' Bujang announced. We listened, but heard nothing. 'Motor boat,' he insisted. Moments later, the dead of night was broken by the faint chug of a launch coming upstream. It sounded a long way off. We could also hear the splash and occasional bark of crocodiles disturbed by the boat and slipping from the mud banks into the safety of the waters.

Dave was all for letting the motor boat go on its way. 'After all, we're only intending to do some ambushes.'

'Shit, let's ambush this bastard, then,' I said. 'It can only be bad news and it must be taking something into Song.'

It was quickly agreed we would do just that. I grabbed the Bren gun from the Sea Dyak who had been kind enough to carry it. Slung around your neck, a Bren could be used like a submachine gun, but it's normally operated by a two-man team, both lying on the ground. With the barrel resting in a bipod, one man holds the stock at his shoulder to aim and fire while the other feeds the spring-loaded ammunition magazine clips as required. When the barrel becomes too hot from sustained firing the second man changes it, removing it with a wooden handle. On this occasion limited visibility meant there was no point lying on the ground, so I slung it over my shoulder and had one of Bujang's warriors stand by to hand me ammunition clips and the spare barrel.

The chugging of the Japanese motor boat grew louder as it headed upstream towards us.

Suddenly the moon came out and almost turned the night into

daylight. Now we saw a large launch with the Japanese flag flying from a masthead and the top deck crammed with soldiers. They were obviously reinforcements for the Song garrison. Some were smoking and there was a murmur of voices. Obviously they hadn't been drinking, because when the Japanese drank they tended to make a hell of a noise.

The launch travelled slowly, very close to the bank on our side of the river. When it drew alongside I emptied a full magazine into the wheelhouse. As I grabbed another from my Sea Dyak helper, I heard the others open fire. A couple of grenades would have been tossed on board, but they take five seconds to go off.

The boat was a screaming commotion. My shots at the wheelhouse had obviously been successful; the motor cut out and the launch ran aground on the bank. I emptied another magazine, this time into the mob on the deck. Our grenades exploded and we ducked as some of the debris blasted towards us. Someone lobbed a couple more grenades and I finished my third magazine. The launch was on fire now, and the last two grenades blasted it back into the water. It was sinking rapidly. All we could hear were groans and a few words in a language we couldn't understand. I didn't even have to change the barrel on the Bren gun. Finally the launch and its contents disappeared beneath the waters of the Rejang River forever.

The moon was shining bright and everything was quiet and still once more. There was no sign of what had taken place.

Bujang touched my arm and smiled. The other Sea Dyaks were smiling too, quietly discussing what they had just seen. Bujang had successfully instilled into them the need to keep the noise down.

Captured Japanese documents later revealed that sixty soldiers had been on the launch and that we killed fifty-seven of them. I don't know how three escaped, unless they were washed to safety in the fast-flowing current.

We left immediately. Although it was highly unlikely the enemy would come after us in the dead of night, we were in hostile territory without any backup and there was no point in taking unnecessary risks. Deciding that we'd now accomplished the downstream ambush, we would now backtrack around Song and worry them upstream, hoping to convince them that they were surrounded. The Sea Dyaks agreed to take us through the jungle for about an hour before we'd all stop for the night. It was a harrowing business. Bright as it was, the moon didn't penetrate the jungle and visibility was zero. Only the sheer skill of Bujang and his friends got us through. I told him when the hour was up and we stopped, God knew where, but it seemed to be in the right direction.

I said the Sea Dyaks could do what they liked as long as they didn't make any noise. In the morning there would be more heads, I promised. Bujang smiled and slipped away to pass the message on.

I went to sleep sitting up, which wasn't a problem to me because I'd slept under far worse conditions in New Guinea. The others had a few complaints in the morning, but I pointed out we were lucky there was no rain, let alone a Japanese wake-up call. The Sea Dyaks had been ready to move for some time. After breakfast we cleaned our weapons. I told Bujang that, without being noticed, we had to get somewhere near where he had taken the heads after the air raid. 'Do you think you can do this?' I asked.

Surprise registered on his face. 'Of course I can.'

'Can we can avoid the old penghulu we met before?'

He nodded and, with the Sea Dyaks in the lead, we took off at a brisk pace through the stifling jungle. After three hours we stopped briefly for a quick bite to eat, just long enough to get our breath back and for Brick Fowler to radio in our movements. Travelling in silence like this for long periods was tedious and wearing and we had to keep jolting ourselves so that we would stay on complete alert.

Two hours later Bujang put his hand on my arm. 'Soon,' he said quietly. We slowed down and shortly came out on a spur overlooking the area of our previous temporary base. What incredible navigation skills these Sea Dyaks had!

We were not stupid enough to return to the exact scene of our previous actions. Our current position was an even better base camp, anyway. However, before we made the decision, Bujang sent Unting and another warrior down to check the old site for any signs of Japanese activity. Had they found any we would have moved on, but all was clear. Obviously the Japanese had put the attack entirely down to Sea Dyaks, and knew there was no point trying to track them in the jungle.

From our vantage point we could see Song further off, and a lot of

Japanese walking about. There was about an hour and a half of daylight left. Bujang touched me on the arm again, full of smiles, and brought forward another smiling Sea Dyak, one of the locals who had stayed behind after our air raid-headhunting episode.

This man had important information. The Japanese had smartened up their act and dug slit trenches, not in the jungle but on the outskirts of Song. These had roofing to safeguard against bullets from strafing planes. A quick scan with our binoculars revealed these structures stood exactly where Bujang and his friend indicated.

The Sea Dyaks were master tacticians. After talking with his friend, Bujang had the following proposition. Another air raid would coax the Japanese into their new slit trench shelters. When they were safely ensconced, but before the planes arrived, the Sea Dyaks would creep onto the roofs. After the sirens sounded the all clear, the Japanese would emerge from the slit trenches to go back to Song, and the Sea Dyaks would jump down and cut their heads off.

It was a fabulous idea that would have terrified anyone. Brick Fowler radioed a request for an air strike as early as possible the next day and was told to tune in and expect a reply in exactly one hour. The radio was battery operated, so you had to send and receive messages at set times in order to conserve power, although battery power could be generated by some poor bastard madly pedalling a bicycle-like arrangement.

One hour later our air strike was confirmed for noon the following day. While waiting for the reply we had a few rice wines and studied the slit trenches through our binoculars. Each one seemed able to hold three or maybe four Japanese at the most. Quite a few of them were on the fringe of the jungle. Three, closely grouped together, were some distance from the others and directly in front of our previous ambush position. I suggested we just concentrate on these three shelters and not be too greedy. Three warriors could sit on top of each one and we could use our new ambush position, because we hadn't made ourselves known to the Japanese. Dave agreed with this.

'You organise the Sea Dyaks,' he told me. 'They understand you better anyway.'

That was fine with me. It was almost dark now. Calling Bujang over, I began to arrange a headhunting raid for the first time. Bujang grinned from ear to ear and shook with excitement at the news. It was a difficult and tedious process to explain the raid to someone from a completely different culture and way of life and in a foreign language. Fortunately Bujang was smart, but it still took quite a long time and a lot of patience. No wonder Dave preferred to drink the rice wine and leave the explaining to me!

Bujang was to select eight other Sea Dyaks to accompany him. I stressed they should be as quiet as possible in order to terrify the Japanese more. They could celebrate all they wanted tomorrow evening when it was over. He agreed to do it as quickly as possible, then return via our old ambush position so we could protect them if the Japanese took chase.

'What do you think of the plan, Bujang?'

'Very good,' he smiled. I asked him to repeat it back to me and once again he did it almost word for word.

'Do you need anything?' I asked.

'No.'

'If you want something, come and see me any time. Otherwise I'll see you in the morning.' Bujang gave me his usual cheeky smile and said something like 'good'. As he turned to go, I stopped him and asked, 'Have we got guards?'

'I show you.'

'No. No need to. See you tomorrow.' I smiled and put my hand on his arm again, which he seemed to take as a sign of my confidence in him. I went over and joined Dave and the others and had a couple of rice wines. I had some catching up to do.

We woke to sunny, clear skies – an ideal day for an air strike. I had a bit of a hangover, which cleared during breakfast and a serious talk with Bujang. The others felt worse, but then they'd been drinking while I was working.

Bujang had Unting and seven others ready to go. I asked whether they had all eaten and he told me, 'Oh yes, a long time ago.' It was only seven o'clock in the morning and we weren't leaving for another three hours or so, after which there'd be another a couple of hours wait for the air strike. I asked if the others knew what was happening.

'They understand. I have told them three times,' Bujang announced gravely, adding, 'You only told me twice.'

The cheeky bastard! I almost laughed, but I didn't because he was deadly serious and proud that he was smarter than the rest.

'That's good. Are their parangs sharp enough?'

'Yes,' he said. He arranged to come back before we had to move to our positions.

When the time came to go, we left Brick Fowler behind with his radio, along with our Sea Dyak carriers and several reluctant warriors, disappointed at being left out. Taking up the ambush position, I watched Bujang and his warriors evaporate into the jungle just behind the slit trench shelters. Then there was nothing to do but wait on full alert. No room for complacency if you wanted the best chance of staying alive.

The jungle was always host to strange noises. Sometimes it sounded like animals screaming and fighting; other times I fancied they were just indignant at our presence. Then there was the creaking of overburdened trees and dead branches thumping to the ground. We were lucky it wasn't pissing down with tropical rain. Looking right into Song, we could see the Japanese walking around and hear the murmur of their voices and occasional laughter. I hoped we would soon cause them a severe upset.

The planes were slightly late, but it didn't matter. At exactly 12.30 I heard the rumble of their engines. We smiled and I could imagine Bujang and his mates jumping out of their skins with excitement.

The air raid siren made its peculiar noise and the Japanese made their way to the new slit trench shelters, glancing over their shoulders as if trying to see the planes which were yet to come into view. Some carried rifles, but they didn't look too comfortable with them. They all seemed to head straight for designated positions. Five went into one of our target slit trenches, and four into each of the other two. Two trenches had one rifle each. Not much to worry Bujang and his warriors, I thought.

The three RAAF fighter bombers now soared overhead. What a mess they made of poor little Song! They shot the place up, returned to drop their bomb load, then turned around to strafe a second time for good measure. It was lovely to watch from our secure position. At last they finished, gradually disappearing until only three vapour trails were left in the sky. Bujang and his warriors quickly nestled on the roofs above the three slit trenches, ready to go. They must have counted the number of Japanese in each trench, because they waited until all of them had emerged in response to the all-clear siren.

Stretching, laughing and talking, the Japanese soldiers were in no hurry at all. Bujang and his mates pounced. Sensing something behind them, the soldiers turned to look and I saw the horror on their faces. Most of them got their first hack on the neck before they could utter a sound. The rest just took off, screaming. To my amazement, five men from an adjacent shelter – not one of our targets – came over to see what was happening just as the Sea Dyaks had finished attending to their first lot of victims. The visitors screamed and turned to run, but only two of them made it.

Japanese from other slit trenches began to move away and a few shots were fired by one or some of them, but to no effect. The Sea Dyaks gathered their loot together and were making their escape when some distance away a Japanese officer began shouting his head off. He was organising an armed patrol to give chase, but it was too late. The Sea Dyaks had already merged with the jungle.

We waited in our ambush position in case the Japs persisted with their pursuit. I didn't think they would, figuring they'd be too frightened of the invisible warriors, and I was right. They stopped to examine their dead comrades, rolling them over with their boots, and four soldiers stayed to guard the bodies when the others moved on. Shortly, a larger crew arrived with local natives dragging a couple of large handcarts. The bodies were taken away.

By the time we reached our base camp the Sea Dyaks were already there, celebrating with great joy. Bujang raced over to me, grinning from ear to ear. He went to put his hand on me but pulled back, realising he was covered with mud and gore. Almost too thrilled to speak, he proudly announced he had taken two of the twelve heads. I smiled and congratulated him, saying I thought it was marvellous and that I'd watched him do it.

'We made no noise again,' Bujang said.

'I know, and it's much better that way.'

He kept nodding his head, very excited. It must have taken a lot of work to stop the others whooping wildly as they attacked.

I asked him to put a couple of lookouts on the alert in case some eager patrol decided to venture after them. If they did, we could quickly resume our ambush position. After all, the Japanese had only seen the Sea Dyaks, not us.

Rice wine helped us celebrate, although by now I'd developed a preference for the local arak mixed with water and wild lemons. The Sea Dyaks milled about Dave with their grisly trophies and he made a good ceremony of presenting the one Straits Settlement dollar per head produced. We were all very pleased with ourselves.

I suggested to Bujang that it would be good if he and his friends got themselves tidied up. This was no slur, because the Sea Dyaks were fastidiously clean people and Bujang knew he was somewhat on the nose from the fight.

We had a few more rice wines and araks with lemon and water and Brick Fowler radioed in our result. It was only late afternoon. Activity in Song was much diminished, with only a few troops carrying rifles, so we decided we might as well stay for the night. Bujang and his warriors came back clean as whistles, still grinning their heads off. We all sat down and talked for a while, because the Sea Dyaks loved recounting their adventures. We listened to a couple of stories out of politeness and then excused ourselves, explaining to Bujang that there were things we had to organise.

To maintain the element of surprise our next strike would have to be from a different location. There was sufficient room for us to move closer to the Rejang River, while remaining upstream of Song and we fixed on this before deciding to have an early night after a few more drinks and something to eat. It was just beginning to get dark. Before turning in I told Bujang our intentions and finished up by placing my hand on his shoulder. 'More heads, Bujang,' I said. He almost shook with delight at the prospect.

I went back to Dave and the others and, because we reckoned we had earned it, we had another nightcap. Then we settled down and hoped for a good night's sleep.

21

Song and Dance

During the blackest of times in New Guinea, I found that by listening closely and trying to decipher the million and one mysterious noises that continuously poured out from the jungle at night, half my mind would stay alert while the other half snatched a desperately needed doze. It was a technique that served me well in Sarawak.

The alert half of my mind woke me a fraction of a second before Bujang gently touched my shoulder. Normally I'd have woken up well before a hand could get anywhere near me. Maybe the alert half of my mind made an exception of Bujang on this occasion because I trusted him.

'All the Japanese, they leave now,' he whispered. I was immediately on my feet. It was still dark and the illuminated face of my wristwatch indicated five in the morning.

Two local Sea Dyaks had raced up from Song with the news. The Japanese were loading the launches moored at the jetty on the Rejang. They were taking a lot of gear and it looked like they were evacuating downstream to Kanowit.

There wasn't much we could do. No point stumbling around in the dark in unknown territory. Who knew what we might run into? If we'd been downstream of Song, where we had sunk the launch a couple of days ago, it would've been a different story. I woke Dave, who in turn woke the others. He agreed it wouldn't be sensible to try anything before daylight. Bujang understood, but was disappointed.

There was no point trying to sleep now. We heated some water over a can of instant heat, drank black coffee and waited for daylight.

A new sight greeted us with the dawn. Local people were back in town, walking around and talking without any worries. We couldn't see any Japs, but it was hardly safe to assume that they'd all gone.

Brick Fowler radioed headquarters that we were going into Song so that if something went wrong, at least someone would know what we were trying to do. We cleaned our weapons again. They were the most valuable items we carried and our best friends. In fact, needing to be as mobile as possible, we weren't carrying anything else into Song. The party consisted of Dave, Ross Bradbury, myself, Bujang, Unting and four warriors Bujang chose. Brick and most of the Sea Dyaks stayed behind to guard our base camp.

Avoiding the places where we had previously attacked, we passed several deserted shelters that looked like sentry posts. They were in the usual filthy condition. Local people spotted us as soon as we reached the outskirts and after a split second of dumbfounded silence, they screamed and raced towards us.

We were mobbed. They were laughing with delight and their screams brought others who joyfully surrounded us too. It was a nice feeling. The poor bastards had copped the Japanese treating them like shit for four years. I would have been happy, too.

'Everything is all right now,' we told them.

As it turned out, all the Japanese had departed. But we still had to confirm this ourselves for our own protection. We entered the central part of town on our way to the jetties, our entourage growing all the time. Bujang took half of the Sea Dyaks to check the houses or buildings on one side as we moved down the main thoroughfare, while the others checked the opposite side.

At the riverside we found the jetties clear of motor boats. Now we could breathe easy – the Japanese had obviously gone downstream to their garrison at Kanowit. They certainly wouldn't have walked out. The jungle had too many ears.

There were so many things to do and so much happening at the one time. More and more locals milled around. A lot of the people who had gone bush to avoid the Japanese were already returning to town. Some had been horribly abused, many looked starved and beatings seemed to have been commonplace. A particularly heartrending sight was a little boy whose arm had been almost severed by a Japanese sword. We applied a field dressing and tried to reassure him that the Japanese weren't coming back. Dave and Ross Bradbury stuck to the PR work, talking to locals, while I arranged to bring Brick Fowler and our gear down. We also had to organise sentry duty and accommodation.

Brick didn't know the local languages, so I wrote him a note explaining what had happened and what he should do. Unting, who carried the letter, helped organise the other Sea Dyaks according to what needed doing. It was just as well I had some patience. Firstly I had to get Bujang to explain everything to Unting and when Bujang was able to assure me that Unting understood, we sent him on his way with the note. Meanwhile Dave and Ross Bradbury were happily drinking with the locals. Rotten bastards, I thought, leaving me with so much to do.

On a hill overlooking the jetties on the Rejang was a large dwelling, used by the Japanese for administrative purposes. It needed a thorough clean and airing before we could move in. Flashing some good Straits Settlement dollars instantly got us a team eager to start work. I think they also took it as a welcome indication that we were here to stay.

I had a drink with Dave while I waited for the cleaning to be done and for Brick to appear. It was refreshing but I didn't really relax. Dave told me the locals were going to put on a special opera performance for us later.

'Oh, good,' I said, although I'd rather have heard some trad jazz. We learnt how the Japanese had changed since our raids began, becoming increasingly worried and then plain terrified, wondering where we would strike next. They had estimated 200 Allied troops and over 2000 armed locals were in the area.

About 200 Japanese were stationed at Song before our arrival, but it's no wonder they took off. Our ambushes must have made them feel surrounded. On leaving they had the mental anguish of having to pass the ambush position downstream where we had sunk their previous launch.

Bujang arrived and gave me a nudge. 'Come and look at our new house. Very clean! The others have arrived.'

I tossed down my rice wine and followed him there.

And our new home was spotless. The cleaning crew waited for my verdict. Accustomed to abuse for their efforts, they were ecstatic when I smiled, thanked them profusely in their own language and produced some good money. I probably paid them far more than their work was worth, but it wasn't my money and it was good public relations. Anyway, they deserved it after what they'd been through.

Brick radioed the good news that we had occupied Song without casualty. Headquarters replied they would relieve us from Kapit in two days time, when we were to follow the Japanese downstream and capture the next township, Kanowit.

Dave, nicely mellow from the rice wine, announced he'd accepted the kind invitation to the locals' banquet and opera performance. There was time for a couple of hours sleep beforehand. That sounded good, because it was still early in the day and we hadn't had much sleep the night before.

I pulled him aside and warned him it was essential that we had sentries watching in case the Japanese sent some troops. I knew it was highly unlikely, but New Guinea had taught me how unpredictable they were.

'You're right. I'll leave it to you to organise,' he said.

There was another thing, too. I'd been thinking about our Sea Dyak team. It appeared they'd be with us for some time and there was no doubt they were very good. There had to be some sort of recognised pecking order among them. They seemed to accept Bujang as leader, so I suggested we make Bujang a corporal and Unting a lance corporal in the Sarawak Rangers that headquarters was trying to reform.

'It'll be good for morale,' I said to Dave. 'All you have to do is signal Sochon, say you've done it because it was necessary, and ask him to kindly confirm by return signal.'

'I'll write a signal out later,' he said.

'No problem.' I grinned. 'I've done it for you. Sign this and I'll get Brick Fowler to send it off.'

'Oh, shit.' He laughed, scrawling his name on it.

'Will you tell Bujang, Unting and the others?'

'No, you do it, Brian. I'm going to get some bloody sleep.'

The confirmation came back shortly, but I didn't wait for it. I found Bujang and told him immediately. When he finally understood he was very surprised, then so overjoyed that he could hardly stay still. Finally settling, he put his hand on my shoulder and smiled his thanks.

I asked him to tell the others that Unting had been promoted to Lance Corporal, one rank below Bujang's rank of Corporal. That would save me from going crazy having to explain it to the rest of the Sea Dyaks. Bujang got them all together and Unting nodded wisely and smiled his thanks. I went through the whole story with Bujang's help, stressing the importance of being alert night and day. The Japanese would hate us for what we had done, I said, and might attack.

'Do they understand?' I said to him.

'Yes, everything is all right.'

'We need sentries down by the jetties all night.'

'I know. I show you.' The little bugger had beaten me to the punch.

'That's fine. Have you got enough food?'

'Yes.'

'Tell me if you need anything, then, or if anything happens.'

He nodded, so I touched his shoulder and left. He'd know where to find me. He knew everything. It really was uncanny.

By now I was worn out. Everything I'd done had taken a lot of time, concentration and patience. It was already time for the banquet and I'd had no sleep at all.

The banquet was a cosmopolitan affair, the local populace being a mixture of Malays, Chinese, Indians and others. This generally did not include the Sea Dyaks, who mostly lived in longhouses up in the wild headwaters.

A large crowd waited for us. We apologised for arriving fully armed, but it was unavoidable. They had gone to so much trouble and gave us pride of place near the specially-built stage. From then on it was food, drink and non-stop conversation. There was even Scotch whisky, which I gratefully accepted with water. It tasted more like home than the arak with lemon and water. Questions were fired at us from all directions. Although I knew the local language, I still had to mentally translate a conversation into English and the sheer pace and number of questions made it far from easy. But they seemed happy with the answers they got.

After a lot of fussing about, it was time for the opera. Although I'd never been to one, I knew the type of music and it wasn't to my taste. But I was determined to appreciate what these nice people were turning on for us.

It was a funny kind of opera. A trumpet player and violinist began with 'Stormy Weather', a good number, but they played too slowly and the trumpet player had difficulty reaching the high notes. Then six young ladies, all heavily pregnant, danced and swayed in time with the music.

'What's the local word for "pregnant"?' I whispered to one of the dignitaries. He didn't know, so he asked a couple of his friends and none of them knew either. It appeared they didn't have a word for it, but I soon realised they probably hadn't understood me and didn't want to admit it.

An Australian phrase came to mind: 'a bun in the oven.' That was a bit tricky to put into Malay, but I came up with 'bloom masak', meaning 'not yet cooked.' They laughed as they whispered it through the audience. People turned to point at me and smile. Life of the party, that was me.

The Scotch and lack of sleep were making me a bit pissed, so I eased off the grog and put some more food into myself. The band struggled on with 'Stormy Weather'. It was the only number they knew.

When the 'opera' finished, the band and dancing ladies were brought over to meet us. We greeted them enthusiastically and told them how much we'd enjoyed their performance.

'It was excellent,' we said. Of course I had to go a step further and added, 'Come to Australia when the war is over. You'll have no trouble getting on stage there.'

After mixing with the people for a while, having more drinks and snacks, it was time to go and learn via radio what had been happening elsewhere. Before leaving we thanked the townsfolk for their kind hospitality, reassuring them the Japanese would not be coming back to Song. We returned to our building, smiling and waving like royalty. Or maybe not – you don't often see royalty stalking about warily with guns draped all over their bodies.

I was thankful to get back. We were all buggered, me especially. I went to find Bujang, and he materialised as usual. Thinking I'd play a joke on him, I said imperiously, 'What is there to report, Corporal?'

This took him by surprise and his face filled with consternation and uncertainty. I felt awful and quickly put both my hands on his shoulders and smiled in the way he was used to. I explained that I was only joking because I was so pleased at his new rank.

'We're still friends,' I said. 'We always will be.'

He smiled, hesitantly at first, and then finally placed his hands on my arm. I made a mental note never to do it again.

I started over. 'Is everything all right?'

'Yes,' he said. 'I've checked the sentries.'

'I'm going to sleep now, but if you need anything come and wake me.'

He nodded, but as I turned to leave he put his hand out to stay me for a moment.

'Is everything all right?' he asked. The poor little bastard, his mind was still ticking over. I put my hand on his arm again, which always seemed to add assurance to whatever I might say. 'Of course it is. We'll get some more heads soon.'

That clinched it. 'Good, good!' He laughed.

I resolved never to put myself in this position with Bujang again. Apart from thinking of him as a friend, he was practically indispensable.

By the time I got back to our building the others were all asleep. I found my own bit of space and decided to flake out. I wasn't worried, because I knew half my mind would stay alert. And there were always Bujang and his mates keeping watch.

Young Brian off to war, 1941

I was supposed to have had some kind of sporting future

Young Brian wins a golfing trophy, late 1930s

In Perth, 1944, while training with Z Special Unit

The legendary George Warfe. Drawing by Ivor Hele, official Australian war artist, at Missim 1943. (Reproduced by permission of Australian War Memorial ART22499.)

Sleeping Beauty commencing submersion

Almost under

My trusty knuckleduster knife

Sea Dyak longhouse

Sea Dyak chief, or penghulu, in full dress

Sea Dyak Ladies dancing with heads

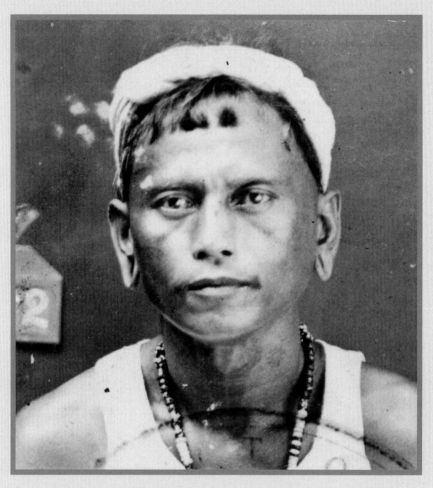

Bujang, September 1945. I took photos of Bujang and Unting at Simanggang with the Japanese commander's Leica camera. Unfortunately the rotten bastard only had a few exposures left on his film.

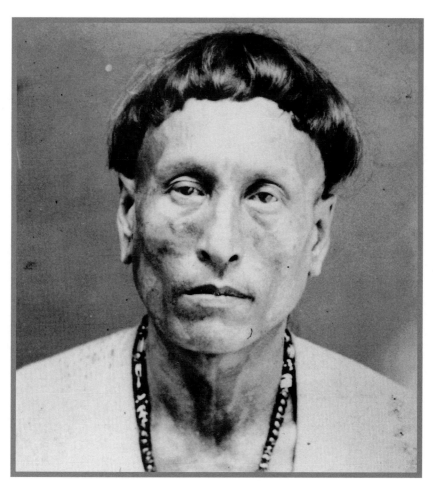

Unting, a fine warrior and Bujang's right-hand man

Sea Dyaks on verandah outside longhouse

Lena Ricketts, 'the Little Rose of the Batang Lupar', photo taken 1952

Together again, Lena and Brian, 1998

22

The Sea Dyak Longhouse

I woke before five in the morning and felt pretty good. The others were still sleeping, so I went to see Bujang. We greeted each other warmly and I breathed a sigh of relief to myself, because everything seemed back to normal.

Dave and Ross were slightly hung over from all their drinking and socialising. We ate and had coffee, while Brick had his morning chat on the radio. Headquarters congratulated us for taking Song, but asked us to go as soon as possible to Kidd's Estate, a plantation about one-and-a-half miles east of Kanowit occupied by an uncertain number of Japanese. We were to ascertain their strength and endeavour to capture a Japanese for interrogation purposes. Dave, Ross, myself and some Sea Dyaks were to do this, while Brick Fowler stayed with his radio at Song until headquarters arrived.

This was a two- or three-day job, minimum. It was about thirty miles from Kapit to Song and another forty-five from Song to Kanowit. But travelling through virgin jungle in a straight line was impossible and the river wound too as it followed the terrain. So the actual distance was probably double.

It was decided the Sea Dyaks would take us downstream by prahu as far as they could. They had moorings for their prahus at all sorts of odd spots along the river banks, places only they knew about. River travel was relatively easy. They guided the prahus with expert hands down rapids and around obstacles. They paddled madly through calm water to speed the trip up, if required. If the rapids were too steep to negotiate, they took the prahus ashore and carried them around the trouble spot, then put them back in the water and continued.

To take a prahu upstream, the Sea Dyaks manoeuvred it into the sluggish-flowing area of the river, avoiding the fast-flowing rips that were ideal for downstream travel. If rapids covered the whole width of the river, they would drop their paddles into the bottom of the prahu and pick up long flexible poles, which they used in perfect unison to force the prahu against the current.

They always sang as they went, splashing playfully and making fun of one another. They would even rock the prahu to tip an unwary passenger into the river. Spoilsport Brian stuffed up their little games. I told Bujang he'd have to ensure they didn't do things like that while we were fighting the Japanese.

'The Japs must never know where we are,' I said. 'We want to surprise them, not let them surprise us.'

Bujang nodded, smiled and touched my arm as if to say, "Yes of course, you poor stupid bastard" – but I don't think Bujang thought that way. As I walked away, I said, 'Tell them more heads soon,' which extracted a hearty laugh.

Departure was fixed for early in the morning and that gave us all a day to clean and check our weapons and get a good rest. The Bren gun was staying behind so we could travel light. All we needed were survival rations, weapons and Sea Dyaks. Six warriors came with us and there were others to man the prahus. Of course, we didn't know how many prahus or paddlers were needed.

'Brian, would you organise everything we need?' Dave asked. 'Make sure the Sea Dyaks have got enough ammunition and food. You seem to know them all pretty well.'

'Yeah, sure.' And there was something extra that needed explaining to Bujang. 'We need to bring one live Jap back with us, to ask him questions,' I said. 'Apart from that, you can take all the heads you want.' I had an afterthought. '*Japanese* heads, that is.'

'We should take Unting,' Bujang said, adding that he had four more special – very good – warriors. 'We take two prahus. We need eight Sea Dyaks to steer each prahu.'

He agreed to pick ten more to complete the party and have the two prahus ready to leave in the morning. He nodded his yes with utmost gravity.

'Make sure your warriors have cleaned their rifles the way that we've shown you.'

He interrupted me. 'Already done.'

'Well, check if you need replacement ammunition and get enough rough food for three days from Brick Fowler. We might even be lucky and get a meal on the way down.'

Bujang straightaway got excited. 'I know a longhouse where we can stay and eat.'

'Excellent. Do you need anything else?'

'No. We'll be ready before first light.'

I gave him a few dollars, which I reckoned he had more than earned. 'Buy something,' I said, touching his arm. 'See me if you need anything.'

Explaining this was hard going, although sign language helped, and when I'd finished I was gasping for a drink. At least I could trust that Bujang understood me. Back at the building the others had just finished off the last of the Scotch, so I fixed myself an arak, lemon and water. And another. That was better.

I explained what had been organised and told Brick he could expect a visit from Bujang and others wanting ammunition and food. Dave agreed it wouldn't hurt to be generous. He told me he'd been approached three times by local Sea Dyaks in Song, heads in hand, hopeful of being paid the bounty.

'Of course I had to refuse them. The heads weren't Japanese. Christ, why me?'

I couldn't help bursting out laughing.

'What's so funny?'

'Well, you're famous, aren't you? The man with the head money, just like I said.'

It wasn't the sort of reputation he wanted. 'I can't see the funny side of it,' he said unhappily.

After cleaning my weapons, I checked all my gear, including my emergency rations and L pill. Then the rest of the day was free, so I filled in the time with one of our new 'toys'. While outfitting myself from the stores at Kapit, a new invention had caught my eye: an MCR short wave radio receiving set. About three-quarters the size of a hardback novel, it was battery operated and received, but couldn't transmit. Brick Fowler was only able to speak on his radio in Morse code, but the MCR could pick up American short wave news and entertainment broadcasts and also the Japanese propaganda broadcasts in English. These were specifically designed for the ears of Allied service people in the southwest Pacific area and were most amusing, especially when the famous Tokyo Rose was on air. She was really something to listen to: so charming, so seductive and so sincerely trying her very best to make her listeners believe her false information.

Tokyo Rose had two pet subjects. The first was that we were losing the war and horrible catastrophes were befalling us. The second was how terribly sorry she felt for all us overseas Allied servicemen. 'Your wives and girlfriends – even now, as I tell you this – are being unfaithful to you. You have been abandoned, you poor things,' she would cry.

This was first class entertainment to poor bastards like us in the jungle. The MCR only had one set of earphones, but we overcame this by turning up the volume to maximum and covering the earphones with something metallic. Although it made the reception tinny, it was still quite clear and a lot better than nothing at all. And so we kept up with the latest songs, but took the news with a large grain of salt, whether American or Japanese. Neither side was going to broadcast anything helpful to the other. Nevertheless the MCR was a definite asset and I was glad to have one.

Before dinner I saw Bujang again. The Sea Dyaks had collected their food and ammunition and he'd already spent some of the money. I didn't ask what he'd bought – it was nothing to do with me – but he seemed pleased with himself. Everything was ready for our departure at first light in the morning.

Back at the building a couple of the locals were cooking us something to eat. The others quietly enjoyed some rice wine. I felt worn out. I joined them and quickly disposed of an arak, lemon and water while I reported the finalised arrangements to Dave.

It was still dark and chilly when we arrived at the riverbank the next morning. Bujang had the two prahus ready to go. A heavy mist lay over the water, and the jungle was deathly silent. We didn't stuff around. With a few whoops of glee, the Sea Dyaks took us into the fast current. The prahus whisked downstream like a couple of corks, our paddlers expertly steering us around obstacles which we could barely glimpse as we flashed past. The Sea Dyaks were relaxed and having a ball, but we gripped the sides like grim death, trying to keep out of the river. We were only two or three inches above the water.

At length the sun appeared and burnt off the heavy mist. Now we saw clearly where we were travelling. The sight of the huge boulders the Sea Dyaks had been dodging in the dark made us grab the sides of the prahu even more tightly.

The trip continued for well over two hours before Bujang told me we were approaching the longhouse he'd mentioned. These Sea Dyaks were friendly, Bujang announced. They had Japanese heads of their own. That was apparently his indication of complete assurance, meant to remove all doubt from our minds.

The Sea Dyaks broadsided our two prahus around a riverbend. It felt like we were surfing. The longhouse immediately came into view, high up on the bank. Prahus were drawn half out of the water and a crowd was gathered in front of the longhouse, waving to us. Their intuition absolutely amazed me. I could understand how Bujang knew we were approaching the longhouse from familiar land features along the way. But how on earth could our Sea Dyak hosts predict our impending arrival? Bujang often informed me of something that was about to happen, always with complete accuracy. I didn't believe in the supernatural and don't now, but it was simply uncanny. Whenever I asked him how he knew these things, he just smiled and shrugged. I toyed with the idea that it was some kind of mental telepathy, but finally decided it had to be an acute inherent intuition, honed over many generations. Whatever it was, I hoped that he continued to supply me with his solid information and, fortunately for me, he did.

The Sea Dyaks greeted each other happily with rapid-fire conversation. It was too fast for me to translate completely, but I got the gist of it, particularly when they traded news about heads. Smiling, Bujang pointed at me and boasted about all the heads I'd taken. There were smiles all round and a muttered chorus of admiration. Hang on, I thought, what's going on? Then I recalled the yarn I'd spun about taking heads in New Guinea when I first had to gain Sea Dyak approval. I may have been a lying bastard, but I had killed a lot of Japanese, so I had no qualms about letting this head furphy stay. It bolstered my prestige and made my job easier, and that was what mattered. Anyway, who was I to ruin such a good story?

The local penghulu invited us inside to drink and eat. We accepted graciously, though I wondered if this was how they greeted their enemies, all the while sizing up their heads for a place on the longhouse wall.

Entering the longhouse via the notched tree trunk, we were taken into the penghulu's own quarters. I supposed it was only natural that he had the best space. He offered us a drink and seemed ready for a long and pleasant talk.

'Dave,' I said, 'We've got to set some sentries and see if we can find out what's happening downstream where we're going.'

I had already guessed his answer. 'Yes, but you do it. You do it better than me.'

I took a couple of arak drinks and climbed down the notched tree trunk, not an easy task with hands full and carrying weapons. Bujang had already posted sentries, so with his help I found two local warriors who knew what the Japanese were doing at Kidd's Estate. After a lot of conversation I ascertained there were quite a few Japanese there, but they didn't seem to be expecting trouble. More interesting was the news that every dawn about ten of them transported something – *what* I couldn't discover – from Kidd's Estate to Kanowit.

I asked Bujang if we could get to where these Japanese left Kidd's Estate without being seen before dawn, so we could wait for them. There was more rapid-fire conversation, of which I only got the gist, but Bujang explained more fully to me. He reckoned if we left by prahu just after two in the morning we could negotiate the river safely. We'd have to go slowly to avoid obstacles, but he assured me it was going to be a moonlit night. How he knew this on a sunny afternoon I had no idea, but there was no doubting him. After about two hours we'd go ashore where a track would take us to our destination in another hour. The two local Sea Dyak warriors would guide us.

'Do you trust this information?' I asked Bujang.

'Yes, I'm sure,' he said. I thought it would be okay, too. I didn't think this pair would trifle with Bujang. He was getting quite a reputation and they knew full well they'd get the chop if they led us into a trap.

Back at the longhouse, I found I had a bit of catching up to do and I fixed myself another arak drink.

'We're going to eat soon,' Dave said. Earlier I had noticed a couple of chickens tethered by the leg to a tree or post, with their necks ring-barked. The poor bastards were squawking and flapping themselves to death and pumping blood everywhere. Inside the longhouse were several little smouldering rock fireplaces. After the chickens were plucked and cooked we had an excellent chicken dinner, served with sweet potato and tapioca on wooden plates. We ate with our fingers, sitting on the rattan mats. It was delicious.

The penghulu asked us if we would stay the night in his longhouse. 'Stay as long as you like,' he said. 'You are welcome.' We explained we were going downstream in the early hours, but would be back.

He then asked courteously if we would each like a young lady to share our beds. This came completely out of the blue, but we soon learned it was standard practice. At first we were shocked. This wasn't distaste – it was more like amazement that all our Christmases had just arrived at once. To tell the truth we'd all been perving, for want of a better word, on the young ladies, anyway. No normal male would have done otherwise – most of them were very appealing.

As I've said before, the Sea Dyaks appreciated a quick decision.

'Thanks for the offer,' I said, 'but we're going downstream tonight. Perhaps another time.' I smiled at the lovely ladies nearby. Dave and Ross Bradbury didn't voice an opinion at the time, but I felt they looked at me with mixed feelings.

I guess my New Guinea initiation had given me a different perspective. I was certainly not prudish or reluctant to take up the penghulu's kind offer. After all, I'd already become an opportunist as far as lovely ladies were concerned. But I'd seen enough war to respect the unpredictability of the Japanese. I don't mean in any way that I respected the Japanese. But I knew they could easily get cheesed off with retreating downstream and decide that enough was enough, muster a large force and come after us with the help of indigenous collaborators. There's no backup behind enemy lines – if you get into trouble you're on your own. There's no front line either. They can come at you from anywhere. You have to watch your back constantly and be at least one move ahead all the time. So there was no way the Japanese were going to surprise me with my pants down in bed with a lady.

Dave and Ross Bradbury saw my reasoning, but seemed doubtful. They had obviously never experienced any real danger. We decided to go to bed early and be ready to leave at two. I said I had to clean my weapons first and they suddenly remembered that they had to do their own.

After final checks with Bujang, I went to get some sleep in my part of the longhouse. Elsewhere I could hear murmuring voices, and I thought of the lovely young ladies nearby, one willing to share my bed. Beneath the floor the dogs, goats, chickens and pigs were jostling and making their usual noises. Above me a row of smoked heads adorned the wall, and I wondered idly who they were. Eventually the animals settled and it grew quiet. I dozed off, careful to keep my mind on its half-alert.

23

A Drinking Problem

My mental alarm clock was absolutely accurate. My wristwatch said 1.55 and as I stirred, Bujang appeared. He didn't have a watch, but he didn't need one to know what I meant by 2 am. I never learnt how he did it, but he always knew precisely when to be up and ready.

We grinned at each other, then I went to wake the others. But when I found Dave, he was curled up with one of the young ladies! She was already awake and looked at me with frightened eyes. Suggesting gently that she should leave, I nudged Dave awake. He was almost cross-eyed and couldn't speak properly. We needed this like a hole in the head. Not only was the raid set to go, but we couldn't afford to lose face by letting the locals see Dave rolling drunk.

'He has to come with us,' I told Ross. 'I'll tell the Sea Dyaks he's got a bad dose of malaria and a very bad stomach upset. I'll say we know he'll come good in a short while, because it's happened before. If we can get him into the prahu, I'll pour water over his fucking face until he either drowns or sobers up.'

I felt really dirty on him. He was designated party leader, yet he had placed us in jeopardy with no consideration whatsoever. What a joke!

Ross, ever the careful one, said, 'What if he rocks the prahu and we end up in the river?'

'I'll knock him cold before he can do that,' I said, but Ross didn't seem to be too happy about it. I felt like telling him to stay behind, but it wasn't up to me. The only reason I was willing to look after Dave was that he was such a nice bloke. At that moment, however, he was on the bottom of my list and I felt like thumping the crap out of him, even though I knew I wouldn't. The Sea Dyaks accepted my story and took it in their stride, and while I hated having to deceive Bujang, I felt I had no choice.

The rest of the longhouse residents didn't stir. They were no doubt used to war parties going out at odd hours during the night. It was quite a job getting Dave and all his gear down the notched tree trunk in the dark. He must have been covered in bruises from all the knocks he received, but like a typical drunk he was completely relaxed and quite pliable. Every time he began to groan or grunt I nudged him to shut up. It was a bright and clear moonlit night, just as Bujang had predicted. Eventually Dave lay flat on his back in the prahu with his head between my knees, giving me sufficient control over his movements.

'Keep still and shut up,' I told him, but I don't think he heard. Fortunately we hadn't lost too much time. As we progressed downstream, speeding along the rip section of the river, I occasionally poured cold river water over Dave's face despite his spluttered protests.

And we made good time. After one-and-a-half hours Bujang turned to me.

'Soon!' he shouted, his voice almost drowned out by the roaring river. I could just make out his smile in the moonlight.

Dave was starting to show a few signs of life. It was time to decide what to do with him.

I gave him another dose of cold water, a few pats on the face and some nudges with my knees. If he was still *non compos* when we hit the river bank he'd have to stay with the prahus. Who knew what would happen when he sobered up to find himself surrounded by ten Sea Dyak boatmen in the middle of the night!

The prahus slid up the river bank and the Sea Dyaks pulled them out of the raging water. We moved to get Dave out, but he was able to help himself a little so we just steadied him and sat him down.

There was no time to waste. I pulled Bujang aside to double-check that the Sea Dyaks knew what we were doing. I reiterated that we had to bring back one live Japanese. 'Of course,' he nodded wisely.

Dave looked shocking. 'I'm sorry, I couldn't help myself – '

I cut him off. 'Look, we've got to get to our ambush position in time or else we've wasted our trip. You better stay here.'

'I'm sorry. I –' he continued.

'Shit, I'm sick of hearing that!'

'I want to come. I'll be okay after a bit of a walk.'

'If we run into an ambush or if you make a noise you could get us all killed,' I said.

'Let me walk at the rear until I come good.'

Admittedly he was improving, so I had Bujang ask Unting if he would accompany him right at the rear. We were still well within our timetable, but I wasn't going to tell Dave that. We set off at a pretty fast pace, with our two Sea Dyak guides leading the way. Bujang gave me his usual 'Soon' before the guides turned to tell him. There was time for a quick break to see how Dave was. He managed a smile and said he felt a lot better (which wouldn't have been too difficult) and that he would be okay.

Moving forward with caution, we shortly reached the main track from Kidd's Estate to Kanowit. It was a marked-out track, unlike our jungle route known only to the Sea Dyaks. The rubbish littering both sides of the way showed that it took a lot of Japanese traffic. We settled into ambush position. After thinking about it, I could see only one way of taking our prisoner alive. If I went with Bujang to the end of the ambush position closest to Kidd's Estate, when the tail end of the Japanese patrol was nearly level with me I would open fire – the signal for everyone else to open up – making sure that I didn't hit the last one in line. A grenade rolled midway through the group with any luck would kill them all except the last in line, who would be too far back to be injured, but might be concussed. Almost certainly he'd make a beeline back into Kidd's Estate, and when he did Bujang and I would tackle him. I had brought a length of thin special-strength rope to tie him up with while we ratted his mates' bodies.

'Sounds good,' Dave said. 'Organise it.'

Bujang and I had come to understand each other pretty well by now. My Sea Dyak was gradually improving, so relaying the instructions wasn't quite as laborious. He in turn briefed the other Sea Dyaks in rapid-fire conversation, which didn't take long at all. Maybe he was talking in Sea Dyak shorthand.

I thanked our two Sea Dyak guides, and they asked if they could come back to the longhouse with us. Maybe they had lady friends there. I asked

Bujang to tell them to stay in the jungle behind us and keep very quiet. He would tell them with greater impact than I could. Apart from their parangs they had no weapons and I was sure Bujang and his mates didn't want them getting any of the heads.

Still concerned about noise, I reminded Bujang that it was more terrifying for the Japanese if we kept silent rather than whooping and screaming during the attack. He put on his hurt look. 'I've already told them,' he said.

The moonlight faded into the deep grey of dawn. We'd been lucky to have such a bright night. If it had been the normal pitch-black, or even worse, pitch-black and raining, we'd still have been stumbling along in the jungle. As we waited, the animal life seemed to stir and wake for the coming day. Rustling came from the jungle floor, birds flapped and scratched at their feathers and monkeys screeched high in the trees. Any minute.

24

The 'Elderly Jap'

We heard them coming just before daylight: a dozen armed Japanese soldiers, talking and laughing as they walked and behind them five unarmed local people carrying goods. Through binoculars they looked close enough for us to reach out and touch.

'Not long now,' I said, passing the news around. As the second last soldier came level with me I opened fire and rolled a grenade in among the Japanese. The locals were too far back to be hurt. I ripped the pin from another grenade and rolled it in, too. The others were shooting by now and the jungle rang with the chatter of submachine guns, grenade blasts and a couple of weak, quickly fading screams.

The first eleven were in no state to cause trouble. The twelfth man was in a bewildered stagger, like a drunk trying to dance. I nudged Bujang and we raced out to drag him into the bushes. A quick rabbit-killer chop kept him bewildered for a while longer, and we trussed him up to stop him escaping while we finished our business.

The five locals, who looked like Malays, had just stayed put, stunned with fear. They got another surprise when I addressed them in their own language.

'Wait here. We won't hurt you if you don't try to do us any harm,' I said, as pleasantly as I could under the circumstances. They probably thought that sounded ridiculous, because they had no way of hurting us. But I wanted them to do as I said, and they did.

The ratting of the dead soldiers turned up nothing of any interest – just

photos of wives or girlfriends and quantities of worthless Japanese
invasion money. We took the bolts out of their rifles and threw them into
the jungle, then dumped the bolts some distance away so that even if they
found the rifles they couldn't use them. I told Bujang we were done, and
he led his mates on Sea Dyak business, thankfully unaccompanied by
whoops of victory.

The Malays had been delivering produce, obviously grown at Kidd's
Estate, to the Kanowit garrison. We wondered why this required an armed
guard of a dozen soldiers, but questioning revealed that on the return
journey they took military gear to the soldiers at the Estate. Well, today's
delivery had been cancelled.

It was hard to gauge how many Japanese were at Kidd's Estate. The
Malays weren't evasive, but it was always difficult getting accurate
numbers above two or three from any of these people, even when
counting fingers. However, after using hand gestures for a while I guessed
at least sixty.

We were too close to Kidd's Estate to hang around, because the other
Japanese would have heard our bullets and grenades. And if they came
looking for us, we weren't interested in a firefight.

'There's a lot more Australians back there,' I told them, pointing vaguely
into the jungle, and counting on my fingers over and over. 'The whole lot
will be coming back very soon, so if you hear us attacking or planes
coming over, hide in the jungle because we don't want you to get hurt.'

We didn't have to tell them what to tell the Japanese. As soon as they
got back they'd be talking, hopefully with a lot of exaggerations and lies.
And they'd definitely be taking other Japanese to see what remained of
their twelve missing soldier mates.

Thanking the Malays for their help, we said our goodbyes and watched
them go, not wanting them to see which way we went. We left minus a lot
of cartridge cases and two grenades, but we had gained information, one
live Japanese, and eleven Japanese heads.

Speaking in Malay, I told the Japanese that we wouldn't hurt him and
that we'd feed him after we'd eaten. He seemed to understand, but said
nothing. That suited me fine; I didn't want conversation with the bastard
anyway. I tied a length of rope around him with a slipknot, which would
tighten if he tried to run away, and anchored myself to the other end. Not

that he'd get far in the jungle with six athletic Sea Dyak warriors around him. He had the use of his hands as well as his feet, which helped him balance and thus keep up with us more easily.

Dave was a lot better by now. He could even talk and smile again, but he kept trying to tell me, 'Brian, I just couldn't help myself.'

'Okay, but let's talk about it when we get back into our own territory.'

As we made our way to the prahus, Dave and Ross kept saying that the Japanese 'looked like a pretty old bastard' and they always referred to him later as 'the elderly Jap.' But I'd seen a hell of a lot more Japanese than they had. In fact he was probably the first one they'd seen up close. He was much like the others I'd encountered, wearing a scruffy uniform with its peculiar cap, and looking like he needed a shave. But to Ross and Dave he was always 'the elderly Jap.'

Back at the prahus our excited headhunters showed off their spoils, which the other Sea Dyaks examined keenly. Bujang said his lot wanted to go straight back to the longhouse. They couldn't wait to brag about their new heads, and good luck to them. It was still morning. We were going to be back in time for a few drinks before lunch.

I told our prisoner that we were going for a prahu ride. 'I'm going to tie your hands together,' I said in Malay, in a matter-of-fact, non-threatening tone. 'Play up and I'll knock you cold.' This I demonstrated by thumping my knuckleduster knife into a tree, right near his head. He stared at the four deep indentations it left in the trunk. He didn't cause any trouble in the prahu.

We had quite a bit of music on the way back. The Sea Dyaks were happy and I gave Bujang the okay to make noise, as there were no Japanese about. They whooped vigorously and sang as they poled the prahus upstream.

When we arrived the whole longhouse was down on the river bank, waiting for us. As we came into sight they laughed and waved and jumped up and down. I wondered what they would have said if we had come back with a hard luck story.

It was marvellous to watch our Sea Dyak mob recount what happened and boast about their new Japanese heads. Bujang and his mates were so proud and satisfied with themselves as the longhouse people listened carefully and examined the plunder in minute detail, green with envy.

'Time to be the big fellow again,' I said to Dave. He did this with his usual ceremony, and Bujang and Unting were among the recipients. I had a quick look around for Dave's young lady, but soon realised that I wouldn't recognise her anyway.

Our Japanese prisoner drew a lot of attention. The Sea Dyaks couldn't understand why he hadn't got the chop. Bujang, whose standing was at an all-time high, explained that we had to take him to someone who spoke his language to ask a lot of important questions. They nodded their understanding but continued to gawk at him, fascinated.

I didn't know his bloody name and didn't want to. I just called him Jap. Gradually the irony of me, who hated the bastards, looking after this one started to hit home. I thought and thought about it, then decided I was really only doing it out of perverseness, because honestly I'd rather have seen him dead. But headquarters wanted a Japanese to interrogate and show off, and I wanted to prove myself capable of getting one. I was sure it was all a waste of time and that this flunky wouldn't know anything worth the effort. But it wasn't my job to argue.

It was still morning, but we were all tired, hungry and thirsty. We decided to stay the night and had a few drinks while downstairs our meal squawked at its post. Bujang was having the time of his life big-noting himself, but he deserved every minute of it. I asked him if they were all right for food and he said there was plenty. He'd put the sentries out, too. Next the rotten little bugger would be telling me what to do, I thought fondly.

Our prisoner was tied up near where I had slept the night before. Bujang had one of his most trustworthy warriors stand guard, under threat of his own life if he let anything happen to him. This might seem unfair and harsh, but it had to be done in case someone in the longhouse had designs on an easy Japanese head. I assured the Japanese he would be perfectly safe as long as he behaved himself. He didn't say a word, but his eyes showed his understanding.

I joined Dave and Ross for another arak. We were going to be eating soon; our meal had fallen silent. As I told them what was happening with Bujang, the sentries and the prisoner, I couldn't help wondering why I had to do all this by myself.

The food was excellent. The old penghulu tried to be friendly, but there wasn't much to say and we were pretty tired. We told him what had happened, although I think he'd already heard a few versions from the guides.

After dinner Dave apologised for getting drunk. 'I just couldn't help myself,' he said again.

I had to say something, so I said, 'I suppose you can't do much more than apologise, but you endangered our well-being and that's inexcusable. Well, I've said my piece and I only work here. Speaking of which, someone's got to feed the bloody Jap, and I suppose that's me because it doesn't look like anyone else will.'

I put some food together for the prisoner. It didn't look too bad; we'd been eating the same stuff ourselves. I made him a black coffee as well. Too bad if the bastard wanted it white or with sugar.

He was quite surprised to get anything at all. I hated doing it, but I didn't dare let the Sea Dyaks do it – Christ knew what that might lead to. I watched while he ate, because I'd let him have the use of his hands to eat and didn't want to give him the chance to cause trouble. I occupied my time by cleaning and checking my weapons.

When we had both finished I led him outside, still tethered, and indicated he could relieve himself in the jungle. Bujang's guard took over again, and I went back to see the others and to have a nightcap or two. I wanted to get a good night's sleep, because we were leaving for Song at first light.

Dave was still full of apologies, but I cut him off politely.

'Look, it's all over and done with now.' I felt pretty confident it wouldn't happen again. 'We've got other things to do. If there's a lesson to be learnt it's best to learn it. I've worked hard at keeping myself alive fighting these bloody Japs over some years now, and I've no intention of letting them get the better of me.'

'Yes, well I'm sorry,' he said. 'And we'll leave it at that, then.' And we did. But at least we had got it all off our chests.

We chatted for a while and the time moved on. I said, 'I'm going to see Bujang and check if everything's okay. Then I'm going to get some sleep. Don't forget to clean your weapons.'

'Oh shit!' they exclaimed, as they both remembered.

'I'll see you in the morning, then.'

'Where are you sleeping?' Ross asked.

'Near the fucking Jap, so no one can knock the bastard off. I'll see you at dawn, unless we get an alarm.'

Bujang had everything organised, as usual. Overnight I became aware of a couple of small scratching sounds. Carefully opening one eye, I saw him surreptitiously checking that the sleeping Jap was okay.

At five in the morning the moonlight seemed almost as bright as daylight. Bujang came to wake me, but I waved to him that I was already up. Our captive was still sleeping, his body making occasional twitches. Maybe he was having a nice dream.

The other Sea Dyaks were ready to go and waiting down by the prahus, so I went to wake Dave and Ross. Dave didn't want to stir and I didn't blame him, but at least he was sober. I didn't know whether he'd been with his young lady, but that was nothing to do with me.

Next I untied the Japanese, tethered him with the slipknot and had him descend the notched tree trunk. I indicated where he could avail himself of a jungle lavatory, and he did. After tying his wrists again we all got into the prahus.

The journey upstream was silent, except for the gurgling river and the splash of paddles. The wildlife seemed fast asleep. But after a while we came across some vigorous rapids. The Sea Dyaks switched to poles and whooped while they pushed us through. The sun emerged slowly and took the chill from our bodies. Daylight brought birds of all descriptions, screeching from the thick forest. We saw monkeys chattering and watching us from trees on the bank. Crocodiles lazed on the mud and slipped into the river at our approach.

Suddenly there was a piercing scream as our prisoner propelled himself, with tied wrists, overboard into the rapids. He almost tipped the prahu over as he jumped. Barrelling downstream, he bounced from rock to rock. It was so frustrating after all the time we'd wasted keeping him alive.

He had no hope of surviving the rip. The flow was incredible and there was no way to turn the prahus around to catch him. It would have put all our lives in danger. If I'd had a rifle, I'd have taken a shot at him, but I only had my Owen submachine gun. Bujang's rifle was at the other end of the prahu and there was no time to grab it. Our prisoner was long gone.

A couple of crocodiles had glided into the water; maybe they would finish him off.

Dave and Ross were still calling him 'the elderly Jap', but there was nothing elderly about the way he launched himself from the prahu like a first-class gymnast. They also seriously suggested that I had nudged him overboard, which was ridiculous. After all, I'd been the only one taking any trouble to keep him alive. To set the record straight, it was all the Jap's own doing.

Trussing him up like a pig would have prevented the escape. A few bullets in his legs would've done the trick, too, and made capturing him easier. But then the Sea Dyaks would have had to carry him, thus endangering our lives by restricting our mobility. Also, knowing how much they hated their Japanese oppressors, I didn't want them demeaning themselves by doing that. The Sea Dyaks were my friends, and I couldn't ask them to do something I wouldn't do myself.

Bujang, of course, just grinned and shrugged. 'Sometimes we win, sometimes not. We tried,' he said, echoing my exact thoughts. What a character he was!

25

Cruising Down the River

Song was now Bill Sochon's headquarters. He had moved in during our absence and was nicely set up. The village appeared much more tranquil and safe since we'd last seen it.

After telling us what a rugged time he'd had of it, he listened to our news. He had received no reports, because we hadn't carried a radio. After we put him in the picture he radioed our achievements back to Labuan.

It seemed obvious that Kidd's Estate would have a similar effect to the raids on Song. Eleven headless, bullet-ridden, grenade-shredded soldiers and wild stories from the Malay carriers would have to make the Japanese wonder what they were in for next. Therefore the decision was to go downstream and do to Kanowit what we had done to Song, hopefully prompting another Japanese evacuation. Sochon had other plans for Ross Bradbury this time, so the party was Dave and myself, Bujang, Unting, four other warriors and enough boatmen to handle two prahus. We needed spare supplies and I wanted to take the Bren gun with its accessories. We were to leave first thing in the morning.

I had a chat with Dave about it. 'Look, you fix it,' he said. 'You know what to do. Then we'll have a drink.'

I didn't really mind. Doing it all myself made me more confident of staying alive. As I went to find Bujang I realised we'd probably get current information on Kanowit and a reliable guide from the penghulu back at the longhouse. Dave will be able to see his young lady again, I laughed to myself. I wonder how that'll grab him?

Bujang was laughing away, telling the locals about our exploits. I listened for a while and heard 'Brian' and 'Australia' come up a few times. He never ceased to surprise me. Obviously he remembered my name from when I met him at Kapit, but he'd never used it. In fact he'd never called me anything.

I told him what we were thinking of doing and he nodded wisely. I'd have to call this the 'Bujang look', because I've never seen another quite like it. It turned out he'd already organised everything – his Sea Dyak team had cleaned their weapons, replaced their ammunition and collected their rations.

'I'll see you before I go to sleep,' I finished off. 'But we'll leave at dawn.'

'Everything will be ready.'

Over a couple of drinks, Dave told me we'd be eating with Sochon as soon as his local conscripted servants had it ready. Sochon had probably never been waited on in his life, but now he had a little power he thought he'd better use it while he could.

'There's no way I'm having a long sit-down meal with Sochon,' I said. 'I'm leaving the minute I finish eating.'

'Don't like him, eh?' asked Dave.

'He gives me the shits.' I went on to explain everything that Bujang had organised for tomorrow's expedition. 'All you need to do is bring yourself. I'll even wake you. What more could you want?'

Before Dave could say a word, Sochon appeared, obviously having overheard the last part of our conversation. 'Are you sure your native can do all that?'

'Bujang is most capable,' I said, containing my anger at his patronising arrogance. 'He's done it all before.'

'Oh,' he said, then regally commanded one of his servants. 'Bwing me another dwink!' I nearly pissed myself trying not to laugh. He's made my day, I thought.

Now, I'm not one to make fun of anyone's disability, if speaking like that is a disability. But here was this pedestrian, pompous oaf pretending to be something that he most certainly was not. His attitude towards Bujang, who left him for dead, eroded any sympathy I might have mustered for him.

Soon dinner was ready and we moved to Sochon's dining room to eat.

I was hungry and really enjoyed the meal, but it wasn't a patch on the freshly cooked chicken at the longhouse. I had a couple more drinks and excused myself. After checking my own gear, I found that Bujang had been busy. He proudly showed me all the supplies I'd previously ordered, including the Bren gun, spare barrels, extra ammunition, grenades, emergency rations and other items. It was all stacked neatly undercover with a fierce-looking Sea Dyak warrior standing guard. Nearby our prahus rested on the river bank.

I put my hand on his shoulder. 'Well done. More heads soon.'

His eyes shone as he nodded eagerly. 'We have everything we need.'

'Good. See you at dawn.'

It was time to settle in for the night. Draping the aerial of the MCR along the wall, I put the earphones on and unwrapped a couple of chocolate bars I'd knocked off from the emergency rations. The chocolate took a fair bit of munching, because it was dehydrated and concentrated. There was some good music on the American overseas broadcasts, but I felt like a bit of Tokyo Rose before turning in.

'You poor boys,' she cooed in her sexiest voice, 'There you are suffering, facing danger and death every day, while the Americans sleep with your wives and girlfriends in the comfort of your own homes. They are doing this now, even as I speak. I feel so sorry for you, my darlings.'

I woke to a sliver of moon casting an insipid light. Our gear was already in the prahus and the Sea Dyaks were standing by quietly.

'Good,' I said to Bujang. 'I'll go and get Dave.'

I wondered what sort of condition he'd be in, but a few quiet nudges of my boot found him awake and sober.

'Wakey, wakey,' I said, 'Everyone waits for you so we can leave.'

'Shit,' he said, but he had no problems getting his gear together. He was, however, most surprised to see everything ready and waiting for him.

'It's all Bujang's work, you know, the one your friend Sochon referred to as "your native".'

'Sochon's no friend of mine.'

'You seemed pretty chummy with the little Pommy shit.'

'For Christ's sake, I agree with *you*,' Dave replied.

Well, at least we have something in common, I thought.

A slight mist rose from the raging water in wiry tendrils. Soon we were racing downstream in the rip. Apart from occasionally whooping with pleasure at avoiding a rock or other obstacle, it seemed that Bujang had them thoroughly trained to keep the noise down.

The sun took the mist away and the jungle slowly came to life. As we passed some crocodiles I couldn't help wondering if they'd lunched on our escaped prisoner. The song 'Cruising Down The River On A Sunday Afternoon' began to play in my mind for some reason. Bujang quickly brought me back to reality, telling me we were nearing our target. The river was too loud to hear him but I read his lips. Sure enough, after careering madly around two more bends, we found the longhouse with all the inhabitants out to welcome us.

The penghulu was all smiles and was very hospitable, but I was sure the good money Dave was paying for the privilege had something to do with it.

It was still quite early in the day, but we accepted the penghulu's offer of a drink, which tasted good after those long hours in the prahu. Bujang went to enquire around the longhouse for a couple of likely guides to Kanowit. If they knew anything of Japanese movements there, all the better.

The penghulu said quite a few of them knew about the Japanese at Kanowit. I thought I'd better ask Bujang to help question our prospective guides and decide who to take. It proved a wise move.

The Sea Dyaks were still able to move fairly freely around a lot of Japanese-occupied territory. Their headhunting activities terrified the Japanese, who tended to think of them as a nightmare from way up in the headwaters, but not likely to come into the towns. Also, some Dyaks who visited or lived in the towns were prepared to work for the Japanese, as were some other indigenous people. After the war these collaborators received terrible retribution. Of course, the overwhelming majority of Sea Dyaks were only too happy to help us fight the invaders.

Apparently we could safely go further downstream than we had gone when raiding Kidd's Estate. Then, a modest half-hour walk down a Sea Dyak track unknown to the Japanese would bring us to the outskirts of Kanowit, just behind a guardpost. This was manned by twelve Japanese soldiers who were always laughing and talking. Three Sea Dyaks repeated these facts separately. Bujang chose two of them to come with us, making it clear that if they tried to lead us into trouble they would get the chop, but if their information was good they would be well rewarded.

Dave and I talked it all over. 'What do you think?' he asked.

'Sounds good,' I said. 'It'll have to be a surprise attack, not an ambush, but that shouldn't be a problem if we do it before dawn. They won't be expecting anyone to come out of the jungle at that hour. Then we can sleep all day.'

We decided to leave at two in the morning again to give us time to get a feel for the place before the attack. Also, we needed more time to take the Bren gun and extra stores.

'But you'll have to be sober this time,' I told him, half-joking. 'There's no way I can get you down a notched tree trunk and into the fucking prahu on my own. I had Bradbury to help me last time.'

'That won't happen again,' Dave said. 'Now, will you fix everything?'

I was glad we took the extra stores and the Bren gun, because we never went back to the longhouse and I ended up needing them. I translated all our decisions to Bujang, asking him not to spread them around, because although it was highly unlikely, we couldn't risk someone going into Kanowit and telling the Japanese what we were up to.

He told me that everything would be ready, including enough Sea Dyaks to carry the extra gear. 'They have enough food and everything is all right.' He grinned. I told him I'd see him later.

I wondered if Bujang had got onto a young lady. It wouldn't have surprised me; he had a lot of prestige by now. All those heads would have greatly enhanced his reputation. I didn't like to embarrass him by asking, but good luck to him, I thought.

Our meal was coming, but it wasn't the usual squawking and flapping chicken. I had heard the animal being knocked off, but it wasn't until it was served that I learned what it was – pork, and delicious too.

When the penghulu kindly offered us young ladies again, I told him no thanks and looked over at Dave, but he avoided my gaze. The rest of the day was spent looking around. Bujang ushered me towards a group of smiling Sea Dyaks, all ready to put on a cockfight for me. I talked my way out of it, but they insisted on showing me the fighting birds. Large and vicious-looking, these roosters strutted like boxers before a bout, eyeing me as though they would have liked to have a go at me, too.

Bujang showed me the workings of the longhouse and it was a real eye-opener. The Sea Dyaks were such smart and industrious people. They had market gardens on the sides of nearby hills, which they planted in seven-year cycles to rest the soil. Time seemed to just disappear and the evening was almost upon us. Deciding to have an early night, I told Bujang that I'd see him at two unless there was anything he wanted me for.

Dave and I dined with the penghulu, who was a bit too friendly. In fact it was difficult to get rid of him. That's probably unkind, but we would rather have eaten on our own. Finally I said my goodnights and went back to my space, where I cleaned all my weapons as my friend Tokyo Rose played some music and told me how sorry she felt for me.

This time I was just getting my gear together as Bujang arrived.

'How do you always know when it's two in the morning?' I asked.

'I know,' he shrugged, a little surprised I should even ask.

There was no sign of Dave's young lady when I woke him. The moon was not as bright tonight, but bright enough for us to see by. The Sea Dyaks, of course, knew their way even in complete darkness.

The journey downstream was much like the others. The raging waters belted against an obstacle course of enormous rocks, and I marvelled at the ease with which our boatmen steered us around them. Before long we were beached on the river bank and stepped out without even getting our feet wet. Planting our stores nearby under Sea Dyak guard, we set out on the secret track.

26

The Road to Kanowit

To the untrained eye there was nothing but jungle. No wonder the Japanese knew nothing of the route. Our two guides and Bujang led the way with me at their heels. Dave and the others moved twenty yards behind, leaving space to move in case of trouble.

The moonlight had no chance of penetrating the jungle's umbrella of vegetation. It was pitch dark and we had to travel slowly to keep the noise down. This was no problem for the jungle-bred Sea Dyaks, but to me it was wearing.

Suddenly Bujang and the guides stopped.

'Do you see anything?' I asked.

We crept forward to where the edge of the jungle revealed the Japanese outpost, bathed in open moonlight. It was a small house, just off a fairly wide track which was the main road to Kanowit. Astride the track was a sentry box, clearly set up to control traffic to and from the town. A light shone weakly inside, where a lone figure sat reading at a table. Through the binoculars I saw more chairs, some cabinets, a phone handset and a rifle on the table. Outside the sentry box were two phone cables, one leading down the track to Kanowit and the other to the outpost.

It was reasonable to assume the sentry was doing his night-shift while others slept in the outpost, where the lights were out. Our army generally changed sentries on the hour, but even if the Japanese did it on the half-hour they were unlikely to do it in between. I decided we'd make life too difficult for ourselves if we attacked when they were all awake for the changeover. It was now four thirty. The sentry didn't look like he was preparing to change, so I figured acting quickly would provide a brief safe period. If we disposed of him with complete silence we could then crash the outpost and catch the others with their pants down.

My first thought was regret that I wasn't carrying my Wellrod, the silenced pistol. My second was that I could probably get him with the knuckleduster knife. But then the obvious solution hit me. Bujang was born in the bloody jungle and would do it much better than I could. He was keen when I told him; in fact he appeared insulted that I hadn't asked him immediately.

'There's no time to take his head,' I said. 'You can come back for it later, after we've attacked the outpost. Tell one warrior to watch at the sentry box for more Japs. And tell him to leave the sentry's head alone until you get back. Okay?'

'Yes.'

'I'll be behind you. If there's any problems I'll kill him with the Owen gun.'

'We won't need that,' Bujang said.

Quietly we moved back to the rest of our party. There was no time to waste. We agreed that if I had to fire, Dave would immediately crash the outpost himself, before the occupants were fully awake. Otherwise he would wait for Bujang and me to return and let me lead Bujang and Unting in first, seeing as I had experience kicking in doors going back to Operation Colt. It was time for Bujang to keep his unscheduled appointment with the Japanese sentry. We had about twenty minutes to do everything before the guards changed. The sentry was still reading, while scratching vigorously all over the upper part of his body. He didn't look up once as Bujang and I approached the open door.

Bujang was on him. The parang slammed down, removing all his worries and feelings in an instant. He was meant to be on guard duty, but all his attention had been on a girlie magazine, and a pretty tame one at that. His rifle lay on the table among old food containers. Dirty bastard, I thought. When we got outside I threw his rifle into the jungle.

Bujang smiled at me, flushed with his success. I touched his shoulder quickly.

'Good. Now get your warrior guard and we'll go.' I uncocked my

Owen gun and cut both telephone cables. We'd rat the place later if there was time. There was fifteen minutes left to crash the outpost before changeover time.

The Sea Dyak guard set up watch from the fringe of the jungle. I went back to Dave and we moved under jungle cover towards the outpost, then approached the front door. There was not a sound. They were probably all asleep. The door was unlocked. Gently, I pushed it open and felt for the light switch, but didn't turn it on. Easing the door open a fraction more, I could now discern what appeared to be a large space.

I drew two grenades from my belt and pulled the safety pins out, holding the release clasps down so that they wouldn't go off until I wanted them to. I waved Unting and the three other Sea Dyak warriors forward and indicated that everyone should get down. Showing them the grenades, I mimed what I was about to do.

Pushing the door open again, I rolled them in as far as possible, closed the door and got down. Five seconds, then the deathly quiet was shattered by a tremendous blast. Flashes from the explosion momentarily lit up the night. The wall we huddled against trembled.

I jumped up to open the door. The fucking thing was jammed by the explosions. Luckily, one kick did the trick. I hit the light switch, but only got a weak light from somewhere inside the house. The grenade blast had broken most of the light globes. I hadn't expected that, but you live and learn. It was one to remember for the future.

There was enough light to see that the interior was shredded to bits. It was a large L-shaped area with a corridor leading to more rooms. No one was asleep now. A couple of Japanese lay dead, while others twitched or staggered about. Bujang, Unting and the other Sea Dyaks raced past me down the corridor, with Dave hot at their heels. I could hear outbursts of screaming, groans, thuds and scuffles, but not a single victory whoop. Bujang had taught them well.

The Sea Dyaks emerged all smiles moments later, with trophies in hand. With them were three indigenous young ladies, screaming their bloody heads off. They were pretty scruffy-looking; the ladies back at the longhouse left them for dead. But as my mother said, there was no telling another person's taste. I was surprised that the Sea Dyaks hadn't made them into trophies as well. Maybe they had some gentlemanly instinct that I wasn't aware of. I made a mental note to ask Bujang about it.

The three of them were hysterical, off the planet with fear. It was understandable after what they'd just seen. The Sea Dyaks hadn't touched them, but they were all bleeding from cuts and one had a badly gashed arm.

I asked them in Malay if they were there willingly or unwillingly. They looked surprised at hearing their own language, but their only reply was to keep screaming. I assured them they were quite safe. They thought about this for a couple of seconds and then started to scream again. There was no getting any sense out of them at all and time was running out. I said to Dave, 'Maybe they were having a good time and we broke it up. Who knows?'

I put a field dressing on the arm of the woman with the bad gash, then made a quick inspection. The dividing wall of the two back rooms had been blown open. Pieces of furniture, clothing and bodies were strewn and plastered everywhere. We quickly ratted the place but there was nothing of value except their rifles, which we rendered useless and dumped in the jungle as we left.

The Sea Dyak information had been completely accurate. We counted twelve dead Japanese. I gave Bujang the okay to collect the sentry's head before we cleared out.

'I come straight back,' he said happily.

The three young women were still hysterical, but the screams had died down to moans. Ushering them to the road, we said a polite goodnight. When they arrived in Kanowit their field dressings and exaggerated stories would make a marvellous advertisement for us. After Kidd's Estate and now this, the Japanese would be shitting themselves.

Dawn was just breaking when we got back to our stores plant. Dave and I had brought some local grog, rice wine for him and premixed arak, lemon and water for me. We sat down and quickly enjoyed one and then another. It was only just after six in the morning, but we reckoned we'd earned it.

Dave gave the Sea Dyaks their head bounties and paid the guides as well. You'd have almost thought the old skinflint was using his own money. We were all quite pleased with ourselves, having achieved our goal without casualty. The Sea Dyaks animatedly compared their new heads and dollars, telling and retelling everything we'd done. Jesus, I was hungry. We had some high-energy emergency rations with another drink and cleaned our weapons.

We got to wondering what the Japanese reaction in Kanowit would be. After all, bad news had a habit of travelling fast. I suggested sending a Sea Dyak into town to have a look around. Bujang wanted to go himself, but I didn't want to risk losing him.

'I go,' he insisted. 'I only take a short time, find out and come back.'

'I'll talk about it with Dave,' I said. We decided to let him do it, but I gave him my Browning pistol first, and showed him how to use it. He caught on fast, as usual, though I didn't let him fire any shots because the sound of gunfire is unmistakable and carries too far.

'Hide it in your loincloth,' I said. 'Only use it if you're in a lot of trouble and there's no other choice. And make sure the safety catch is on. We don't want you losing the family jewels.'

That drew a weak, embarrassed smile. Maybe it wasn't funny to the Sea Dyaks.

'Well, be careful. We'll be waiting for you. And more heads soon – but not on this trip.'

He nodded his okay and moved like lightning into the jungle. He could travel a lot faster when not burdened with Dave or me.

Two hours later he was back. I had spent the time cleaning the Bren gun and its two spare barrels. He appeared as if from nowhere and sat down in front of me, looking content with himself. He hadn't even raised a sweat.

'Shoot anyone?' I asked.

He handed me the Browning and sadly shook his head. 'The Japanese are leaving. They're all very frightened and they carry guns. They have packed up a big boat and they leave tonight for Sibu.'

Sibu was the second or third largest town in Sarawak after the capital, Kuching. It had a large Japanese military base, headquarters for the garrisons we'd been forcing downstream.

'Can we bypass Kanowit in the jungle and ambush them on the other side of town?'

'Oh yes. I have a friend who knows a track. I go and get him.'

While Bujang went for his friend, I told Dave what had happened.

I was becoming quite cheesed off at having to repeat my conversations back and forward between Dave and Bujang. I asked him to be present in future when plans were made with Bujang. He agreed the ambush was a good idea and this time came with me to see Bujang's friend.

All the gear had to go with us, as we weren't intending to come back this way. We had enough Sea Dyaks to carry it. We were going to hide both prahus in the jungle, but I had an idea to send one back to Sochon with a message.

'You said you've spent the whole war writing reports,' I said to Dave. 'Tell him we expect to be in possession of Kanowit tomorrow. Say we'll have to stay there initially to stop looting or tribal fighting, and we anticipate he'll want to come down and take over now that everything's safe. We need supplies. We advise no casualties our side. PS – hope you're well.'

We were on the move just after twelve and it was going to be a long day. Once more the Sea Dyak track was just thick jungle. I couldn't see a bloody path anywhere, but the Sea Dyaks never stopped once as they took us around giant trees and through deep open faults in the terrain. At least we could be sure there were no Japanese floating about. They wouldn't be game to venture too far after they'd seen the outpost and talked to the three ladies who had been there.

There was no movement of air. The jungle smelt stale and we sweated like pigs. The only noise, apart from the odd creaking of a tree branch, was the occasional scream of wildlife. After a couple of hours, more light began to seep through the tree canopy. The air freshened, and the cascading water of the Rejang River sounded ahead.

Bujang sent two Sea Dyaks to scout around before we emerged from the jungle. They gave the all-clear and we approached the river bank. It was an ideal ambush position, elevated and near a bend. The fast-flowing rip was on our side of the river, which meant the Japanese craft would pass near our bank to gain more speed. It was a beautiful day, but we weren't here for the weather.

I decided to use the Bren gun, with Bujang changing the barrel for me when it got too hot. Dave would drop some grenades into the boat and then use his submachine gun if there was time. Double-checking the site, I realised we had to set up further back. We were close enough to spit on them, and could easily have copped shrapnel from our own grenades.

Bujang rehearsed changing the barrel of the Bren and passing me fresh magazines. We sent a couple of Sea Dyaks upstream so we'd have advance warning of the Japanese approach. Everyone knew what to do, so we decided to have a feed and something to drink.

It was likely the Japanese would think it safer to travel by night. If so, we'd just have to wait on the alert all day. Suddenly it occurred to me that Bujang might have been wrong – maybe they weren't clearing out at all. I thought I'd better keep that to myself, because if I told Dave, there was a chance he'd give the ambush away. It was only three o'clock and there was a lot of waiting ahead of us.

Sure enough, Dave became restless. 'We're wasting our bloody time. Let's go,' he said.

'Why, got a date with a bird, have you?' That brought on an unhappy look, but at least it shut him up for a while. But we had a hell of a long wait. The daylight turned to dark, which in turn dissolved into a beautifully moonlit night.

It was spot on ten when our two Sea Dyak observers appeared from upstream.

'They come, they come!'

We jumped into position, all fully alert. Dave appeared to have bucked up. A faint motor slowly became louder. We heard the murmur of voices, which gradually became recognisable as drunken laughter. They weren't just pissing off, they were pissed to the eyeballs as well.

A large motor launch rounded the river bend, conveniently hugging our side in the rip. It was lit up like a Christmas tree. They were drunk as skunks, drinking and singing, having the time of their lives. It sounded a crook sort of song to me.

The others knew they had to wait for the Bren gun to get things rolling. Concealed by darkness, I stood up with it slung around my neck like an Owen gun. Bujang stood by with the spare magazines. The launch drew closer and I emptied two magazines into the wheelhouse. Dave lobbed a couple of grenades on board and they exploded simultaneously.

We were real spoilsports. We completely stuffed up their party. The engine stopped and the launch went aground on the river bank. Most of their lights were out, but the moonlight showed there weren't many of them left standing. Those who were screamed wildly.

I'd fired more magazines by now, so I motioned to Bujang that it was time to change the barrel. Unfortunately, in his excitement he forgot the wooden handle and grabbed the barrel before he remembered it was red hot. I changed it myself while Bujang nursed his hand, but he still supplied me with magazines. Dave blasted the launch free from the river bank with another grenade or two. It careered through the rip and ended up mid-river, wallowing like a wounded animal in the still water.

Its lights were out and nobody was moving. Water lapping its sides, the launch slowly disappeared beneath the surface. Soon only a few bubbles betrayed its presence and the night fell silent. The whole operation had taken twenty minutes. With smiles across their faces, Dave and the Sea Dyaks gazed in wonder at the bubbles. I wished I had a camera to take a photo of them.

Bujang's left hand had a very nasty burn. Fortunately he was right-handed. He smiled ruefully and didn't appear too put out, but I knew a burn like that would've worried me. I cleaned it, then applied ointment and a field dressing.

'Dave, how about letting Bujang and his mates have a quick look for some heads?' I said.

'Yeah, why not?' He almost laughed, snapping out of his reverie.

This time I went with them, carrying the Bren in case there were any survivors armed and dangerous. But there was no need. I didn't watch the head-taking business; it wasn't an especially entertaining sight and I'd seen it all before. When they finished I had them throw the decapitated bodies into the river, hoping the rip would carry some downstream to Sibu. I counted thirty-five bodies on the shore, but the Sea Dyaks presented thirty-eight heads to Dave for payment, so I must have missed some in the dark. Of course there were plenty more at the bottom of the river.

After the Sea Dyaks collected their spoils we retreated to a clearing in the jungle. We didn't anticipate any Japanese coming after us, but couldn't afford to be complacent.

'I'll pay you for the heads in the morning,' Dave announced to the Sea Dyaks. 'As soon as there's enough light to count the money out.'

The Bren gun had done an excellent job. I stripped it down and cleaned all the pieces thoroughly. This was a bit difficult in the moonlight, but I'd been trained to do it in pitch dark. Bujang watched closely. Dave got himself a couple more grenades. After a meal we found we only had a few of our premixed drinks left. Mine tasted out of this world and we vowed to take a more lasting supply on future expeditions.

There was no sense going into Kanowit at this time of night. We had no idea what kind of reception we would get and we were all very tired. We decided that five in the morning would be better, when it was lighter and most people were still asleep. Our wake-up call was at four, giving us plenty of time to stumble there in the dark.

There was no longhouse to sleep in tonight, but that didn't worry us. It was a lovely night anyway. Before I dozed off I went with Bujang to look at the river. There was no evidence of the ambush, apart from a few cartridge cases glinting in the dark. The Rejang River had swallowed everything else. I thought of all the atrocities the Japanese had committed, of the disgusting cruelty they had meted out to these lovely Sea Dyak people since invading Sarawak. Our ambush was a job well done, I thought; it meant good riddance to a lot of shits. It was like stamping on vermin. Then I decided there was no point dwelling on it any further. After all, I thought, it was what we were here for.

I put my hand on Bujang's shoulder, motioning that I was ready to go back. He looked at me and at that moment I could've sworn he knew what my thoughts had been. Back at our camp I said goodnight to anyone who might have been listening, curled up under a tree with my Owen gun in my lap, and went to sleep.

27

Trouble with the Boss

'How's your hand?' I asked Bujang in the morning, as I applied a fresh field dressing.

'Good,' he answered, but I knew he'd say that anyway. Still tired, we were reluctant to start work so early, but figured on getting a feed in Kanowit. Before we left I asked Bujang to make sure our guides kept checking that we were keeping up with them in the dark.

The outskirts of Kanowit appeared after just over an hour of travelling. It was still pitch black and we couldn't see any movement about town. I suggested making our base near the wharf area, figuring we'd be safer where we could make life difficult for any Japanese river traffic. If they came back to Kanowit it would probably only be by river. Dave agreed, so we moved down towards the Rejang.

As daylight emerged we stole through the town, alert for any stray Japanese. There were no motor launches at the jetties and it turned out they had all gone, but for now we had to be sure rather than sorry. On the way we noticed several buildings potentially suited to our purposes, except that they were filthy.

Soon the town was stirring. No doubt the first local to see us had passed the word and now more and more were coming out to gawk. Before long a delegation of five local business people approached with smiling faces, wishing to cement their standing with us.

A lot of these townsfolk were two-faced bastards. They'd run with the hare and hunt with the hounds. All they wanted to do was to stay in business, make money, and have protection from the Sea Dyaks and others they'd been ripping off for years. They always did their best to cosy up to whoever happened to be in the box seat. Now the Japanese were gone it was us. So we took them with a grain of salt, but they proved useful.

They told us how pleased they were to see us. 'Are you English?'

'No. We're Australians,' I said, adding facetiously the obvious comment, 'And our associates are Sea Dyaks.'

'The Japanese all left last night.'

'That's good. How many were there?'

'A lot.'

'Yes, but how many?' I imitated counting with my fingers. They exchanged glances and tried to work it out between themselves. Not too astute for businessmen, I thought.

Finally they agreed that over seventy Japanese soldiers had left on the launch. We never relied on the locals' numbers. Unlike the Sea Dyaks, whose estimates were generally spot on, they could be way off the mark in either direction. Anyway, it didn't really matter. However many there were, they were all dead in the river now.

'Where are the Japs going?'

'Sibu.'

'Why?'

They told us the Japanese had been attacked at Kidd's Estate and the Kanowit guard post, and bodies had been found without heads. The Japanese thought a large force was attacking and they were badly rattled. The rumours were working perfectly.

'Are they coming back?' I asked, keeping up the pretence.

'Oh yes, very soon, with more soldiers.'

That was enough crap to listen to. We were hungry, thirsty and tired, although our success had boosted our energy quite a bit. Arriving in the town so early under cover of darkness meant that no one knew where we had come from. As yet they had no idea whether we had been involved in the altercations. Nobody knew about the sinking of the launch, either, although they would soon enough. News would soon reach town via the Sea Dyak grapevine, but greatly distorted as usual. One of the three women from the guard post might spot us. And there was always a chance someone would recognise one of the Japanese faces dangling from a Sea Dyak waist. But it wouldn't matter anyway.

We offered the business delegation money if they would clean up three buildings we needed and arrange some food for us. Their eyes lit up at the prospect of being paid for their efforts; they were accustomed to the Japanese forcing labour and stealing whatever they wanted. No doubt they thought we were idiots for paying, but Dave would make sure we got value for money. We settled on a menu and two of them raced off to get things started.

'Will you be staying long?' one of them asked.

'Yes. And others will be arriving soon.'

I rechecked Bujang's hand. The burn didn't look anywhere near as bad as it did last night. The Sea Dyaks had remarkable recovery powers, and our ointment was very good for healing and preventing infection. I'd used it myself.

Shortly a large team of locals descended on the buildings with all kinds of cleaning gear. Bujang arranged sentries and we stacked our stores nearby. Leaving the Sea Dyaks to watch them, we took Bujang and Unting with us for a stroll to make our presence better known in the town.

A lot of people watched us, but most kept their distance. We smiled and addressed them in Malay, which surprised them. Suddenly I realised why everyone had been staring at us so apprehensively ever since we arrived. It was the severed heads Bujang and Unting wore, tied to their waists with bits of vine. I guess we'd become blasé about that sort of thing by now, but the townsfolk found it quite upsetting.

The locals made us a lovely meal. They were extremely courteous and continually questioned us, though we fended them off as politely as possible. At one point I tossed in, 'How did you get on with the Japs?'

This took them aback. Exchanging glances, after considerable thought one of the businessmen smiled and said, 'We tried to get on as best we could,' as if they were martyrs. I bet you did, I thought.

The five businessmen who ate with us couldn't keep their eyes off the Sea Dyaks and seemed bothered by the fact that we were unperturbed at our friends' grisly trophies. Perhaps they were worried that they would be next. The Sea Dyaks remained unaware, of course, and tucked happily into their meal. It was just another day to them.

'Are you worried about the Japanese coming back?' one of them asked.

'No, I don't think they'll come back,' I said. 'But we'd like them to.'

He nodded, but I don't think he quite understood what I had said. Just then someone arrived with news that the buildings were now 'very clean.'

They were spotless. Dave paid the cleaners, who bowed and smiled their pleasure at getting their hands on the money. I was getting sick and tired of all the false smiles. In our new headquarters I claimed a piece of space with a window overlooking the river. Bujang and his crowd settled in, too, and I put some more ointment on his hand. He'd already placed his sentries and cleaned his weapons, of course.

The local delegation returned with three flunkies carrying food and cooking utensils. They introduced us to a local man who was to be our cook.

'I very good cook,' he said. 'You see.'

'What's your name?' I asked.

'Jim,' he said. Lying bastard, I thought, but he turned out to be all right, and soon added an assistant who called himself John. I got Bujang to check the food brought in for the Sea Dyaks and he gave it the okay.

Dave and I decided to relax over a quiet drink, then have another walk around town. We agreed we'd achieved a good result – fortunately without injury, apart from Bujang's hand. Soon our Sea Dyaks would talk to local Sea Dyaks, who would in turn talk to the townsfolk and then everyone in Kanowit would know that the Japanese who said they were returning soon were actually dead in the water. That would surprise them.

'I bet Sochon turns up tomorrow,' I said. 'As long as the report you sent him was sufficiently enticing.'

'Well, I wrote it pretty much along the lines you suggested,' Dave said.

'He'll be down,' I replied.

There wasn't a great deal for us to do. We had to wait for Sochon to arrive before we could move on, mainly to keep the peace. It was obvious that a lot of the people didn't like each other, but were happy to see us in charge. They had been very badly treated by the Japanese and many were in need of medical attention. Like Song, some had been bashed, some hacked by swords, and a lot looked half-starved. Unfortunately we didn't have the training or supplies to do much more than offer sympathy.

Jim and John proved good investments. Dinner was excellent and we told them so. We fixed a couple of pre-dinner drinks and watched the power of the mighty river flow past us. Everything seemed so peaceful, almost as if the war had finished. It had been a busy few days and we'd had little sleep. We decided to sleep in until six, unless there was an emergency. Bujang told me he had eaten well, patting his stomach, and his sentries were all fixed for the night. 'I wake you if something happens,' he said.

First thing in the morning, Bujang arrived with a grin on his face.

'Let me look at your hand,' I said.

'It's good,' he replied. 'It's a lot better.'

The improvement in such a short time was almost miraculous. I told him to keep it clean and show me if there was any problem. 'Some of the others will arrive by boat from Song today. Ask the sentries to let us know as soon as they hear anything.'

'Of course.'

'After we've all eaten, we'll go for another walk around town, but I'll come and get you,' I said.

Dave was still fast asleep. Let him sleep, I thought, and then another thought told me no, wake him up. So I nudged him with my boot and told him it was almost time for breakfast, which Jim ensured was far better than emergency rations. I asked Dave if we could take Jim and John with us when we moved on and he agreed straight away; Dave liked his food.

Afterwards we bathed in the river. The water was fresh and the current racing over us was very cleansing. The Sea Dyaks regularly washed in the river and every time they saw us do it they would point and laugh and have great fun. This morning was no exception and I waved to them.

Everything around town appeared quite settled. Many locals told us that they hoped we would stay so the Japanese would not come back. We had nothing else to do so we talked to them, assuring them they were safe.

At eleven thirty one of our Sea Dyaks whispered something urgently to Bujang, who sent him away and came over to me, holding up three fingers.

'Prahus come from Song,' he said.

Well, it certainly wouldn't be Japanese coming from Song, unless something very strange had happened. It would have to be Sochon, or someone on his behalf.

'When do they arrive?' I asked.

Looking puzzled, he replied, 'Not long.' He had only ever said 'Soon' before, so I asked him again and he concentrated hard then said again, 'Not long, I think.'

Anyway, I was happy to go along with that. Given my experience with Bujang, it was good enough for me. It was almost certainly Sochon, but when I reported to Dave I suggested we set up an ambush in case it wasn't.

'We can sit in the sun and drink grog while we wait,' I added with a laugh.

'Very good,' Dave said. 'You organise it all.'

'All right, but you organise the drinks,' I said. He agreed and we went about our respective jobs. I sited everyone comfortably, so we could easily be in the sun or the shade as desired.

The prahus could only berth at the jetty and our concealed ambush position looked straight down on it. We had a clear view upstream at least half a mile to the closest bend. Bujang assured me he could change the Bren gun barrel this time without burning himself. So we practised a few times and he was fine.

It was a lovely day. Dave arrived back with John, who carefully carried a few drinks for each of us. What a lazy bastard Dave was, I thought, not carrying a bloody thing. We waited an hour. It was just as well we had a few drinks, because after an hour doing nothing became very boring and Dave went back to replenish our supply.

I asked Bujang again when the prahus would arrive. This time a quick talk to his warrior mates resulted in a very serious 'Soon'. I kept examining the river bend through binoculars, but there was nothing apart from raging water. We had a couple more drinks and waited. Then at one thirty Bujang whispered, 'Very soon now.'

Jesus, these Sea Dyaks were uncanny bastards – Bujang in particular. Sure enough, at that moment the binoculars revealed three prahus rounding the bend.

'It's Sochon, all right.' I laughed. 'I can see the fat bastard. Doesn't look like he's enjoying his trip very much.'

He was twitching and moving himself around on the hard bottom of the prahu. It made me think of a constipated pregnant turtle. I heard a noise and turned around to see Dave laughing too.

I wanted us to wait until the prahus pulled up at the jetty, then rise from our ambush positions and say 'g'day'. Dave quite sensibly vetoed this, pointing out that Sochon wouldn't find it at all amusing. Instead we strolled down with our weapons to greet them as they disembarked.

Sochon was there with Pip Hume, Brick Fowler and a couple of others. Hume had brought some of his jungle warfare students, and others appeared to be Sochon's conscripted servants. There was a lot of supplies and equipment. Everyone said their hellos, but apart from Brick there was not much enthusiasm in the greetings.

I think Sochon was somewhat surprised to see us all grouped together, thinking we should be out guarding against an attack. Of course he didn't know that Kanowit was secure. There was a lot that Sochon didn't know.

Sochon's conscripted servants lugged his gear into the headquarters. Dave asked Jim to prepare a meal and offered Sochon a drink from our supplies, but our glorious leader declined because he had his own Scotch, which he didn't offer around.

We went to have a drink while they settled in. 'I'll bet you we'll be out of here tomorrow,' I said. Dave shrugged.

Finally we were summoned for our meal. It was good tucker and Sochon said so. 'I'm yet to learn what's happened here in Kanowit,' he said. 'It certainly seems quiet. Now we're here I think you people should have a feel around further downstweam. Dwaw what you need from supplies and see if you can get away by morning.'

I looked at Dave with a told-you-so look as Sochon continued. 'Now, tell me what you've been doing since I weceived the weport you had the natives deliver to me.' For some reason he refused to call them Sea Dyaks.

Dave had already told me that his entire war experience was writing 'fucking reports', as he put it. Now he transferred that skill into words. He was very good at it, too. He related, with graphic and accurate detail, everything we had achieved, which was far more than anyone could have reasonably expected of us. He even praised me, and Bujang too.

It was intriguing how Sochon's facial expression changed as he listened to Dave. The small toothbrush moustache on his upper lip began to twitch uncontrollably. I had to work hard to stop bursting out with laughter.

Dave went right up to our ambush position above the jetty where

Sochon's three prahus had come in. ' ...we then saw what we considered to be friendlies,' he finished, joking gently.

Sochon could contain himself no longer and poured out all his pettiness and resentment. 'How could the bloody natives know there were thwee pwahus coming downstweam?' he scoffed.

'I don't know, but they were spot on,' Dave said. 'But we had our ambush ready in case the prahus carried Japs.'

'I don't believe it!' Sochon blustered.

'I'm afraid that's exactly what happened,' said Dave.

Instead of congratulating us for a job well done, Sochon was furious. He looked as if he was about to have a fit. 'I sent you down to do a weconnaissance of Kanowit,' he almost snarled – there's no other word to describe it – 'and now you tell me all this!'

I couldn't contain myself any longer. 'Christ, you wanted to take Kanowit! What was there to be gained by letting the Japs escape to come back and try to kill us another day? And another thing, you didn't have enough bloody brains to give us a wireless operator to keep in touch if we got into trouble and needed help, let alone an air strike or supply drop. And stop calling Bujang a bloody native. He's worth several of you!'

His mouth was wide open. I found myself wishing he'd swallow a fly, but then maybe no self-respecting fly would enter his bloody mouth. I considered threatening him with offering Bujang two dollars for his head, but something told me that was going too far. Apart from Sochon's lack of humour, there was a very real risk the Sea Dyaks would take it literally if word went around. I walked out instead.

'By the way,' I said as I left, 'have you ever killed any Japs yourself?'

Taken aback, he closed and opened his mouth. Then, surprisingly, he just said, 'No.'

'Well, you should try it some time.' I went to find Bujang, as I'd said I would see him later.

'Everything is all right,' he told me. 'We ate nice food and the sentries are out.'

I don't know what transpired between Sochon and Dave, but later Dave asked, 'Don't you think you were a little bit rough on Sochon?' Honestly I thought not; he could have done with a few more home truths.

This was actually my second big run-in with Sochon. The first one happened after returning from our first Song recce to find that Sochon and his mates had demolished our grog ration. It was a lousy thing to do however you looked at it, especially considering the hard circumstances we were living under, and I had abused him mightily.

I wasn't worried about Sochon doing anything to my detriment, because our achievements spoke for themselves and he'd only make a fool of himself by complaining about us. Time proved me right on that one. I suffered no repercussions from my altercations with him, except maybe his personal enmity and I didn't give a stuff about that. The useless prick wouldn't have lasted five minutes in New Guinea. I had a pretty good idea what George would've thought of him.

I asked Dave if we were still leaving in the morning. 'Yes,' he said, 'But we're going downstream by land this time, almost as far west as Sibu, keeping as close to the river as possible. We're supposed to find out what's happening, ambush any Japanese and make sure none come upstream towards Kanowit.'

'Who's going?'

'The same bunch of us who took Kanowit.'

'What about Jim?'

'No.'

'Do we get a radio operator?'

'No.'

'What time are we leaving?'

'How about seven in the morning?'

'Whatever – it's not for me to say. How long are we going for?'

'We're taking three weeks' supplies. Maybe we can stay at longhouses on the way.'

'That fucking stinks,' I said. 'It's just the stupid type of planning you'd expect from an idiot like Sochon.'

'Why?' he asked quietly.

'Because there's no way we can watch for Japanese coming upstream to Kanowit when we're travelling by land. You can't just follow the river bank like you'd walk down Collins Street. There's too many obstacles. Even within spitting distance of the bloody river we wouldn't see it through the jungle. And another thing, we'd want to be behind the jungle anyway. We don't want to stand out like dog's balls and be a perfect target to anyone who sees us. I wouldn't walk downstream in the open anyway, orders or no orders. And there's another thing you can tell your idiot mate – '

'He's not my mate, but go on.'

'If the Japs did come upstream, what are the odds we'd hear their launch and be able to race down to the river bank and ambush them? The roar of the waters would probably drown out the motor noise. Or they might come by prahu and we wouldn't hear a bloody thing.'

'You're right. It's a real fuck up,' said Dave. 'What would you suggest?'

I poured myself another premixed arak and thought for a moment. Then it occurred to me that a prahu of Sea Dyaks could keep an eye on the river while posing as fishermen. They could travel downstream at the same pace as our patrol, hugging our side of the river bank. The man at the tail end of our patrol could keep in verbal contact with them. A Japanese jungle patrol wouldn't hear them. If any Japs came up the river, the 'fishermen' could warn us in time to set up an ambush. Dave agreed it was the way to go.

'We'll need a prahu and about four more Sea Dyaks to man it,' I said. 'And a long talk to explain it all to Bujang and his mates.'

'Good,' Dave said. 'I'll go and see Sochon.'

'Tell him it was your idea. He won't like it coming from me.'

'I'll just tell him. I'm bloody annoyed about it myself.'

Dave came back shortly with a satisfied smirk on his face. 'As long as we do it, we can do it which ever way we think best. And we can help ourselves to a prahu and extra stores within reason.'

'What's "within reason" mean?' I asked.

'He didn't say, so I guess it doesn't mean a bloody thing. What do you think?'

'I think Sochon just wants to get rid of us.'

'Well then, let's piss off before he changes his mind.'

While Dave rustled up three weeks supply of drink mixes and kept Sochon occupied, I told Bujang what needed to be done. As an incentive, I said the quicker we got going the more heads there'd be in it for him. When I had him repeat to me all I'd told him he was word perfect. I also said we'd pay good money for anything we had to buy.

Bujang assured me he'd arrange the prahu and four Sea Dyaks to pose as fishermen, plus four extra carriers ready to leave first thing in the morning. I knew he was as good as his word, and felt slightly embarrassed because my promise of more heads was far less certain. But he knew I'd do my best, and you couldn't do more than that. Bujang suggested Unting was the most reliable man for the crucial job of maintaining contact with the prahu at the tail of the patrol.

I made sure we had more than enough food, plenty of spare ammunition and grenades. We were not depriving Sochon and his team; there was more than enough left for them and they had additional supplies from the town and a radio if they needed anything else. My medical kit had to be restocked, mainly because of Bujang's burn, and I packed a good supply of batteries for the MCR radio. I grabbed at the large supply of emergency ration chocolate bars, taking the lion's share like a starving Billy Bunter. I was sure we'd put them to better use than Sochon possibly could. Chocolate was not only a handy snack, it made a good bribe for someone who had never tasted it before. Very few people in this neck of the jungle knew what a chocolate bar was.

Satisfied my commandeering was 'within reason', I stored the goods in my space overlooking the river. Dave was already there, proudly displaying a hefty stockpile of drink mix. I showed him what I'd commandeered. 'It's all within reason,' I said.

'Of course.' He laughed.

Bujang spoke up. 'I'll get the prahu and more Sea Dyaks.'

'Have you all got enough food?'

'Oh yes.'

'We'll leave about seven in the morning,' I said. 'And, Bujang – '
He turned around. 'More heads.' Laughing wildly, he raced off.

'What's that all about, Brian?' said Dave.

'The "more heads" bit?' I said. 'It's like an aphrodisiac to Bujang.'

28

The River with no Name

We left Kanowit at about seven thirty but there was no farewell party. I didn't see Sochon and that suited me just fine. Brick Fowler wished us luck, our cooks Jim and John said goodbye and we left in high spirits. It was a fine, sunny day and the jungle was alive with animal and bird calls.

The humidity was so thick it felt like we were wading through it. The dense foliage blotted out the sun and the air tasted rotten. We walked through a perpetual twilight. Bujang and a guide took the lead and I was close behind. Unting was at the rear, in touch with the 'fishermen.' We couldn't move very fast, because we were almost forcing our way through the jungle. I couldn't see a track anywhere, but as usual the Sea Dyaks knew where to go. After an hour or so we stopped at a riverside clearing and gulped in some fresh river air. Unting and the prahu drew level with us at the same time.

I asked Unting if he had any trouble talking to the 'fishermen'.

'No trouble,' he said.

'If you do have trouble or if they spot something, tell me straightaway.'

'Oh yes,' he replied, as if to suggest I was stating the obvious – although Unting was far too polite to have meant that.

'Okay. More heads soon, Unting,' I said, and he smiled in anticipation. We would have to find something for them.

Just as we were about to move off, Bujang grabbed my arm and pointed. A family of orang utans had emerged from the jungle behind us. There were four of them: Mum, Dad and two kids. We tried to approach them slowly, but they didn't like that and moved away, so we didn't persevere. They were lovely to watch.

I grabbed four of the chocolate bars, unwrapped them and made a big show of pretending to eat and really enjoy them. Then, plucking a large green leaf from a nearby shrub, I laid them down on it and retreated to the jungle fringe.

Dad led the family forward, with Mum holding the two kids by the hands. They sniffed at the chocolate bars and started to eat them. When they finished they looked down at the empty leaf, then up at us as if asking for more. We left some more titbits for them to find, although no chocolate, and continued our way into the stifling jungle. As we slogged through the bush, our Sea Dyak eyes on the river continued alongside us in the prahu.

Our new friends followed at a discreet distance for the next couple of days. They were fascinating to watch, but backpedalled every time we tried to approach them. Given time, we might have been able to get closer and interact with them, but unfortunately we had other things on our minds. I was glad I'd taken most of the chocolate bars from Kanowit, though. I much preferred our orang utan friends enjoying the chocolate to Sochon cramming it into his fat gut.

Travelling by land was much dirtier and more wearing than racing comfortably downstream in a prahu. But it was also a lot safer – on the water we would have been as vulnerable as the Japanese launches we had ambushed so successfully.

We stopped the night at a friendly longhouse. After accepting the penghulu's invitation to stay, we set up an ambush position under cover of a large tree, just in case any Japanese showed up on the river. I told Bujang we needed sentries watching all the time. He smiled and said, 'I know. It's done.' And, sure enough, I could see them.

The penghulu had not seen any Japanese river traffic for at least a week. But he told us that over the years of their occupation they had brutally ransacked his longhouse many times. They always came by river; he had never seen them bashing through the jungle as we had done. We told him what had happened in Kanowit and why they had stopped coming along the river. He digested the news slowly, nodded his head, and then broke out with a huge smile.

Dave and I bathed in the river to wash off some of the musty smell of the jungle. The water was marvellous, so clean and refreshing, and made me feel almost brand new. The river bank filled with enthusiastic barrackers and as we came out of the water I saw our evening meal flapping under the longhouse.

We cleaned our weapons and checked and laid out our gear in case it was needed overnight. Over a pre-dinner drink the penghulu asked a favour. He wanted our considered opinion of a certain head that held pride of place in the longhouse. Jesus, I thought, now they reckon we're connoisseurs! Obviously Bujang had been talking us up. The penghulu led us to a special alcove where we admired the bloody thing politely from several angles and told him that, yes indeed, it was a particularly fine head. He beamed with pleasure at our approval. It was always good public relations to try and make someone happy.

We had an early night so we could start out first thing. Before I turned in, though, I made sure Bujang and his mates were all right and knew when we would be leaving. They had eaten well and would all be ready in the morning. Bujang showed me his hand and it seemed to be fine. I explained that we needed a sentry watching all night in case a Japanese launch or prahu came upstream. But he'd already organised it.

Back at my space, I grabbed my Owen gun and decided to flake out. I was rooted. There would be no Tokyo Rose tonight. She could get stuffed.

⌒⌒⌒

We got away early in the morning, thoroughly refreshed. Dave paid the penghulu for food and board and he seemed quite surprised to be paid at all. 'Stay here any time,' he said.

Then it was out of the lovely fresh air and bright daylight, and into the dim and mouldy jungle. It was another world and, as always, quite eerie. Our fake fishermen were in their prahu, waiting for Unting to give them the sign to move.

We soon looked as though we'd never had our bathe in the river the night before. Wildlife screeched everywhere and the river's roar only added to the pandemonium. Behind us the orang utan family kept following at a safe distance.

After three solid hours I asked Bujang to find a clearing near the river where we could stop for a breather and a drink. Five minutes later we were on the bank. Dave and I drank in the fresh air, gasping away like a couple of fish just pulled out of the water. The Sea Dyaks looked on with polite amusement. It was a few minutes before we were ready to eat.

After half an hour or so we pressed on, but not before leaving some titbits for our orang utan camp followers. An hour or so later Unting materialised beside me and Bujang. 'Japanese boat, it comes now.'

'Did you see it or hear it?' I asked him.

'We heard motor.'

'Two warriors need to guard our front on the track,' I said to Bujang. 'Tell them to keep watch and not be distracted by whatever happens.'

Our front – the direction we were travelling – now became our rear, because we broke through the few yards of jungle to the river bank, where a small, flat clearing a short way downstream seemed ideal for our purpose. The river's noise blocked the sound of our movements and it was only now that we heard a faint motor working its way upstream.

Grabbing the Bren from its Sea Dyak carrier, I sited it and placed a pile of magazines, the spare barrels and a pack of grenades alongside. Our position was not too bad. The boat had to negotiate a river bend well downstream of us before it would come abreast.

I raised the binoculars as a large launch, Japanese flag fluttering in the breeze, came into view around the bend. A number of soldiers stood on the deck, admiring the scenery, smoking and talking, quite unconcerned. From their clean clothes they had obviously not been traipsing around in the jungle.

The launch struggled upstream against the current, hugging the opposite river bank where the flow was not so rapid. They were too far away for our submachine guns or grenades.

'The Bren's the only weapon any good to us,' I said to Dave. 'I'll aim for the wheelhouse. When I open up, throw some grenades as far as you can. You won't reach them, but the explosions will worry them.'

I reckoned on firing when the boat was about fifty yards downstream. If we couldn't stop it before it came abreast of us, we'd lose it, because there was no way of stopping it if it got past us. We'd also be unable to warn Sochon what was coming his way, which was his stupid fault for refusing to let us carry a radio.

Bujang came alongside to help change the magazines and barrel. I hoped he wouldn't burn his hand again, but suspected he had too much sense to be caught twice.

I switched the Bren gun to automatic fire, took careful aim, a deep breath, and then emptied three full magazines into the wheelhouse. The launch staggered and the screaming started.

'What can you see?' I shouted to Dave, who was studying the devastation with binoculars.

'Oh shit, it's bloody marvellous!' he exclaimed.

'Throw some fucking grenades!'

I fired two more magazines. The boat's motor was sounding like a bad smoker's cough. Then there was one, two, three, four explosions from Dave's grenades, each one blasting great spouts of water into the air. The grenades couldn't do any damage, but the Japanese had no way of knowing the next one wouldn't land on board.

By now the launch was turning around. We changed the barrel quickly and I shot two more magazines into the wheelhouse as it swung around momentarily to face us. Completing the turn, the launch started downstream. I sent two more magazines up its arse before checking with the binoculars. Bodies were strewn across the deck while others staggered about, clutching arms and legs. Smoke poured from somewhere and the cough from the motor was enough to make you want to give up cigarettes. The stricken boat disappeared around the bend in the river.

The Sea Dyaks chattered excitedly among themselves. I smiled at Bujang, who had been a big help. 'How's your hand?' I said.

He laughed and showed me. 'No burns today.'

'Shit, what a mess!' said Dave. 'They won't be back. Good thing we had the prahu on the water. I'll have a go at Sochon when I see him. I wonder what he'd have done if the Japs got to Kanowit unannounced.'

We had a good laugh. I was pleased that Dave was coming around to my opinion of Sochon, and very pleased that my 'eyes on the water' idea worked out. I wondered whether the Japanese had fired any shots in retaliation. Although they were heavily armed, I didn't think they had, but then I was busy lying on the ground with my head alongside the Bren gun, which made a hell of a din as it fired. If they had fought back I probably wouldn't have heard the shots or seen any muzzle flashes.

None of the others knew either. Generally if someone shoots at you, the bullets make a distinctive crackle. You'll also hear them rustling through the foliage and see flashes coming from the direction of the firing. But no one had seen a thing, so we just didn't know. At least, though, none of us had been hit.

We never did find out exactly how much damage we caused in this attack. Later some Sea Dyaks told us gleefully about dead and wounded Japanese being taken from a badly burnt launch that limped into Sibu. 'How many were there?' I asked, and they showed me handfuls of fingers. When I asked Bujang how many that meant he just smiled and said, 'A lot.'

Normally after an ambush we'd have disappeared as fast as possible, in case of reprisal. But here we felt quite safe – not that we were going to stay for long. Dave organised drinks while I cleaned the Bren and its spare barrels. Bujang watched keenly as I unscrewed the butt to remove the flannel and oil, which I used to wipe down every part of the gun. There was also a rod to clean the barrels. When the cleaning was complete I refilled the magazines with new bullets.

The drinks were excellent and it was nice to relax in the sun after our concentrated activities. All too soon, however, it was time to move back into the fetid jungle dark.

Our orang utan friends waited for us on the fringes. Apparently the firing hadn't frightened them off or maybe they felt safer with us around. The two kids held Mum's hands and looked at us longingly. I grabbed four more chocolate bars, pulled the wrappings off them and offered them up on another large leaf. Their eyes followed my every movement and I gave them a friendly smile, but I don't know how they interpreted it. We moved into the jungle and Unting gave our eyes on the river the signal to start 'fishing'.

After about three hours of pushing through the jungle Bujang told me there was a longhouse not far ahead.

'How far?'

'Not far.'

'We'd better make sure it's clear of Japs. Maybe the launch pulled in there.'

'I look,' said Bujang and he raced off. We sat down to wait, acutely alert for anything that might happen. An hour later a few gentle rustles in the jungle made me swing my Owen gun around, ready for action, but it was only Bujang with a smiling penghulu and his retinue of bodyguards.

'No Japanese,' the penghulu said, but he had seen the damaged launch go by. 'Plenty of smoke and makes funny noise. You stay at my longhouse.'

After about half an hour we stopped at a riverside clearing where his longhouse stood. After savouring mouthfuls of beautiful fresh air, I explained to the penghulu what we had to do and went with Bujang to site the Bren gun downstream. Bujang placed a couple of his sentries on the river bank. By the time we returned, Dave was already having a drink with the penghulu, with one poured and waiting for me. The penghulu showed us our bit of space and invited us to stay for as long as we liked. Dave had learned that the Japanese had only come by boat, never by foot, and every time they just stole whatever took their fancy. Surprise, surprise. How to win friends and influence people. This appeared to be general Japanese practice all along the river. Up until now, that was.

Dave also learned that about half a day's walk downstream was a large longhouse near the junction of the Rejang and a large unnamed tributary leading south. This tributary carried a lot of Japanese water traffic. Checking a map, we saw that Sibu was only a short distance beyond the junction of the two waterways. We would go no further downstream than this junction.

By now we were becoming accustomed to – but never bored by – the pleasant welcome ritual that followed our arrival at a longhouse. There were the smiling faces to greet us, the penghulu's welcome and the cheering multitudes who always came to watch us bathe. Even our evening meal squawking under the longhouse was a sideshow for us.

Talking to the locals, always an enjoyable experience, revealed that they knew what had been happening. Our Sea Dyaks wasted no time boasting of their feats, and news in a longhouse spreads faster than a special edition newspaper. After a few drinks and a good meal, the old penghulu began to regale us with his reminiscences of yesteryear. I quickly excused myself – lying bastard that I was – on the grounds of feeling a fever coming on, and left Dave to do the talking and listening.

The next morning I was greatly refreshed and a wash and a meal made me feel even better. Dave paid the surprised but delighted penghulu for our board, and the whole longhouse came to bid us farewell. Bujang pointed out the orangutan family, concealed where the foliage began to thicken. It felt good that so many people – and even orang utans – seemed happy to know us.

So here we were all nice and clean, only to enter the jungle and get filthy all over again. I asked Unting to leave some titbits for our simian followers when we moved off, in case they hadn't had breakfast.

It was the same old grind through the dense jungle. Quickly getting covered in muck, we just ploughed on until well after midday, buggered from the lack of fresh air. Then suddenly Bujang turned and whispered, 'Longhouse soon. You rest. I look for any Japanese near.'

'You be careful,' I whispered back. Of course we couldn't rest; we had to be ready in case something happened.

Bujang was back in under an hour with a big smile on his face. 'No Japanese. Penghulu wants to meet you, but he's old and can't walk far. He waits to welcome you and wants us to stay with him.'

More slogging through the jungle brought us to the largest longhouse we had seen so far. Facing the Rejang River, it sat well back from the south bank in an elevated position and had a commanding view of the tributary running south a little further down river. People of all ages crowded the shore, waving and smiling. It was a fantastic reception.

The old penghulu moved forward. 'Good to see you. You must stay here as long as you can.'

'Thank you.' I smiled.

'A Japanese boat went downstream. It's not very well and makes funny noise. I don't think they'll come back.' He laughed.

'No,' I said. 'And we're very glad to be here.'

We were more pleased than the penghulu could have known, just to have some respite from our daily grind of tramping through the jungle. But the old penghulu was keen for a long talk so Dave did the honours while I took Bujang out to position the sentries and the Bren gun. Again, there was no history here of the Japanese hacking their way through the jungle as they had in other countries. They were obviously shit-scared of the Sea Dyaks and found the waterways quicker, cleaner and safer – and they were, as long as you didn't bump into some bastard with a Bren gun.

We hid our prahu in among the local fleet. If we were too conspicuous, an alert Japanese sentry downstream might have spotted us through binoculars or telescope. Far better to let them assume we were no closer to Sibu than where we had stopped their launch.

The Bren gun looked clean, but I decided to give it another scrub to make sure. We couldn't risk a stoppage at a critical moment. The Bren gun was dependable and trouble-free, so I told her there were no hard feelings and I loved her. She didn't talk back.

Bujang's attention never flagged as he watched me work on the Bren. The devastation it caused fascinated him. Then it hit me – what an idiot I was! He'd probably have given his last Japanese head to fire it himself. I'd have to see if I could organise it.

Dave was on his own when I got back up the notched tree trunk. 'Here's your drink,' he said. 'Accommodation's sorted out and food's on the way.'

We decided to take it quietly for a couple of days, now we'd come as far as we were supposed to. Dave let the penghulu know, and showed him some money, which made him even happier.

I looked to edge of the jungle for our orangutans, but there was no sign of them. Unting told me he hadn't seen them since we left the titbits out that morning. I asked him to let me know if anyone saw them.

The penghulu was a nice old bloke, even more polite than the others we'd met. 'May I join you?' he asked, even though we were in his longhouse. He told us repeatedly how pleased everyone in his longhouse was to see us, and what a delightful surprise it was to speak with us in his own language.

His story was the same we'd heard at other longhouses. The Japanese only came by water and always looted whatever they wanted. They used the tributary river, mainly at night, where they had an outpost upstream. It had made his people very happy to see the broken Japanese boat. Just wait until our Sea Dyaks start gabbing about our other activities, I thought.

'What do you call the tributary?' I asked him.

He shrugged. 'It has no name.'

'Tidah Nama – no name,' I said, translating the phrase into Malay. And that's what we called it.

After eating I checked that Bujang and his lot were okay. 'We need sentries watching every minute of the day and the night,' I said. 'And whatever happens, even if it's a false alarm in the middle of the night, I want you to wake me.'

'I fix all that and I know where you sleep.'

I hadn't yet seen my own piece of space that Dave had organised, but Bujang had already made it his business to find out where it was.

The next couple of days were almost a holiday. We bathed and kept clean, we ate and drank well, and had many pleasant talks with the locals, who even coerced us into watching a cockfight. Three times each night, and several times during the day, Bujang's sentries fetched me to watch a Japanese launch traversing the Tidah Nama. It was quite a distance away and wasn't causing trouble or going up the Rejang where it might have upset Sochon, so I could see no point in giving our position away by attacking. I just noted down the times and direction they travelled, figuring that their schedule would be handy to know.

Each time Bujang called me out I congratulated him and his sentries for being so observant. They always appreciated praise, and my blokey more-heads-soon farewell even more. This promise of more heads often made them literally shake in anticipation, just as someone else might have shivered from the cold.

29

The Would-be Soldiers

On the second day of our 'holiday' two things stuffed up our rest and caused considerable inconvenience for the next couple of weeks. First, Dave woke to find his stomach and groin covered in ulcers.

'You haven't been drinking enough rice wine,' I joked, but it was no laughing matter. He was extremely uncomfortable and just looking at the mess was enough to make you feel uneasy. I helped him bathe it with antiseptic and apply ointment. But he wasn't happy and I wouldn't have been, either.

Second, later in the afternoon Bujang brought news of two prahus coming downstream from Kanowit way. He didn't know who was in them.

I said to Dave, 'You take it quietly. I'll see what it is.'

'Okay, but let me know what it is as soon as possible,' he said.

I raced down to the river bank with Bujang, slung the Bren gun around my neck and passed a couple of magazines to him. I didn't think they were Japanese, but I had no intention of being unprepared if they were.

Through the binoculars I saw that the prahus carried a mix of Sea Dyaks and other indigenous people. That was strange; they generally hated each other's guts. Bujang shrugged. We kept half-concealed as the prahus pulled onto the bank and Bujang recognised some of the Sea Dyaks. I counted ten indigenous men carrying rifles and wearing green army shirts. Some of them had been with Sochon when he arrived at Kanowit. A big recommendation.

'Who are you?' I asked as they came forward.

One of the indigenous men gave me a courteous half-bow and handed me an envelope. With the Bren gun I motioned for him to step back. His smile vanished and he retreated.

The envelope was addressed to Dave, but I wasn't too proud to open it.

'Shit,' I said to myself. Bujang looked on anxiously. 'It'll be all right,' I added for his benefit.

The letter was from Sochon. It informed us we now had reinforcements: ten soldiers trained as guerrillas. Corporal Abu was in charge of them until they came under Dave's command. They had supplies with them.

Sochon was just compounding his stupidity. Apart from the fact that the Sea Dyaks and these people didn't speak the same language, he had forgotten the difficulties their mutual enmity would cause. In a township like Kanowit we'd be able to keep them separated, but here we were shacked up in a Sea Dyak longhouse, deep in Sea Dyak territory. I figured I'd let poor old sick Dave sort it out. After all, he was the boss.

'Which one of you is Corporal Abu?' I said.

The man who had handed me the letter stepped forward, a little more warily this time.

'Right,' I said. 'I'll take you to Captain Kearney. He'll decide what to do with you. Unload the prahus and bring the stores and supplies with you.'

'Yes, sir,' he replied.

I placed the Bren gun back on its siting and turned to Bujang. 'We're going up to sort things out, but if the sentries hear or see anything let me know immediately.' He nodded and ran off. There was no yes-sir-no-sir crap with Bujang.

I had the new arrivals wait a distance from the longhouse, with the new stores and supplies, while I sent for Dave. He didn't look the best when he arrived.

'Surprise, surprise,' I greeted him. 'Gifts from your mate Sochon – and it's not even Christmas.'

'What?'

I handed him the letter and pointed to Sochon's guerrillas. 'The corporal called me "sir". I wonder what he'll call you.'

'Shit, this is the last thing I need! I feel bloody awful. You've always got an answer – what do you suggest?'

'Frankly, I'd keep the supplies and send the men back to Sochon.'

'We can't do that. Any more bright ideas?'

'Well, we'd better get the penghulu and Bujang used to the idea. The Sea Dyaks won't want them here. I suppose we can blame Sochon and say we don't want them either, but we're stuck with them. You could also probably drop an extra bribe to the old penghulu. I'm sure that'd ease his pain and suffering.

'We really need to keep them away from the Sea Dyaks as much as possible. Let them build a shack in that clump of trees over there where they can eat and sleep without interruption. It's sheltered and there's plenty of ferns and leaves to lay down for a roof. Your mate Sochon said – '

'He's not my bloody mate,' Dave interrupted angrily. 'I've told you that!'

Christ, he must be feeling crook, I thought. 'Okay. Sochon, who is *not* your mate, said in his letter to you, which I read, that these are "well trained, very good guerrillas". If that's the case, they won't have any trouble building a shack. A boy scout could do it on his ear. We just have to make sure the penghulu and Bujang are onside before they start building.'

'Okay, let's do it.'

To my surprise, the arrangements worked out. It proved good politics to put the Sea Dyaks in the picture. Dave passed the old penghulu more money for looking after us so well, and straightaway he asked us to stay as long as we liked. And yes, it was all right for the 'would-be soldiers', as I dubbed them, to build their shack. He understood it wasn't our fault that they had arrived. None of the Sea Dyaks were happy about their presence, but at least they realised we didn't approve either.

We warned Corporal Abu to keep his men away from the longhouse, and said we'd give them their duties tomorrow. A quick check of their supplies showed they had everything they needed. They weren't unhappy, but they weren't exactly ecstatic to be there either. Their stores included more food, ammunition and medical gear for us, but unfortunately no chocolate bars. Luckily, I still had a decent supply.

Dave went up to the longhouse to organise drinks while I had a quick word with Unting. I asked him whether he'd seen our orang utan family, but he told me he hadn't. He looked for them several times, but the food we left them was untouched and there were no tracks. It was a pity because they were such a lovely family and so intriguing to watch, but we never saw them again. I would've liked to take photos of them, but naturally cameras were taboo on our type of operation.

Over a drink Dave and I discussed what we should do with the newcomers.

'Maybe send them out on a patrol somewhere, and they might get lost,' I suggested. But we decided not to worry about it until morning. Our evening meal was screaming under the longhouse beneath our feet, so I decided to check on the would-be soldiers and see Bujang before dinner.

Abu's men had finished their shack and were settling in. It was makeshift, but it had three sides and a roof to keep out any rain. I told Corporal Abu that we'd see him in the morning. Bujang was his usual self again, so I felt less concerned about the newcomers.

'Everything's all right,' he said. 'No boats yet.'

'Don't forget to wake me when you or the sentries hear one, see one or anything else.'

'No.' He smiled. I clapped him on the shoulder and went back to Dave. I knew it wouldn't be long before I'd be called out.

Dave didn't look too bright when I got back. He had a look on his face as if it was the end of the world. He only picked at the meal and didn't even seem to enjoy his rice wine.

I fetched him a couple of painkillers and he went to lie down, looking very sad and sorry. Knowing I'd be getting up a few times during the night to look at boats, I fixed a large arak, lemon and water and went to my space. Propped against the longhouse wall, Owen gun in my lap, I put the MCR earphones on and listened to some jazz on the American station and then tuned in to good old Tokyo Rose. This is the life, I thought, and life is for living.

That night I remember dreaming of orang utans, chocolate bars and boats. Half-alert, I was on my feet just seconds before a smiling Bujang came into view. Beat you again, I smiled to myself.

'We hear boat,' he said.

This time the boat was chugging upstream on the Tidah Nama, hugging the far bank. I noted the time and told Bujang that we might cross the river one night and stop it. I was called out once more that night, and again I simply logged the time. As I dozed off I realised I was getting a bit jack of this boat disturbing my sleep. As soon as Dave felt better, perhaps we could knock it off.

His ulcers didn't look any worse in the morning, but they were still revolting. I helped him bathe them again and applied the ointment. 'I feel really crook,' he kept saying. Fortunately I was still clean as a whistle.

'I might have to go back and get some medical treatment,' he said mournfully.

'Well, that's your prerogative,' I said. 'But I'm sure they'll heal up, given time.'

Going back meant to Kanowit at least, and then being flown out by cat boat if they could get one in. We had no medical people with us at all. At least he would have the luxury of travelling upstream by prahu instead of bashing through the jungle again.

Another boat was spotted on the Tidah Nama that morning, but early in the afternoon Dave made up his mind. 'I've decided to go back. I hate to do this to you and leave you on your own.'

'Oh, don't worry about that,' I said. 'I'm used to being on my own. I've got Bujang and the Sea Dyaks here, anyway, so you look after yourself. I'm sure you'll be okay.'

He decided to leave by prahu first thing in the morning, with the same Sea Dyaks who had brought our 'reinforcements' downstream.

'Why don't you take them all back with you?' I said. 'No one wants them here.'

'That wouldn't be very wise, Brian. Sochon would have a fit. I'll take four of them and leave six with you, because I'll need some armed people with me.'

'For Christ's sake, tell Sochon not to send any more. We'll stop the Japanese going upstream to call on him, but if he sends any more of these people I'll just ship them straight back.'

That got a laugh out of Dave.

'I mean it,' I told him.

'I know you do.' He laughed again.

It didn't take him long to get organised because we didn't have much gear and most of it was staying with me. Another Japanese boat was on the other side of the Tidah Nama. I wasn't sure yet if it was the same boat each time or whether there were several different ones. However many of you there are, I thought, you're getting one hell of a surprise in the not-too-distant future.

The whole longhouse woke very early to see Dave off. We made a big noisy business of it, in order to suggest to any enemy observers that all foreigners were departing upstream. There was no sense keeping a low profile anymore – not after Corporal Abu's arrival by boat. Overnight there had been two more boat calls, and I promised myself that as soon as Dave left I'd do something about it.

I wished him good luck and reassured him that his ulcers would soon heal. I suggested future supplies include batteries for the MCR and chocolate bars for any more orang utans. That raised a small chuckle.

'Take this,' he said, handing me some of the money he carried for expenses.

The prahus moved out into the river and over to the far side, where the current was more sluggish. I missed Dave's company, but his departure did not occasion me any disquiet. Life was much the same, except that I had no one to speak English with. Our watch on the river continued and as I was regularly called out day and night, my antagonism towards the boat or boats only increased.

Most of the time I spent wandering around the longhouse chatting with locals. A special cockfight was held in my honour. It didn't interest me, but I had to join in as they barracked and cheered just like we would have at a football match back home.

The river bank on the other side of the Tidah Nama was dense jungle and there was no traffic apart from wildlife. It was a good spot for an ambush and allowed us to keep the Rejang River covered in case other Japanese tried to go upstream towards Kanowit.

Unfortunately I had to take the would-be soldiers along. I couldn't leave them at the longhouse in case they caused trouble with the Sea Dyaks, or vice-versa. I suppose I was lucky there were only six left from the original ten.

'Tomorrow night,' I told Bujang, 'we paddle across as soon as it's dark.' I pointed out where we would land. 'And we have to take Corporal Abu's men with us.'

He wasn't happy about this last bit, but nodded his understanding.

Next I let Abu know our plans. I told him to ensure his men had their weapons properly cleaned and that they had some cold snacks. It could be a long wait and there would be no fires. He gave me a sloppy, 'Yes, sir, we will be ready,' but didn't seem too pleased. I couldn't have cared less anyway, because I certainly wasn't counting on his help. I'd be relying on Bujang and his mates.

The following afternoon we prepared for our sortie. The boats had kept coming, obviously to a rough timetable. Among the supplies Sochon had sent I found a Verey Light Pistol, a very cumbersome flare pistol capable of turning the blackest night into broad daylight. I gave it a good clean.

The Sea Dyaks were ready, with two prahus concealed in the trees. We decided to put half of the would-be soldiers into each prahu. Corporal Abu knew we were to move in complete silence, but his men muttered and argued as we approached the prahus. I realised I'd have to make something very clear before we got out on the water.

'Bring your men over here for a minute,' I said to Abu. 'Now, it's essential that no one make any noise whatsoever, because it endangers all our lives. Do you understand?'

There were a few nods, but I wanted to make a bigger impression. Pulling out my knuckleduster knife, I slammed it into the side of a small tree, splintering the trunk. They exchanged surprised looks. 'That's how I'll silence the next man making too much noise. Without warning. Understand?'

As I put my knuckleduster knife away, they all said yes and I knew I'd made my point.

30

Across the Tidah Nama

The moon had not yet shown itself, but darkness suited our purpose as the Sea Dyaks paddled us silently across the water. When we got to the other side they hid the two prahus in the jungle and I positioned everyone in a perimeter with instructions to let me know about any strange movements. I sited the Bren gun to cover the Tidah Nama and also the Rejang, in case someone was going upstream to pay Sochon a visit. Bujang put his sentries a short distance away, watching in both directions.

By now I had no trouble communicating with Bujang and he was so smart he often anticipated me. However, I still had to be patient with my instructions. Corporal Abu, for example, was slow to catch on and I had to explain everything to his crew separately.

If the boat kept to its timetable, we had a four-hour wait ahead of us. I warned Abu's men it was essential we remain quiet the whole time. When the boat approached, they were to line up beside me and when I opened fire – but not before – they should then fire at the boat with their rifles. Abu seemed to follow – so I explained further.

The boat was likely to be coming from the direction of Sibu. If it was going up the Rejang on the far side, it would be in the sluggish water and no doubt going Sochon's way, so we would have to stop it as we had the one further upstream. But if the boat was on our side of the Rejang and going against the current, then it would be going to turn into the Tidah Nama, which was where we were waiting for it.

Confident they had understood me, I announced I was going to wait by the Bren gun. Actually I was going to have a drink and a quiet doze. I added that any strange noises were to be reported immediately.

When Bujang sidled up to me four hours later, I was just waking and getting to my feet. 'Sentry heard boat,' he said. 'All the soldiers ran away. We go and get them?'

I nearly asked if he meant dead or alive but I didn't, because I knew which one he meant.

'No,' I said, smiling at his eagerness. 'How long before the boat arrives?'

'We have time to get them before boat arrives,' he urged.

'No, the boat's more important.'

'They left their guns.' Bujang sounded most indignant. I went to see. Sure enough Abu's men had dropped their guns and most of their gear before they fled.

'Where did they go?'

He shrugged and pointed vaguely into the jungle, but I figured he'd know exactly which way to go if I let him give chase. The would-be soldiers would be very likely lost in the jungle by now, but I wasn't worried about that.

According to Bujang, the boat was coming from the Sibu direction on this side of the river, meaning it would come right past us. Even I could hear it now. It was obviously still a fair way off, because noise travels a hell of a long way at night, particularly over water.

'Forget about Abu,' I told Bujang. I decided to use the Verey Light Pistol and warned him not to look directly at the flare. He briefed his warriors and they lined up slightly behind me.

The boat's chug got louder and we began to hear voices and laughter. They were soon going to have something new to laugh about. Now we could see the boat, moving as close to the river bank as possible. I slung the Bren around my neck and had one of Bujang's warriors stand by with spare magazines and grenades. I fired the flare cartridge up into the air. It flew upwards, leaving a trail of sparks behind, exploded and slowly descended to earth, illuminating the whole sky. In the split second before opening up with the Bren, I saw some of the Japanese and most of Bujang's warriors staring upwards at the flare. I fired at the wheelhouse, grabbed another magazine from the startled warrior holding them, emptied that and grabbed a third one.

The boat's occupants fumbled about, their night vision lost. The motor stopped chugging and the occupants staggered under the fire of the third magazine. As I grabbed a fourth, the current forced the boat towards the bank and it stayed there. No one was at the wheel.

Bujang was overjoyed. 'We fix! We fix!'

Before I could say anything he quickly spoke to his warriors. They put their rifles down, drew their parangs and raced down to the boat.

The Sea Dyaks attacked in complete silence but there were cries and protests from the people on board. I went to have a look. The Sea Dyaks proudly held up six Japanese heads. The corpses all wore military uniforms.

The boat was still afloat, but it was too heavy to paddle and the motor was useless. The crew had been armed with rifles and the cargo included food, clothing and ammunition. It looked like a delivery service between Sibu and the Japanese outpost further up the Tidah Nama. If there was another boat it was due in four and a half-hours, but I was pretty sure we'd been watching just one boat going backwards and forwards on a supply run.

Even so, I decided to wait and make sure. I told Bujang immediately, since it was always a good policy to keep the Sea Dyaks informed of every decision. It made them feel part of what was happening, and they naturally needed reasons to do what was wanted of them. He passed the word to his warriors. Bujang even told me in a weak moment that they liked being with me, which was a big compliment. Maybe it was all the heads I'd helped them obtain.

He said his sentries would report any noise to me, even if it was from Corporal Abu's men. That was fine by me, so I settled in to clean the weapons and wash down some emergency rations with an arak drink. I would have liked to go up the Tidah Nama and do over the Japanese outpost, but my orders were to prevent the Japanese going up the Rejang towards Sochon and I couldn't do both at once.

I allowed half my mind to doze off for a while, then got up to stretch my legs. We still had three hours to wait. Bujang was pleased with his night's work, which had compensated for his disappointment at not being allowed to pursue the would-be soldiers.

'Where do you think they ran to?' I asked him.

He perked up. 'They're too long gone in the dark now. When daylight comes we'll get them.'

I thanked him but thought, no, let them go wherever they've gone. I could hardly let Bujang and his mates grab their heads, despite their sins.

Eventually time proved me right about the boat. No others came, and I decided to return to the relative comfort of the longhouse while it was still dark. Before leaving, Bujang and I went back to the Japanese boat to throw their weapons and supplies overboard. I drained the fuel tank and found a large hammer, which I used to bash the motor and steering gear and anything else that could be wrecked. Finally I lowered the Japanese flag, turned it upside down and shredded it with my knuckleduster knife.

Dislodging the boat from the bank, we coaxed it into the fast current of the Rejang, hoping it would find its way back to the Japanese at Sibu.

Facetiously I said to Bujang, 'We'll wave goodbye to the would-be soldiers, wherever they may be.' I don't think he latched on to this weak attempt at humour, but he smiled.

A lot of people were awake at the longhouse, which was quite abnormal at this time of night. The Bren gun fire and the flare, new experiences for them, were responsible. Gathering around, they chattered excitedly to Bujang and his mates and gave rapturous 'oohs' and 'aahs' upon seeing the new heads. It was almost like a fashion parade.

With Dave gone it was my turn to be the big fellow. Calling Bujang over, I announced loudly, 'Here are six Straits Settlement one-dollar notes for the heads you took. Please give one dollar to each of the brave warriors who obtained a head.' Bujang was all smiles as he took the money, and so was I.

The procedure created considerable interest and I knew there would be lots of stories told that night and the next. No more boats were reported and I slept until morning. In fact there were no more reports, as there had only been the one boat after all. As a matter of courtesy, I spoke to the old penghulu during the morning, a duty previously undertaken by Dave. He knew all about our foray and glowed with pleasure, so I was able to make it brief.

The shack the would-be soldiers had occupied had little in it, except what looked like a heap of garbage. I asked Bujang to have it dismantled, which the locals were happy to do and I never found out what happened to them – not that I cared. I never learnt whether the Japanese boat reached Sibu, either. It would've been interesting to know the Japanese reaction, but it didn't matter much.

From now on the sentries had little to report apart from occasional Sea Dyaks stopping by on their travels. I always talked to them to get whatever information I could.

One night I heard on the MCR that atomic bombs had been dropped on Japan. The news brought a big smile to my face and two extra arak drinks in celebration.

It brought me even more pleasure to hear about the official Japanese surrender on the 14th of August. But the war wasn't over in Sarawak. Sea Dyaks passing through spoke of continuing enemy violence and cruelty, generally further to the south. Some of the Japanese were murdering their prisoners and local people, anxious to remove all eyewitnesses to their atrocities. And the radio news bulletins spoke of many Japanese refusing to surrender elsewhere in the Pacific.

I was quite flattered that in several instances visiting Sea Dyaks would asked after the *orang puteh* – white man – they had heard about. (*Orang utan*, by the way, translates as 'man of the jungle.' The females and children of the species, lovely as they are, don't seem to get a separate mention and are also called *orang utan*.)

I explained to Bujang that despite two big bombs forcing the Japanese to surrender, a lot of them were still fighting. I stressed that we had to stay alert, and that if we encountered any hostile Japanese it was still 'more heads'.

Boredom was creeping in at this point. My assignment restricted me to this area, but I longed to visit the Japanese outpost on the Tidah Nama. There were no more Japanese boats about and even the sentries were getting restless. Bugger it, I thought, we will do the Japanese outpost over. I sat down with an arak drink to plan it and felt much better now that I was doing something. But this all came to a sudden halt.

Later that morning Bujang and one of his sentries came racing up, all smiles, and said, 'Three prahus coming from Kanowit!'

31

The Phone Call

Grabbing my Owen gun, I hurried down to the water so I could appear to be casually waiting, armed and accompanied by armed Sea Dyak warriors. The trio of prahus were in the fast-flow section on our side, and quickly reached the landing area. Dave stood up in the front prahu. He almost fell into the river in his hurry to get out and onto the river bank. 'Brian, the war's over!' he said.

'Yes, I know, but it's not.'

'What do you mean?'

'I'll tell you later,' I said. 'But it's good to see you.' And it was, too. I hadn't spoken my own language to a fellow Australian for some time. It was like old home week.

Ross Bradbury and Brick Fowler were with him, along with Jim the cook, more Sea Dyaks and a whole stack of supplies. Jim was pleased see me. No doubt he was even more pleased to get away from Sochon. But I was happy to see him, too, knowing that we were about to have a very tasty change of diet.

'Let's go back to the longhouse and have a drink,' I said to Dave. 'You've still got your piece of space. Say hello to the old penghulu and while the others settle in we can talk.'

'All right. I brought you more batteries for your MCR and some more chocolate, too.'

'Hey, that's good. Thanks a lot,' I said.

The old penghulu was really pleased to see Dave again. 'Stay as long as you can,' he told them all. No doubt he was anticipating another nice payout, which of course he got.

Finally we sat down with our drinks. Dave had been flown back to Labuan, where his ulcers cleared up after a couple of days in hospital. I told him what I'd been doing and included the mysterious disappearance of the would-be soldiers.

'Sochon said they were good,' Dave said. 'He was very proud of them.'

'I wouldn't give you tuppence for Sochon or his soldiers. But you know that already.'

I told him my plans. 'Sounds like a good idea,' he said, 'but we'll have to put it off, at least for now. We've got another job to do. What did you mean when you said the war isn't over?'

I explained to him what Sea Dyak eyewitnesses had told me about Japanese activity to the south.

'Shit,' he said. 'Our orders are to move south into the 2nd Division of Sarawak and capture any Japs in the area, administer by the best available means, recruit ex-Sarawak Rangers and examine the food situation with a view to relieving food shortages in the Sibu area.'

I laughed.

'What's so funny – have I missed something?'

'It's all unknown, hostile territory. The Japs are still killing people down there. What are we supposed to do – walk up to them and say, "Please, I want to capture you?" You've got to be bloody well joking! Your mate Sochon's full of bright ideas, tucked safely away and knowing bugger all.'

'I've told you, he's *not* my mate.'

'The stupid bastard should come and see for himself what things are like.'

'Brian, it's not my fault.'

'I know that, but Sochon is such an incompetent, ignorant fuckwit he makes my blood boil. Here's an idea – tell him what happened to six of his crack guerrillas.'

'Don't worry, I will.'

It occurred to me that if I'd stayed at the Canungra jungle warfare school as an instructor, I'd have well and truly outranked all these people by now. I would have been living in comfort and my health would have been better. But really I was glad I hadn't. Sochon wouldn't be game to get rid of me and I had no regrets about the life I'd led so far, filled with intense experiences non-stop. Life's for living, I kept telling myself, and that always settled things and took the doubts from my mind.

There were thirty-seven of us now: four Australians and thirty-three Sea Dyaks, some of whom were carriers, although they all went armed with parangs. We had plenty of supplies and Brick Fowler's radio meant that we had contact with the outside world, even if it was only in Morse code. We decided to leave early in the morning, the day after next.

Several small townships were on our way, but the main target was Simanggang, which was the second or third largest town in Sarawak. It was just over sixty miles away as the crow flew, but actually much further because the terrain was trackless mountainous jungle.

I told Bujang our plans, drawing on the ground to show where and how far we wanted to go. I asked if he could find one or two Sea Dyaks to guide us through this territory, and maybe show us some secret tracks.

'I fix.' He nodded and away he went.

That evening we got together while Jim set about getting us a meal. I was really looking forward to it. Everyone quizzed me about what I'd been doing and they laughed heartily when I told them how keen Bujang was to go after Sochon's would-be soldiers. Apart from our usual local drinks, they'd brought down some Australian beer with them. It was good to have, although my ration had been mysteriously depleted by the time it reached me.

Having someone to talk to again was quite a change, although they didn't know as much as I did about the Japanese surrender and they certainly didn't know as much about the situation in 2nd Division. Anyway, we had to be ready for an early start the day after next. We would, of course, be taking everything with us.

That night the MCR radio news spoke again of Japanese still holding out in various locations after their supposed surrender. Things were different in Sarawak, though. As it was still under Japanese control, there was no Allied army for them to fight except when we chose to sneak out of the jungle to attack. In Sarawak the Japanese were just venting their spleen on their prisoners and the local populace.

As we were busy organising our gear the next day, Bujang introduced me to two Sea Dyaks from the south who could lead us there along safe tracks.

'Very good. We'll pay them and give them food, and we leave early in the morning. You look after them, Bujang.'

'I fix,' Bujang assured me. It was good to have them along, but I was sure Bujang could have guided us himself had it been necessary.

We invited the old penghulu to have a meal and a farewell drink with us that evening, but he politely settled for just a drink. Maybe he wanted to go to bed early, or maybe he had a young woman waiting for him. Anyway, he had his drink, graciously accepted payment from Dave and excused himself to go wherever he was going.

Our departure early in the morning was pleasantly delayed by the occupants of the longhouse, who came out as a group to farewell us. It felt fantastic to have so many lovely smiling people genuinely wishing us luck. I was pretty sure we'd done some good for them, and confident that they'd now seen the last of the Japanese.

We waved our goodbyes and moved into the dense, dark and unknown – to us – jungle. I moved up front with Bujang and the two guides. The rest were strung out in a line behind with Dave or Ross at the tail end making sure no one lagged behind.

Winding our way around the mountainous country, we occasionally came to small clearings where we could gulp some fresh air and have a quick rest break or snack. The first night was spent in the jungle and early the next morning we met two Sea Dyaks travelling towards us. They had come from Penebar, our first objective, which they said wasn't far. That didn't tell us much, because they weren't carrying anything heavy and moved far faster in their home territory than we Australians could.

The Japanese in Penebar knew about the attack on the launch and had decided to leave to join their friends further south. The two Sea Dyaks asked if they could join us. Initially Dave said we didn't want them, but he relented when he realised that staying with us meant they couldn't tell anyone else about us.

We approached Penebar cautiously, but the Japanese had already left. The locals were at first surprised to see us but when they realised who we were, they were overjoyed and welcomed us warmly. Penebar was in the 2nd Division, so at least we were heading in the right direction.

This was not longhouse territory. We grabbed a couple of empty shacks for temporary accommodation, although some locals offered to vacate their homes for us. There were a few local disputes to settle. Accusations of collaboration with the Japanese flew thick and fast, and such complaints were common from this point on. All we could do was explain that others would come after us to act on any information of that sort. And we reassured them they were unlikely to see any more Japanese.

After conferring with the guides and locals it seemed like it would take a full day, without mishaps, for us to get down to Betong. There was no sense in arriving towards dusk and risking an altercation with the Japanese in the dark. Instead we planned to arrive mid-afternoon, which would give us time to look around and if necessary pick our own time and place for any fighting. Unfortunately this meant another night in the jungle, but that was unavoidable. We decided to leave late the following morning, after helping the locals with any of their problems, if we could. We were graciously offered a young woman each for the evening, but I told them I was too busy. This time I noticed that Dave did the same.

After hearing further complaints about collaborators in the morning it was back to the semi-darkness of the jungle. Apart from a couple of rest stops we trudged along without incident until sundown, when we had dinner and curled up under trees to sleep. It was to be the last night I'd ever sleep rough in the jungle.

We reached the outskirts of Betong around midday. After a quick scout, an excited Bujang reported that the Japanese had not long gone. 'We go after them,' he said.

'No, not yet,' I told him. 'But don't worry; we'll catch up with them.'

Again, the locals were pleased to see us, and eager to inform on collaborators. Again we were offered, and declined, ladies for the night. Betong was larger than Penebar and, like many townships in Sarawak, boasted a fort. This one, Fort Lili, was doubling as a kubu, or gaol.

About twenty Japanese had just left Betong, including some from Penebar. I gathered this from a local who opened his hand four times when asked. All were armed, and they had a radio they 'spoke on with funny noises' – in Morse code, I assumed. Their destination was Simanggang, where there were a lot more Japanese.

As we enjoyed a drink while waiting for Jim to cook dinner, I said to Dave, 'What about these rotten Japs – are we going after them?'

'No. I don't feel like getting my bloody head shot off now that the war's over. What do you all think?'

Ross Bradbury and Brick Fowler agreed with him. But I couldn't help thinking of certain incidents, engraved on my mind forever. There was my friend at Wau who had both buttocks carved off to make a Japanese meal. There was my brother, still a POW and God only knew what they'd done to him. There was the catalogue of awful things I'd seen done to harmless local people in New Guinea and Sarawak, some too shocking to write about. Now, having surrendered, the Japanese were hurriedly murdering prisoners and local people, making sure they spared no one who might speak out about their barbaric war crimes.

'Dave, that's okay, but how about I take a few Sea Dyaks and try to capture a few Japs? After all, you told me that's what we're supposed to be doing here.'

I had him stuffed there. He didn't have an answer, but he argued for some time anyway. Finally he relented. 'Oh, go if you want to, but I'm not happy about it.'

'How many Sea Dyaks can I have? What about the Bren gun?'

'Take twenty Sea Dyaks. You can have the Bren gun. No one else knows how to use it anyway. And take what stores you need, but leave us something.'

I stood up to go. 'I'll be back for another drink with you, but I'll be leaving in the morning before you wake.'

Bujang was eager to accompany me and shivered in anticipation. We decided to take Unting, six warriors, one of the guides and eleven other Sea Dyaks to carry our stores and weapons. When we were packed and ready to go I went to see Dave for that drink.

'Now, what exactly are you going to do?' he asked.

'Try and capture some Japs. We'll just play it by ear.'

'Okay. Well, best of luck, but there's no need for you to go. If I had any bloody sense, I'd order you to stay here.'

At that moment I decided to confide my full reasons for wanting to go. When I finished, Dave gave what I took to be a mournful nod. 'Okay, I understand,' he said. 'We'll follow on down a day or two after you. Good luck.'

The radio had no relevant news that night. Before dawn I rose to find Bujang busily proportioning out the loads for our carriers. He smiled a greeting. It was quiet and no one was around.

'Are the sentries still out?' I asked him, not fancying the idea of Dave and the others getting their throats cut while they slept.

'Of course,' he replied. That was good; it was important that the sentries not be visible anyway.

When we got going we moved more quickly than when the other Australians were with us. I suppose I had more jungle experience from New Guinea and the Sea Dyaks, of course, moved like lightning. Bujang and I led with the guide and Unting took the rear to hurry any stragglers along.

The next township was Skrang, at the junction of the Batang Skrang and the Batang Lupar. (*Batang* means 'river', and the Batang Skrang is a tributary of the Batang Lupar, a tidal river flowing into the China Sea just above Kuching. It's a big river, although not as mighty as the Rejang. Simanggang is on the Batang Lupar.)

While gasping for fresh air at our next break, I had an idea for Bujang. 'What about changing into a loincloth and racing on ahead into Simanggang to have a look around? Mix with the locals, see how many Japs are there, how many prisoners they have and what's happening there. Take the guide.'

His eyes lit up. 'I go. No guide. Guide can take you to Skrang.'

'All right. But take my Browning pistol in case of emergency. Just do what you did in Kanowit, and remember all the heads you got there. We'll keep going towards Skrang.'

He nodded. 'I find you soon.' Bujang swapped his green army issue trousers for a loincloth, and I gave him a couple of crumpled dollars if he needed to buy something. He took the pistol almost lovingly, and carefully tucked it into the loincloth. The poor bastard would've given almost anything to own it.

'I see you soon.' Before I knew it he had disappeared.

We had a couple more short rest stops, which I begrudged, because

I was keen to reach Skrang before nightfall. I tried to force the pace as much as possible, and there were no complaints. Maybe the Sea Dyaks thought that if I could keep going like this, then it shouldn't be a problem for them. Finally, very late in the afternoon, the guide stopped and said, 'Skrang soon.'

Taking Unting, I had a good look around the jungle fringes of the township. No Japanese were about; in fact we couldn't see anyone at all. Cautiously moving forward, we surprised a couple of indigenous locals. I smiled hello and asked them in Malay if there were any Japanese there. They were surprised to hear me speak their language. The Japanese, they said, had left for Simanggang that very day.

Unting fetched the others. By this time word had spread and locals were appearing from all directions to welcome us. I asked for a couple of unoccupied huts where we could put our gear and sleep. They found three for us. I took the smallest one, which also accommodated our gear, and left the other two for the Sea Dyaks.

I told Unting to put three sentries out. He was nowhere near as smart as Bujang and it took longer to get the message across. I sited the Bren gun in a good position pointed towards Simanggang, knowing that any trouble would almost certainly come from that direction.

I was buggered. I had pushed myself too hard, and it was my own fault. I had a drink in my hut and went to talk to some locals. The Sea Dyaks were already filling their heads with all sorts of stories.

Skrang was a neat little township and I came across a compact office set-up with a small telephone exchange board. I wasn't familiar with this type of thing, but after looking it over and reading the attached instructions, I realised it had connections to a limited number of locations, including Simanggang.

Picking the phone up, I deciphered some printed instructions and saw that getting through involved connecting the appropriate plugs and then winding a handle, which rang a bell on the phone you were calling. I continued wandering about, talking to the locals, but my mind stayed on that phone. Finally the temptation was too much. I knew I'd never forgive myself if I passed up the opportunity. Besides all that, I felt a bit cheeky.

I went straight back to the telephone exchange and made the

connection between Skrang and Simanggang. The bell handle whirred in my ear as I wound it. I hoped it would be louder at the other end. Finally a voice came on, but nothing distinguishable.

'I would like to speak to the Japanese commanding officer,' I said in Malay, clearly and politely.

'Who?'

'The Japanese commanding officer.'

'Why you want to speak?'

'Just get him. It's very important.'

'You wait.'

Ultimately a voice came on, probably Japanese, which I couldn't understand.

'Are you the Japanese commanding officer?' I asked.

The reply came in Malay. 'Yes.'

'I'm part of an Australian infantry battalion just out of town.'

He interrupted me, in English this time. 'You English?'

'Do you speak English?' I asked.

'A little,' he said.

'Well, I'm an Australian. I'm part of an Australian infantry battalion just –' Before I had finished he began muttering anxiously, probably in Japanese, then repeated what I had told him in English. There was a panicked cry almost of disbelief as he hung up on me.

Rude bastard. I was tempted to ring him back, but I thought, no, I've made my point. I couldn't help bursting into laughter and a couple of the locals watched me aghast, no doubt thinking I was off my rocker. But I couldn't have cared less. That phone call made my day.

Still on a high of pleasure and satisfaction, I was treating myself to some chocolate and an arak drink when Bujang, grinning from ear to ear, materialised beside me. He handed me the Browning automatic pistol.

'I have not fired,' he said.

I was pleased to see him. 'Did you see our sentries?'

'Yes,' he nodded, 'They're good sentries.' That was something, coming from him.

By show of fingers, Bujang indicated that he had seen over thirty Japanese soldiers in Simanggang. Two large boats had pulled up at the docks, and there were a lot of male and female prisoners, too many for him to count. 'I spoke to two prisoners. I tell them we have someone with us and we help them soon and we kill the Japanese.'

He shouldn't have done that, but we couldn't undo it now. Anyway, I'd already gone and introduced myself to the Japanese commanding officer. But Bujang wasn't finished. 'Some prisoners are sick,' he said. 'Some beaten by Japanese, and they kill more. The Japanese will kill them all tomorrow.'

32

The Little Rose
of the Batang Lupar

Darkness was falling. Bujang helped me reposition the Bren gun for an ambush on the outskirts of town. With our sentries watching all night there was no way the Japanese could surprise us now.

In the morning I decided to write a note to the Japanese in Simanggang, demanding their surrender and I put considerable thought into it. I didn't expect they would comply, although there was always a chance they might. More likely they would come after us, but at least I would have tried. Under the circumstances I thought it was probably the right thing to do:

The Officer Commanding Japanese Forces,

Simanggang.

It is advised that the Emperor of Japan has surrendered unconditionally to the Allies and that the Japanese Commander in Chief in Kuching is surrendering to the Commander in Chief Australian Imperial Forces, General Sir Thomas Blamey.

I now call on you to surrender. You with all your troops will proceed upstream the Batang Lupar as far as the Batang Skrang and will arrive there by 9 (nine) o'clock tomorrow, 14th Sept 1945, when you will be met by me.

If you comply with these instructions and these only, you are guaranteed a safe passage here. You are furthermore warned that all escape routes from Simanggang are closely guarded and if you fail to comply with the above instructions I cannot be held responsible for subsequent events.

For D. Kearney, Officer in charge, Australian Imperial Forces, 2nd Division Sarawak.

Adjutant B. Walpole, 13.9.45.

Simanggang had been a large administrative centre before the war, so even if none of the Japanese could read English, plenty of others there would. Bujang caught on very quickly when I showed and explained the note to him, and I left it to him tell Unting.

My idea was for Unting to go down to Simanggang in his loincloth and hand the surrender note to the Japanese. Shortly afterwards, Bujang would have another scout around and see if anything had changed. If they saw each other in Simanggang, they would pretend to be strangers and ignore each other.

It took me a long time to explain this to them both, but they listened carefully.

'Do you understand what to do?' I asked, and they both nodded a vigorous yes and repeated their instructions back to me without hesitation. I congratulated them and told them that if the Japanese didn't come upriver to Skrang to surrender by the next morning, we would go into Simanggang. That bucked them both up. I told them I'd wait in our ambush position by the Bren gun.

It was a long wait until they returned and I imagined all sorts of scenarios: some good; some bad. Unting was back first, looking pleased with himself. He had handed the surrender note to a Japanese soldier, who gave it to another, who found someone else to translate it for him. They talked about it for quite some time and then gave Unting a small parcel to take back to the note's author. I nudged it open with the blade of my knuckleduster knife. Coloured boiled lollies. Poison, or just a joke – who knew? I threw them in the river. Later I learned it was typical of the Japanese to do something strange like this.

When Bujang reappeared he spoke of a lot of movement in Simanggang. People had been relocated within the town and many were upset and crying. The Japanese had beaten some and had killed others.

'A lot of them want to run away but they have nowhere to go.'

'Did you see any Japs?'

'Oh yes,' he said. 'They walk around and make people do things.'

They had both done well. All we could do now was wait until morning, exercising extreme vigilance in case the Japanese came after us, and be ready should they arrive to offer their surrender by nine o'clock. I made sure the Sea Dyaks were packed and ready to move without notice.

We took up our ambush position with the Bren gun at dawn. By nine no one had come to surrender, so there was no point mucking around any longer. It was time to go into Simanggang. Bujang and Unting smiled, raced off and had the other Sea Dyaks ready in a matter of minutes.

Our guides were unnecessary, as both Bujang and Unting knew the way now, but we took them anyway. Bujang led us into the jungle and told me we were following a Sea Dyak track. I took his word for it, but I couldn't see a track anywhere and I knew it was pointless to look for one. This was deadset virgin jungle – with an emphasis on the dead. It was steamy, hot as buggery and deathly silent. We were in an eerie half-light all the time because we couldn't see the sky. Occasionally a weak tendril of light pierced the canopy of foliage, but it was no place to be if you suffered from claustrophobia. There was no movement of air or any sound except for the occasional screech of a bird or a monkey.

For all I knew we were going around in circles, but Bujang was too smart for that. He wouldn't have known what a magnetic compass was, but he didn't need one to find his way.

Several tedious hours later, after leading us around trees and other obstacles, Bujang gave his cheeky smile and said, 'Soon.' Calling a halt, I asked him to scout ahead for Japanese sentries. Soon enough he reported several, but they were only watching the regular track from Skrang to Simanggang.

I thought quickly and sketched my plan in the dirt. 'Could we go around quietly and use the secret Sea Dyak track to get behind the sentries?'

'Oh yes.' Bujang nodded.

'Okay. Unting, take two others to the main track in front of the Jap sentries. We'll get into position behind them and send a runner back to Unting. Then Unting and his two warriors will fire a few shots up into the air and rejoin us. The sentries will think they're being attacked. If they open fire, we attack from their rear.'

It seemed the right choice. They'd still have a chance to lay down their arms, despite already knocking back my invitation to take their surrender. And we had to help the prisoners as well as protect ourselves. Bujang didn't even have to think. He was rapt in the idea. 'We do, we do.' He laughed.

The Japanese put on a real show when Unting fired his decoy shots. A siren screamed and they let loose with what sounded like a lot of heavy weapons – heavier than anything we had. They had obviously been waiting to ambush us and were probably expecting a whole battalion to come marching down the main route from Skrang. Fortunately the stupid bastards directed their fire at our decoy as we watched, unnoticed, behind them.

The sentries were covering for their soldier mates, who, together with some forced labour, were busy loading a couple of boats for a quick departure. They were all out in the open, but we still had cover from the jungle. In Malay I shouted twice for them to surrender. They looked up, surprised, then swung their weapons towards us. So much for the war being over! The forced labour fled for their lives.

There was a torrid firefight, when suddenly, from the corner of my eye, I saw movement near the fort on top of a nearby hill. It was a lady. She must have fixed her eyes on me because she came racing down that hill as fast as her poor undernourished body would allow. She came straight for me, wrapped her arms around me in a hug, and gave me the biggest kiss of all time. I've never been so surprised in all my life. The Sea Dyaks around me all grinned broadly at this unexpected development.

'Down, down!' I shouted to her. The Japanese were still firing bullets. I gently pushed her down. She weighed next to nothing. We finished our firefight and the Sea Dyaks rounded up the rest of the Japanese – those who weren't killed. But the lady probably couldn't have cared less if she had caught a stray bullet. The Japanese were going to kill her and the others that day and she knew it. She was very brave. 'You're safe now,' I told her.

Her name was Lena Ricketts. She was a twenty-seven-year-old nurse, born in Sarawak. Her grandfather had originally come out from England as an administrator. When the Japanese invaded she tried to escape with her father, sisters and brother, but their car broke down and they were taken prisoner.

She had been a prisoner for over four years. Four years of hell. Her father and one sister were dead, and she was in a shocking condition, with a desperate look on her face; her clothes were in shreds, worse than rags, filthy and covered in grime. The Japanese had made her clean out gutters and all kinds of filth but had refused to let her wash. The worst of scarecrows would have looked respectable by comparison.

The Sea Dyaks had the remaining Japanese huddled in a group, about ten of them. They looked most unhappy, perhaps even fearful, and with good reason. The Sea Dyaks' headhunting was well known, and so were the horrible things their own lot had been doing to the Sea Dyaks over four years. Bujang and his mates gazed patiently at the Japanese necks and I soon realised why. They were making their professional assessments and waiting for the okay to take their usual trophies. I had to think quickly. All the Japanese heads they'd taken with me on previous occasions had been in physical combat. And that was fair enough, under the circumstances, because those Japanese would certainly have killed us had they been able to. But this lot had surrendered, finally.

From what I had seen firsthand over several years, the Japanese were worse than animals by our standards and if the situation had been reversed, there was no doubting what they would have done to us. But the situation wasn't reversed and I was an Australian, not a rotten Japanese.

'No, no more heads,' I said to Bujang and the others. 'But you'll be paid for these as if you *had* taken them.'

I explained why and they went along with it reluctantly, only out of respect for previous judgements I had made. But they weren't happy.

The Japanese commanding officer stood out like a sore toe from the others, with his neatly pressed jungle greens, white silk scarf, and highly polished black jackboots. He was Kempeitai, similar to their better known counterparts the German Gestapo, but more brutal. I motioned him forward.

'Why were you going to kill them?' I asked him in Malay.

The answer was blithe, very matter-of-fact. 'Oh, I was ordered to kill all prisoners. They were to be killed today.'

I told him what a little shit he was, as best I could. And I was not too bad at that. I ranted at him in Malay, Sea Dyak and English for several minutes. Then he asked me if he could have his ceremonial sword back. Apparently it had important family connections and historical value. The Sea Dyaks had naturally relieved the Japanese of all their weapons earlier.

'You'd have to be bloody well joking,' I said, this time in English. 'You can go and get well and truly stuffed, you bastard.'

I couldn't tell whether he understood me literally, but he certainly seemed to get the message from my tone of voice. He cringed back into his group and had nothing more to say.

I had them line up and couldn't help giving them a bit of a thump as they stood there. Any red-blooded Australian would've done the same after seeing the shocking way they had treated the poor local people. The sadistic treatment this lot had meted out was beyond the comprehension of anyone normal. I had met a lot of vicious bastards by now, but these easily took first prize.

I offered each of them the chance to hit me back, but none was game. I also ordered them to strip off all their clothing, which they did with some Sea Dyak prompting. This was standard military practice. It deflated their arrogance a bit, kept them from making mischief and, best of all, brought to light any concealed weapons. Sure enough, five still had knives.

Many of the Sea Dyaks had little in the way of clothing and helped themselves gleefully to the cast-offs, though I never found out who scored the black jackboots or the white silk scarf.

I asked Bujang to lock the Japanese in the Fort Alice kubu. This was the fort on the hill from which Lena had made her run to freedom. As the Sea Dyaks hustled the prisoners away, they still cast longing looks at their necks and the Japanese never knew how lucky they were. Later, when the sun went down we made them bow to it, in imitation of the daily humiliation they had forced on Lena and other POWs over long years in captivity.

Lena stood beside me during the whole of my confrontation with the Japanese officer. She looked, listened and watched with a fierce intensity determined not to miss a thing. Never to this day have I seen such an intense expression on anyone's face. But I had no indication of her thoughts, and she didn't say a word. It was fifty-three years before I found out what had been going through her mind. Then I understood why she was so intense.

A large crowd of the locals had also gathered to watch the change of management in Simanggang. Needless to say they were overjoyed with the result. Suddenly my experience with the telephone in Skrang came to mind and I had an idea.

'Lena, is there a telephone connection from Simanggang to Betong?'

She said there was and took me to the Simanggang switchboard. Betong was on that switchboard, so I made the connection. In Betong it had never entered our heads to ask whether there were telephones, and the locals hadn't offered the information. A telephone would've been the last thing we'd have expected to find in the jungle. There were no lines to be seen hanging from poles, the small switchboards weren't operated all the time and I'd only found the one in Skrang by accident. Dave probably had no idea there was a phone in Betong. What a laugh!

I picked up the phone and gave the bell handle a violent twist. It whirred but there was no answer. I turned it several more times and was just about to give it away, when a scratchy voice said, 'Salaamaat' ('Hello' in Malay).

'Get me Captain Kearney, the orang puteh,' I said in Malay as authoritatively and politely as I could.

'Who?'

I repeated it.

'All right,' the voice said, and the phone was put down with a *clunk*. Lena watched me closely as I waited. Finally I heard the phone being picked up and Dave muttering in the background.

'G'day!' I laughed.

'Shit – I didn't know there was a bloody phone here!'

'I know. Anyway, Dave, I've taken Simanggang. Everything's all right here now, but I'll tell you what, I've found the Little Rose of the Batang Lupar.'

The tension that had completely enveloped Lena visibly relaxed and she smiled for the first time. It was a good smile.

'Are you all right?' Dave asked.

'Yes, I'm okay.'

'We're coming down to Simanggang. We'll see you in the next day or so.'

'Okay.' I couldn't resist adding, 'And don't worry – you won't run into any Japs.'

'Good.' He hung up.

Turning to Lena, I said, 'I have to see how Bujang and the others are getting on. After I've finished I want to talk to you. Do you know Bujang?'

'Oh yes,' she said, 'I spoke to him when he was here the other day looking around.'

She showed me where the Sea Dyaks could stay. 'You'll have to stay in the Residency after it's cleaned.'

The Residency turned out to be a beautiful, imposing old mansion administered by the public works department. The remittance boys who had lived in these sorts of places before the war really had it made. Bujang told me the Japanese were locked in the kubu with no trouble. I took him aside and told him we still needed sentries out all the time. It was a big town and although I didn't think anyone would be game enough to attack us – everyone seemed overjoyed – we had to be prepared all the time.

'I fix.' He nodded.

Bujang was happy with the huts supplied for the Sea Dyaks. I told him to see me in the Residency any time if anything happened. We both laughed because we'd been having this same conversation for a while now. I put my hand on his shoulder, but I couldn't say the usual 'More heads, Bujang' on this occasion and I wasn't about to lie to him. I just said, 'You're a good friend.'

Leaving Unting in charge, we took a walk around town and as we came down the hill we saw Lena and her sister attending to some wounded Japanese.

'What on earth are you doing?' I asked her.

'We're nurses,' she explained. 'We must help anyone who is hurt. Even Japanese.'

I wouldn't have touched the mongrels with a forty-foot pole. But that was Lena. Despite her wretchedly emaciated condition, she was doing all she could to administer professional care to people who had spent years bashing and starving her. She is a unique and marvellous person.

After meeting her sister and brother it was obvious that Lena was the firebrand of the family. I suggested we meet for a drink and perhaps a meal after I'd done my rounds and she offered to show us around town. She was fluent in all the local languages and dialects and was well known for her excellent nursing. I learned afterwards that her expertise had saved her from being forced into a Japanese army brothel. Even so it was pretty rough in the hospital – a Japanese doctor, for example, had once punched her in the face so hard that her head struck the wall and she was covered in bruises. That was because she forgot to bow to him. On another occasion two hospital orderlies were beaten up and one almost drowned.

As usual, everyone was ecstatic to see us. The Japanese had given them such a shocking time it made me feel great to be able to help them. Beatings, sun torture, water torture, bayonet cuts, starvation rations – it was more of the same sad tale we'd encountered in the towns along the Rejang. But now the people smiled, giggled and wouldn't stop telling us how happy they were to be free. Many wanted to give me something to show their thanks, but they didn't really have anything left to give. The Japanese had taken it all. Thanking them for their kind offers, I declined politely, giving my best smile and saying I was glad to be here and that they didn't have to worry about the Japanese anymore – which brought a rousing cheer.

Simanggang was the biggest town I'd seen in Sarawak, located in what had once been a wealthy district. Until recently the Japanese had maintained a large military presence. There was deep anchorage on the Batang Lupar and there were wharves and storehouses for river traffic. The streets were properly laid out. There was a hospital, gaol and a large bazaar operated by prosperous *towkays* (shopkeepers and traders). Sadly the bazaar was rather short of *barang* (goods for sale), apart from a little locally grown food.

The Japanese trading company Takashimaya had operated here, apparently on a very one-sided basis. The Japanese had appointed numerous constables, but they were unarmed and there were also some ex-Sarawak Rangers. A large government building had treasury, health, tax, police, land and other departments. Realising I had to take some responsibility for kick-starting a fresh administration, I met a couple of the senior departmental heads and had a chat with them.

I'd had a busy day, it was getting late and I was hungry and thirsty. People frequently approached me to dob in collaborators, but I had no way of knowing who was telling the truth and I hoped Lena would help me out.

I decided to make an announcement to the people surrounding me, a crowd which included civil servants, constabulary and a couple of ex-Sarawak Rangers. 'Everything is back to the way it was before the Japs came. There are no more Japanese. I'm an Australian, but I've been in your country for some time, fighting the Japs with my Sea Dyak guerrillas. I don't want any trouble and I'm sure none of you people do either, but if anyone does make trouble, my Sea Dyaks will lock them up without any argument. Please pass this message around the town. I'll talk to you in the offices here tomorrow morning. I'm glad to be here and everything will be all right now. You can all sleep safely tonight.'

After my little speech we went to the Residency. The post-Japanese scrubbing out had already commenced and a fawning overseer greeted me. 'Very nearly ready, ready soon,' he said repeatedly.

Lena had a bungalow and said she'd be fine there, now that the Japanese had left.

'Would you and your brother and sister come back and have a drink and eat with me a little later?' I asked.

'Yes, we'd like to,' she said.

I offered to walk her back to her bungalow, but she insisted she'd be all right. So I found the overseer and offered him Straits Settlement dollars if he could rustle up a good cook to feed us.

'Oh yes, I can do,' he said eagerly. 'What kind of food?'

'Nice food. Chicken and things.' I gave him some money. 'If the meal and drinks are good, I'll give you a bonus.' Bujang told him where to deliver the Sea Dyaks' food.

Suddenly I remembered Bujang was still waiting to be paid for the heads he hadn't taken. I gave him a bit more, 'For a couple of extra heads,' I said; I thought they deserved it. He smiled shyly, but was clearly very pleased. Bujang arranged to send the rest of my gear over and I told him that I'd check with him later.

As soon as Bujang departed another realisation hit me: I hadn't cleaned the Bren or Owen gun. And after that was done I decided to have a go at cleaning myself. The Residency had three bathrooms, and it was a long while since I'd seen one. I can only use one at a time, I laughed to myself. I had a good scrub and felt brand new. Not having seen myself in a mirror for ages, at my first glimpse I thought, 'Who the fuck is *that*?' But of course I was the only person there.

I chose a large room and put all my gear in a corner, making sure the Bren gun was easily accessible. I still wore the Owen gun because there was no sense in taking chances.

I found a gramophone, some records and a lot of unused needles so I whacked on 'St Louis Blues' and it came out beautifully. Then I looked through the cupboards and turned up some unopened bottles of Scotch and other drinks. I busted the seal on a bottle of Scotch and had a couple. I felt on top of the world. There was still plenty of time before dinner, so I went around to find Bujang.

He reported that his warriors were okay. The huts provided for their accommodation were good, their food had arrived and his sentries were on duty. I asked to see him early in the morning. 'We're going down to the administrative offices,' I said. 'Bring two armed warriors with you.' And he nodded vigorously.

The Residency was a hive of industry when I got back. People were hard at work on our meal and a drink waiter brought me a Scotch and water. Lena arrived with her sister Alice and brother Herbert and I greeted them warmly because it felt as if I'd known them – Lena certainly, anyhow – for a lot longer than just a few hours. We sat down in the reception room and sipped our drinks. Shortly the waiter summoned us into a large dining room decked out with good quality, if slightly worn, furniture. There was a tablecloth and serviettes, and expensive cutlery and plates. This beats the shit out of the jungle, I thought.

'What are you smiling at?' Lena asked me.

'Oh, just the thought that it's a lot more pleasant here than in the jungle.'

'It's certainly a lot more pleasant without the Japanese,' she said.

She and her family spoke of their indescribable excitement when, after all those years, they heard the first shots and finally saw us move in and take over the town. I didn't know what to say. 'Well, it's nice to meet nice people, particularly in the jungle,' I said and we all had a laugh.

'It's been years since we've eaten like this,' Lena said. 'It's like Christmas – except I've almost forgotten what Christmas is like.'

After the superb meal we listened to the gramophone and talked and talked. I told them briefly what I had been doing, but I was more interested in their stories. They had been through a horrific ordeal; it was hard to believe some of the sadistic things the Japanese had done.

After an American air-raid in 1944, the Kempeitai interrogated Lena for eight hours, threatening to behead her with a sword placed on the table in front of her. Her brother Herbert had been tortured by being bound hand and foot for three weeks and locked in a tiny cell with two other men for three months.

We all had a wonderful evening – the most enjoyable evening in quite some time for all of us, although it had been a far longer time for them than for me. When it drew to a close we thanked the people who had looked after us and I offered Lena and her family an armed escort home. She saw no need for that, but when I asked if she would help me out at the administration offices in the morning she said she was only too pleased to and we wished each other goodnight.

I decided not to sleep in the room I'd chosen. I wasn't expecting trouble but I thought it best to be careful, so I left the gear in there and curled up in the corner of the room next door. I knew Bujang would be able to find me if the sentries had anything to report.

I was exhausted, but it had been well worth it. I'd made a lot of people happy and quite a few Japanese most unhappy. That seemed a pretty good balance to me. I put the Bren gun in a corner and dozed off, on the half-alert as usual, with the Owen gun cradled in my lap. What a day it had been!

33

A Day at the Office

I woke early, feeling pretty good. There was no movement around the Residency. The bathroom hadn't been a mirage or a figment of my imagination, so I had a good wash and a shave and felt brand new. The kitchen had a large stove with a smouldering fire underneath and an urn of hot water on top so I had a mug of instant coffee, and then another. Both were very good.

Then it was time to go to the office. Setting off with my Bren and Owen guns, I passed a couple of Bujang's roaming sentries and was about to ask one to carry the Bren for me when Bujang appeared from nowhere and took it from me. 'Everything all right,' he smiled. 'Nothing happened overnight.'

The offices were practically deserted when we arrived. They were well-equipped with plenty of typewriters and duplicating machines, and lots of filing cabinets. I commandeered a large and imposing office with three desks – for Lena, Bujang and me. I was sure Bujang had no use for it, but he was welcome to one if he wanted it, and I knew his decorative presence would give potential troublemakers something to think about. The Bren gun didn't leave a lot of room for papers or documents, but Bujang didn't have much use for them anyway.

I'd given a lot of thought about what to do. The locals would obviously want to know what was happening, and they had a right to know. Still, it was all new to me. School history lessons came to mind. In the old days, when the authorities wanted to get a message across they issued a proclamation. So I sat down to write four of them, signing them all on behalf of Dave, who was nominally in command:

Be it known to all people resident in Simanggang that as from today, 15th September 1945, Captain D. Kearney of the Australian Forces is the Officer-in-charge of the 2nd Division, Sarawak.

Be it known to all people, resident in Simanggang, that as from today, 15th September, 1945, all Government Laws will be adhered to in the same manner as before the Japanese temporary occupation of Sarawak.

Be it known to all people, resident in Simanggang, that as from this day, 15th September, 1945, Japanese currency is not to be used for any purpose whatsoever. Sarawak currency or Straits Settlement currency is the only currency that may be used. Failure to comply with this will be treated as a criminal offence.

Be it known to all people resident in Simanggang that as from today 15.9.45 the following price list has been fixed by the Government of Sarawak. Any failure to comply with this price list will be treated as a criminal offence.

Shortly Lena walked in, all smiles. How different she was from the poor desperate lady who had come racing down the hill towards me only the day before. It already seemed such a long time ago. She was what we Australians referred to as a 'very good sort.'

I showed Lena her desk and asked if she could translate my proclamations into the local written language. She got busy and it was a piece of cake for her. By now the office staff were showing up, looking surprised and whispering about these newcomers who were already at work.

Calling over one of the Department heads, I asked him to have the proclamations typed as soon as Lena finished with them, and to have copies distributed and displayed all over Simanggang.

The Department head told me there was trouble at Engkilili, an outlying township, and I decided to send a former Sarawak Ranger named Corporal Mulinng. I'd spoken to him a couple of times since I arrived and he seemed reasonably smart and capable. Mulinng said he knew Engkilili very well so I offered to put him back in the Sarawak Rangers if he went there to restore order. I promised to send him help.

'Yes sir,' he said. 'I will do that.' That was my first 'sir' in Simanggang, but I didn't let it go to my head.

'Good. Wait here while I get everything ready.' Bujang fetched him a rifle and ammunition and I quickly set about a letter of authority which Lena translated into written Malay for me. The Department head had it typed and duplicated:

The Native Officer

Engkilili

The bearer Cpl Mulinng is proceeding to Engkilili under my instructions, and is to be the temporary Military Occupation Force of Engkilili. You will help him in all ways possible.

Instructions for you:

1. *Capt D. Kearney of the Australian Imperial Forces is the officer-in-charge of 2nd Division Sarawak.*

2. *Japanese currency is no longer to be used for any purpose whatsoever. Sarawak currency or Straits Settlement currency is the only currency to be used.*

3. *All Government laws will be adhered to in the same manner as before the temporary Japanese Occupation of Sarawak.*

4. *The following price list is laid down by the Government of Sarawak.*

Failure for any person to comply with these instructions will be treated as a criminal offence.

Mulinng had no questions, so I gave him his armaments and a few Straits Settlement dollars and he went happily on his way.

The proclamations created great interest around Simanggang. I warned the administration head he would soon have to start answering all sorts of questions from the people. 'After all,' I said, 'that's what you're being paid for, as from yesterday.' That brought a smile to his face. Although I could understand most of the language that the questions came in, whenever I couldn't Lena certainly could. 'You'll have to become my secretary,' I laughed.

We must have looked a strange mob. Two armed Sea Dyaks stood guard at the door. Inside I had the big executive desk with an Owen gun slung on my shoulder and an automatic pistol, two hand grenades and a knuckleduster knife hanging from my belt. Nearby Lena, confident and unassuming, seemed like she had worked there for years. Bujang, rather bored, looked very menacing with his parang and his desk filled with a loaded Bren gun and rifle.

There was a great deal of ill feeling against local Japanese collaborators. I couldn't blame anyone for that, but it was not for me to make judgements. All I could do was log the complaints to be followed up and acted on by whoever came after us.

However, I did lock up two accused collaborators who seemed pretty bad types. But this was mainly for their own safety – the townsfolk wanted to tear them to pieces. It seemed pretty clear they'd been involved in the murder of Europeans at the time of the Japanese entry into Sarawak.

The whole town was dirty and unhygienic, so I asked the Health Department to sanitise the hospital and send inspectors out to arrange a total clean up. Then I dissolved the Japanese trading company Takashimaya, putting all its stores and money under the control of the appropriate administrative departments. There was no real shortage of food at all – it had just not been dished out. The Japanese had a large supply stockpiled for themselves and had been content for everyone else to starve. Now, at last, the department head could arrange for the needy or disabled to have sufficient food. I also had him make sure enough padi (rice) was planted and the market gardens re-established. 'There'll probably be a good market for rubber,' I suggested, 'so maybe you should attend to that too.'

'Yes, sir, we'll do that now,' he told me gravely as he left.

I had the Treasury head pay wages as from yesterday, and told him that no government taxes or rents need be paid until the old government took over. Paying wages, of course, had not been on the Japanese agenda when they could get the same result by using brute force. The effect this had on office morale was immediate.

I asked Lena if she had enough food at her bungalow, but didn't want to make a big deal of it because obviously she was very proud. And although she said they'd be okay, I made her take some instant coffee home. There was a lot in the stores and I knew it would probably be a luxury for her.

'How about we knock off work now and have a rest?' I said. 'Would you all like to come over for a few drinks and a good meal at the Residency later on?'

'Oh yes, we'd like to do that.'

'Good. Dave and the others should be here from Betong by tomorrow.'

Now that things were more settled I decided to requisition what I required and keep a record of what it cost for later reimbursement. This included food and drinks for that night, supplies for the Sea Dyaks and some things for Lena's bungalow.

I told Bujang we still needed sentries out all the time. When Dave and the others arrive I'd like prior notice to welcome them, I thought facetiously.

'What are you going to do now?' I asked Bujang.

'Maybe go and see cockfight. You come?'

'I'd like to, but I haven't got time. Could you get a couple of Sea Dyaks to watch the Residency in case any nasties come walking around? Tell them they can come in and talk to me at any time.'

'I fix.'

Back at the Residency I didn't bother about a proper meal. I just demolished two emergency rations and drank a couple of my special arak mixes. After a short nap I had a look at my share of the Japanese commanding officer's spoils that Bujang had dumped in a corner of my first bedroom.

There was a beautiful Leica camera, but the film was crook and there was very little of it. I took photos of Lena, Bujang, Unting and others. Bujang and Unting came out okay and their portraits appear in this book, but the remainder were blank.

The commander's sword was in perfect condition and bore his Kempeitai insignia. The long hilt had elaborate brown bindings over studded sharkskin and featured an elaborate flowing brown tassel. A perfect blade was encased in a softly-lined, polished metal scabbard. The hilt was attached to the blade by a concealed pin. Removing the pin revealed a hidden parchment in Japanese writing. Although I couldn't read it, I knew it related the history of the sword. No wonder the bastard wanted it back. But it was going to make a good pair with one I'd acquired from some other bastard in New Guinea.

There was also a full-length, silver-tipped cane with an engraved silver knob. The only wording that I could read was '1912'. I'll use this when I get old, I thought with a chuckle. An automatic pistol, which looked like a Japanese copy of a German Luger, had obviously never been fired. Finally there was what was clearly his battle flag. I promised myself I'd have the writing on it translated one day, just to see what he felt the need to boast about.

The Residency staff were keeping busy. Maybe they'd heard the news about being paid; maybe they were just conscientious. Whatever it was, dinner was on the way. I relaxed with another arak drink and put on "I'm Beginning To See The Light", a fabulous number. When Lena, Herbert and Alice arrived I had a wonderful evening of food, conversation and music. After it was all over I again offered to walk Lena and her family home, but they assured me they felt quite safe.

'Would you come to the office tomorrow and help me again?' I asked Lena.

'Oh yes, I'll be there,' she smiled and we all said goodnight.

Now that Bujang had a couple of warriors roaming around outside I decided to sleep in my original bedroom. There was a bed frame, but it was too uncomfortable so I settled into a corner with my Owen gun. I decided to have a word to the head of Public Works the following day about making these beds comfortable enough to sleep on.

Bujang arrived as I was about to leave for work in the morning. First thing was to check that everything was all right at the kubu. It was manned by the local constabulary, who had been bullied mercilessly by the Japanese throughout their occupation. No love lost there.

'Have you been giving the Japs food and water?' I asked the constable in charge.

'Oh, yes.'

'Have they caused you any trouble?'

'Oh, no.'

'Well, when Captain Kearney arrives he'll decide what to do with them.'

'Yes, sir.'

We proceeded to the offices, where there were a couple of minor decisions to make. Lena helped to translate for several people. The morning wore on until one of Bujang's warriors came gliding up to him and whispered excitedly. Bujang turned and grinned. 'They come from Betong.'

'Come on, Lena,' I said and, along with Bujang, we went outside. A stream of office workers and a whole crowd of locals followed us, all wanting to see what was happening.

I met Dave's party near the outskirts of town. They had a couple of hangers-on from Betong with them.

'Welcome to Simanggang,' I said. 'May I introduce you to the Little Rose of the Batang Lupar?'

'Hello.' Lena smiled.

I told them how good it was to see them again.

'Good to see you, too, Brian,' said Dave. 'Are you all right?'

'Right as rain. But let's get you all settled in and I'll tell you what's been happening. It's pretty safe here, although I still carry my Owen gun. Probably habit. Let's go.'

As we walked I pointed out some of the buildings we were passing and Lena filled in any details I didn't know. I asked Bujang to show the rest of the Sea Dyaks their quarters after they had dropped their stores off at the Residency.

'If they need more food or anything else let me know,' I said. 'I'll see you soon, anyway, because we'll take Dave to see the kubu and the offices.' Bujang nodded again.

There was plenty of room at the Residency for each of the others to pick a bit of space. They looked at me like I'd gone crazy when I said I'd organise 'evening dinner, drinks and nibblies' after they had settled in. However, the Residency staff head graciously agreed to put on a special banquet for seven people.

Later I pulled Dave aside and over a quiet drink related to him everything that had happened since I left Betong, which already felt like years ago. But now that Dave had arrived, he could run the town. Actually there was bugger all to do now, but I wanted a few days off.

'You've done a good job and seem to have organised everything,' he said, looking over the proclamations.

'Well, it's all yours now, Dave.'

We still had plenty of time before dinner so I offered to take him to the kubu to see the Japanese prisoners and the constabulary guarding them. Then we went down to the offices so that he could meet the department heads and, if he felt like it, the towkays who ran the bazaar.

'These Japs are real bastards,' I told him at the kubu. 'You only have to ask any of the locals or Lena. I had to stop Bujang and the Sea Dyaks souveniring their heads – and sometimes I feel sorry I stopped them.' If I'd known about the trouble I was going to get into later, I wouldn't have stopped them at all.

Dave was in for a surprise at the offices. 'Bujang has a desk?' he asked, amazed.

'Of course. You can have my executive desk while I have a couple of days off, if that's okay. It's the best one in the place.'

'Yes, of course it's okay.'

After our rounds we met Lena, Herbert and Alice for the big dinner at the Residency. We had good food, imported drinks, and the poor old gramophone worked its guts out. It was great fun and we had a dinner party every night for the next few days.

During the day, Lena showed me around the town. One of the most awesome things was the powerful bore of the river. When the tide changed it gushed and roared upstream like a tidal wave. It had to be seen to be believed. Bujang gave me a tour of the Sea Dyak areas. He took me to a couple of cockfights, which didn't impress me much but made him happy.

I visited the Japanese to tell them my opinion of them again, in a mixture of Malay, Sea Dyak and English – although I found the Australian idiom provided the most appropriate words.

34

Farewell to Simanggang

Five days later Brick Fowler received radio instructions that an Australian navy patrol boat was coming upstream to Simanggang. When it arrived we were to hand over control to a Major Ditmas and 'extract' ourselves from the area to Sibu, either by hired or commandeered boat.

'Extracted' meant leaving immediately after achieving an objective, and there wasn't much more for us to achieve in Simanggang. We continued our dinner parties at the Residency while we could, to make the most of the short time we had left.

Major Ditmas was with BBCAU – the British Borneo Civil Administration Unit – derisively known as B.Cow or BB Cow. It consisted of people trained in Australia to take over administration when it was safe to do so. Few of them were Australian and none had seen wartime action or combat.

The patrol boat duly arrived and disgorged Major Ditmas. Two things were soon apparent: he was a small-minded, obnoxious Pom, and he had little to do because we'd done most of the work. To my relief, Dave dealt with him most of the time. Ditmas actually turned out to be worse than Sochon, and I wouldn't have thought that possible. He was a real shit of a person.

He was strange in other ways, too. The rest of us were known as Dave, Brian, Ross and 'Brick' – but he was only ever Major Ditmas. His initials read 'W.P.N.L. Ditmas'. Did this stand for something too frightful to be revealed? Whatever – there was no way I was going to call him 'Major', let alone 'sir'. If I had to speak to him, I always prefaced my words with phrases like 'Oh, by the way' or 'Excuse me, but'.

He had no authority to order us about, so when he tried I simply give him a smiling, 'I beg your pardon?' He woke up to this pretty quickly and instead concentrated on giving the locals orders, no doubt in preparation for becoming their administrator.

When I was in New Guinea, commando and infantry units did all the face-to-face combat with the enemy. The same people were used over and over again. They had the utmost disdain for people who implied that they had faced such hazards when they had not. This might help to explain some of the antagonism created by W.P.N.L. Ditmas.

To extract ourselves we hired an old boat, the *Merry Jolly*, to take us to Sibu. The pair of Japanese motor boats would have been ideal, but we'd shot them up during the takeover and they were no longer seaworthy. Thinking to make our long journey a bit more comfortable, we transferred some of their armchairs and other amenities aboard.

Meanwhile Ditmas caused all kinds of trouble for the townsfolk. He had probably never had so much power or authority before, and was making the most of it. At least he kept away from us, except for poor old Dave, who was handing over the administration to him. I felt sorry for the people of Simanggang. They were just beginning to get over the trauma of the Japanese occupation and now they had to put up with the Ditmas occupation.

Something else was bothering me, too. I asked Dave to come with me to the Residency for a drink and a talk. 'I'm worried about Bujang and the Sea Dyaks,' I told him. 'We've been through a lot together and they're my friends. They've been loyal and completely trustworthy and never complained. I couldn't bear to see them stuffed around by Ditmas. They'll rebel against him in the end, just like they did against the Japs, and that'll put the poor bastards in all kinds of shit. I think we owe them more than that.'

'What do you suggest?'

'Well, firstly we ought to tell them we have to go back to Australia now the war's over. I'd tell them that now the Englishman is here, they'd be better off going home with all their Jap heads.'

'Fair enough,' said Dave.

'Then I'd like to reward them. It's no big deal. We could give them two or three rifles and some ammo. There's a heap of Jap stuff no one would miss. We could give them all the Sea Dyak stores we brought down. It isn't much and when they've gone no one'll know where they are. Nobody knows where they've come from anyway, except us. I'll even write Bujang a note of appreciation for all his warriors did for us. I'll make it say everything he has with him is his because we gave it to him.'

'Good,' Dave said. 'Do it. I'll say goodbye to them, too, when they're leaving.'

At least Dave didn't muck about. I organised everything and he paid them up when I was ready. Explaining to Bujang wasn't easy. 'Everyone in your longhouse will love you for what you've done,' I told him. He kept nodding and said he agreed they would all go home.

'When will I see you?' he asked repeatedly.

I simply couldn't tell him the truth, weak bastard that I was, so I just said, 'I'll come back to Kapit where I met you.' That appeared to satisfy him.

Bujang was very keen to show me his longhouse. There would be a special ritual for all the heads he had collected, and I was invited. 'You must come,' he implored, over and over again. 'You helped take the heads.'

Even if I had wanted to go, it was impossible, but to be honest I wasn't too broken-hearted about missing out. It was touching to be invited, however. It was as if Bujang imagined Australians were headhunters just like the Sea Dyaks. And if he did, then that was partly my fault.

I gave him all the Straits Settlement dollars I had left. It didn't look like much to me, but I knew he could do a lot with it. I read him the 'letter of ownership' of all the goods and gave that to him as well. In another letter I gave a flowing appreciation of the services he and the Sea Dyaks had provided to the Semut 3 guerrilla operation. He tucked the money and the two letters away carefully.

'Goodbye, Bujang,' I said, placing my hand on his shoulder, the gesture he had always liked so much.

'I see you soon,' he replied, his eyes glowing in anticipation of the heads ceremony. 'I see you at my longhouse.' The Sea Dyaks turned and disappeared into the jungle like ghosts.

I never saw any of them again, but Bujang has remained in my thoughts to this day.

I'd lost a true, trustworthy friend. He was a real warrior. His ancestors would have been proud of him, and I was proud of him, too. The long war years had made me almost immune to becoming upset, but I must admit I found Bujang's departure somewhat traumatic after what we had been through together. What a marvellous people the Sea Dyaks were, and Bujang especially. It hurt having to lie to him, but it was far better for him to leave now.

Dave noticed how I felt. 'Come on,' he said. 'How about a drink?'

We had another dinner party that night. Extraction time was drawing near. I put on the record 'Come To Me My Melancholy Baby', another wonderful song, but under the circumstances I found it depressing and gave the gramophone away for the rest of the night.

Dave told me he was writing a report for Major Ditmas regarding the events that surrounded our occupation of Simanggang.

'That's right up your alley,' I said.

'Yes, well, we'll talk about it.'

'If you want any suggestions from me, don't tell Ditmas too much. That type of bastard tries to find fault with everything. He isn't like us and he won't understand. Don't give it to him until right before we leave, then just ask if he needs anything clarified before we go. Anyway, your bullshit reports always answer anything anyone might ask.'

Dave wrote his report and made a copy for Major Fisher of SRD, the commanding officer at Sibu. Ditmas accepted it without query, so we had a few drinks to celebrate divesting ourselves of the responsibility for the 2nd Division of Sarawak. Then it was time to clean our weapons and prepare for an early departure the next morning. Lena, Herbert and Alice joined us for a final dinner, along with some locals and a couple of the crew from the Australian patrol boat.

It was the best party we had in Simanggang, a very special farewell to the lovely people I'd met there. We talked non-stop, laughed our heads off, drank and danced and listened to the music: 'I'll See You In My Dreams'; 'Have You Ever Been Lonely, Have You Ever Been Blue?'; 'Tonight I Mustn't Think Of Her, Music, Maestro Please' and so on. The contrast between that night and shooting at Japanese only a week before was almost unbelievable. But such is life.

Finally the evening drew to a close. It was a lovely moonlit night and Lena and I strolled down to the Batang Lupar and sat on the river bank under a huge jacaranda tree in full bloom. I had my last look at the incredible river bore surging and roaring past us. We looked at each other and said goodnight.

There was no point stuffing around in the morning. After an early cup of coffee we got all our gear together, ready to be carried to the wharf. Then I had a brainwave and raced back to fetch the gramophone and records. A little music on the river wasn't going to go astray.

It seemed the whole town had turned out to see us off. The crowd smiled and waved. Many of them held their hands out, saying repeatedly, 'Thank you, thank you!'

Bujang should be here, I thought. He had played a major role in liberating the town, but my feeling that it would be better for him to leave early was borne out by subsequent events.

I found it extremely difficult to say goodbye to Lena and the right words just wouldn't come. Although we'd only known each other a matter of days, I felt we had a special bond because of the unforgettable, strange drama of our meeting, and also our adventures administering Simanggang over the following week.

'We'll meet again soon,' I said. What more could I say? Under the prevailing conditions, there was no certainty of anything, except that the Japanese regime was finished.

As we boarded the *Merry Jolly* everyone seemed glad to be getting out of town and on their way home. I was too, but my role in the taking of the town lent a somewhat nostalgic tinge to my emotions as I looked back at the happy crowd. I felt as if I'd known these people for ages.

Memories, thoughts and images flashed through my mind. When I blasted into town the week before, these people were desperate. What a difference a week had made! I felt so good to have been able to bring about such a change. But by far my strongest impression was of Lena, racing down the hill from Fort Alice, emaciated and filthy. Now here she was, smiling and waving from the river bank. Not only extremely attractive and accomplished, Lena was possibly the most courageous woman I've ever met and she has stayed in my thoughts for the rest of my life, just as vividly as the day we met. Her courage was truly inspiring.

The *Merry Jolly* turned its bow downstream into the fast current. As she rounded the first bend in the river, the people at the wharf were lost from our view.

'I'm going to have a drink,' I said, to no one in particular.

35

Court Martial

How strange it was to enjoy watching and listening to the jungle without having to worry about Japanese bullets coming at you. It was still early morning, but already it was a beautiful sunny day. Old habits die hard, though. I kept the Bren ready on deck and continued to wear my Owen gun.

Our first stop was Lingga, a small township where we had something to eat. These smaller places had someone called the Native Officer in charge. We told this one what was happening and said that Major Ditmas would contact him soon. The Japanese armchairs and some other stuff had only been cluttering up the launch, so we left it all for the Native Officer to send back to Simanggang, which he said he would do.

We proceeded downstream and out into the South China Sea. Travelling up the coast, we eventually entered the mouth of our old friend, the mighty Rejang River, and continued upstream to Sibu. Here we joined members of other Semut guerrilla groups who had been operating elsewhere. From Sibu we were to be flown back progressively to Labuan by cat boat. Dave handed a copy of the Ditmas Report to Major JCB Fisher of SRD, who accepted it with thanks. The locals couldn't pronounce his surname and always addressed him as Tuan Pisser, *tuan* being Malay for 'mister'. We called him that as well, in a friendly fashion. He was a jovial and pleasant man.

Dave was on one of the first flights. I followed a couple of days later and found that Labuan was now a vast military base. I tried to find Dave, but he'd already gone home. Much later I found he was flown out very smartly, because charges were about to be laid against him by our own Australian Occupying Forces. This, of course, was the work of that shithead Major Ditmas. And there was more to come.

Now that the war was over, there was no reason to give SRD personnel priority travel, and so we waited as anxiously as everyone else. However, we still remained as a unit, not coming under the jurisdiction of the occupying force, our own Australian 9th Division.

Lieutenant Colonel Courtney was in charge of our SRD base at Labuan. He was always referred to as Jumbo Courtney, though he wasn't inordinately large. He was a Pom, but not at all pompous like many of the others I'd encountered in the military. Having seen action with the Special Boat Section of the British Army Commandos, he understood what it was like on an operation.

While we waited for our turn to go home, one of our operatives, Des Foster, circulated a sendup suggesting we were to swim home using jungle hammocks as rafts! I understand Des became a journalist after the war.

On the 10th of October 1945 I was sent to see Jumbo. With Dave's departure, enquiries about the taking of Simanggang were directed at me. I wasn't next in command or anything like that, but it had basically been my operation. After we'd gone, apparently, locals had been mentioning my name to all and sundry while discussing their liberation. Ditmas was considerably cheesed off that we had left the town in pretty good shape and given him very little to boast of.

'What the bloody hell is this all about?' Jumbo showed me a written complaint from Ditmas which he wanted me to answer in writing.

The content was outrageously trivial, concerning a handful of items not accounted for, including the armchairs left at Lingga and the gramophone and records, which we had left at Sibu with the rest of the stores. Other missing items, such wine glasses and pillows, we had definitely not taken. Ditmas even accused us of stealing cutlery from the Residency, to which I replied that if our Chinese cooks had inadvertently included them with our own stores, they would probably be at Sibu with everything else. I finished my statement by writing that 'Major Ditmas's report that we wished to remove a bicycle but could not find room for it on the launch, is fantastic.'

Life at Labuan was pretty much the same routine as when we had been waiting to go into Borneo. There was extra grog from the Air Force ground crew, fishing with hand grenades, and a lot of hanging around. On the 16th of November 1945 Jumbo called me in to answer more complaints from Ditmas about minor items of missing property. It happened again on the 5th of December.

'Whatever did you people do to Ditmas?' Jumbo asked when I arrived for the third time. 'Now he's lodged his complaints with the Ninth Division. They're asking the questions now.'

'Oh well, fire away.'

'One query concerns missing gold and silver ornaments. The Native Officer at Lingga claims you had them.'

'I know nothing about that. It's news to me.' In my written statement to the Ninth Division's Investigating Officer I declared I had 'no knowledge whatsoever of the ornaments referred to'; that 'they were certainly not handed to me by Corporal Bujang as alleged'; and finally, that the Semut 3 guerrilla group was 'demobilised and I have no idea where Corporal Bujang would be at present.'

I was now glad that Bujang was safely back at his longhouse in the Kapit district. He would have had no idea how to defend himself against these false allegations. But there was more to come. Jumbo told me that Ditmas had recommended Ninth Division interview me about the capture of Simanggang.

'Why? Ditmas wouldn't know a thing about the raid. He only arrived when everything was safe. You just have to talk to the locals to find out what the Japs were doing to them. Even the Jap CO admitted he was going to kill all the prisoners that day.'

'Yes, yes, we know you did well at Simanggang,' Jumbo said. 'The thing is, we don't want any of our operatives interviewed about our activities. Everything we do is classified top secret. So we're putting you on a cat boat in the morning. You'll go straight home and on leave until it all blows over.'

Of course I had no say in the matter, but flying home right away beat the hell out of waiting weeks to sail back. I was the envy of everyone, and ironically I had Ditmas to thank for it. Early the following morning I boarded Wally Mills's Catalina and flew non-stop to Darwin, arriving on the 8th of December 1945.

What a sweet feeling it was to stand on our own Australian soil again! And it was a bonus to still be in one piece. I could only think what a beautiful country Australia was and that there was nothing like it anywhere else in the world.

SRD staff met me at Darwin and arranged a priority flight to Melbourne. Jumbo had radioed instructions that I was to be gone before the 9th Division could get their paws on me. In Melbourne, Z Special Unit base issued me with new gear – the clothes I'd been wearing in Borneo were pretty tatty by now – together with some pay and ration coupons. I was handed an open leave pass and asked to keep in touch, although they knew where to contact me. It was just a matter of waiting to see whether anything would eventuate from the 9th Division's request to interview me. I was particularly glad to have the open leave pass, because it came as a bonus on top of my accrued entitlements.

The atmosphere in Melbourne was vastly different now that the war was over. People were overjoyed, and those with loved ones still overseas could be fairly certain they were coming home. Rationing still applied to most commodities, but that would soon ease and didn't seem much of a problem anymore.

My parents had no idea I was back in Australia. I wondered whether to ring them, but decided to just go and knock on the door, confident that their joy at seeing me would soon overcome any shock my sudden reappearance might cause. And if no one was home I'd just have a drink at the Botanical while I waited.

My mother opened the door. She was momentarily spellbound, then grabbed me fiercely. Pushing me an arm's length away, she appraised me closely.

'I'm all in one piece!' I said, as she hugged me again and muttered all kinds of words. Finally she quietened down and pulled me inside. There, looking utterly amazed, were my father and my brother Denis.

What a fantastic surprise it was for all of us! My parents were overwhelmed. Here were both their sons back home in one piece, although my poor brother was very much the worse for wear. After his unit had obeyed General Percival's orders to surrender, the Japanese took them from Timor to Changi, and from there Denis was sent to slave on the notorious Thai-Burma Railway. He didn't talk much about his experience, but I knew some of it from word that filtered back from SRD Intelligence, which was a pretty reliable source. Today, the story of how they were starved, bashed and degraded is well known. They worked their guts out and were turned into physical wrecks. Thousands of them, of course, never came back.

Denis had been home only a short time. Always highly intelligent, he hadn't lost a thing in that department, but there was next to no meat on him, he had a blood disorder and he was covered with shocking skin infections, including tropical ulcers and their remnants. I became his self-appointed carer, having dealt with this sort of thing many times in the jungle. But I'd never seen anything as bad as this.

My celebratory drink tasted just perfect, more so because I was able to have it with the whole family. No more arak with wild lemon and water for me. My mother belted out a few numbers on her piano. One of them was 'Bye Bye Blues'. How appropriate that was.

Denis and I did a lot of things together, although it took a while for his strength to return. I also began phoning the ladies I had met when I was last in town. They were generally pleased to hear from me and asked after my health, but mostly they now had firm commitments to other men. Some were already married. 'You've been away so long,' they would say. Everyone was bespoken. So I had to start again, but that was no problem.

I was invited to a party by a couple of Z Special Unit people. It was a great night and there were lovely girls, girls, girls. This led to more parties and soon I had no trouble finding all sorts of lovely young ladies wanting to have a bit of fun and a good time. Denis came along to many of these parties and made his own contacts and lady friends.

We had a wonderful Christmas together. My father got hold of a Christmas tree, the first one I'd seen for years. It made me smile with joy just to look at it. We got some good grog from John at the Botanical Hotel, even though alcoholic drinks were still rationed, and my mother somehow scrounged or acquired the ingredients for a proper old-fashioned Christmas dinner. She cooked it to perfection and I found three threepences in my portion of the pudding. My parents were so happy that we were all together after such a long time. And I felt happy for them, because they were such marvellous people and had quietly endured so much mental anguish.

Denis and I went to a riotous all-night New Year's Eve party. Everyone enjoyed themselves immensely and we all agreed in hoping that the New Year would be much better than the old.

My time was pretty much taken up with four very lovely young ladies. Alicia ran a fashionable ladies' hairdressing and beauty parlour. As she had a couple of beauticians working for her, she was able to take time off, but she wouldn't allow me to meet any of her clientele. Lynda was the personal secretary to a General. She was mad keen on the beach. Mary was a lovely, very young war widow. Her husband had been killed in action quite early in the war. Marilyn was unhappily married to a serviceman who was still overseas. They had agreed to separate when he returned to Australia. Later he arrived home unexpectedly to find us in a somewhat compromising situation, which I finally managed to talk my way out of. But that's another story.

Meanwhile, Z Special Unit had heard nothing about the 9th Division's wish to interview me at Ditmas's request. On the 22nd of January 1946 I was officially sent on thirty-three days leave, after which I was to report for discharge. I'd had a pretty good run, having been on leave ever since I came home, and still had thirty-three days to go. My parents were pleased and so were my four lovely young ladies – but separately, of course. They didn't know each other and there was now a fifth: Penny, a third-year law student at the university. She seemed to have plenty of spare time on her hands and had a marvellous tan from going to the beach.

Life continued very pleasantly, with parties, girls, the beach, more girls, more parties and more beach. People often asked if I had any interesting stories to tell about my wartime experiences. They gathered I'd been in some kind of strange Special Operations, mainly from the combination of my Australian Commando colour patch, my Australian parachute wings and Sarawak Rangers badge, clipped to my black beret. No one had heard of that last one before and telling them I was in Z Special Unit would only have created more confusion.

No account of SRD or Z Special Unit operations had been published and none was for many years to come. There were never many operatives anyway and the Official Secrets Act always prevented us from saying too much. So when pressed, I'd recount some incidents, such as meeting

Lena, or I'd describe Bujang and his warriors. This seemed to provoke two reactions. Polite listeners would nod and perhaps say, 'Go on!' – meaning doubtfully, 'Is that so?' Others would glance sideways with a look of disbelief and I could practically hear them think, 'Lying bastard!' Finally my story didn't sound convincing even to me! It all seemed too outlandish to be true. So I stopped talking about it altogether.

Finally, my thirty-three days leave came to an end and I imagined I'd become a civilian soon, but that wasn't to be. Reporting to HQ AMF, I was 'received in on strength,' as the phrase goes. An adjutant called me in for an interview.

'You've been missing,' he said by way of greeting.

Stuff you, I thought, and showed him my two leave passes, which spoke for themselves. He wasn't a bad bloke, however, because he said, 'Thank you. These are fine. They're quite in order, but we didn't know about them. We have orders to send you to Victoria Barracks to be interviewed about some matter. We'll give you another leave pass to go there and a note of explanation.' Ditmas and the 9th Division had caught up with me at last.

At Victoria Barracks there was some delay before a bright-eyed young Major arrived.

'We've been waiting a long time to interview you,' he said. 'Where have you been?'

Nonplussed, I showed my leave passes again.

'I see,' he replied. 'Well, we have a whole list of complaints lodged against you, pertaining to an operation in Sarawak.' He opened a fairly thick folder and proceeded to read to me. As I had anticipated, Ditmas had been busy.

The complaints included the trivial ones I'd already answered, but there were more serious items this time. I stood accused of killing and ill-treating Japanese, and inciting the locals against them after the war's end.

'The killing of the Japanese is tantamount to murder,' the complaint read. When the Major finished he said, 'We have your written replies to some of these questions. Do you have any comments?'

'It's garbage and untrue,' I told him.

This wasn't what he was expecting. 'Would you comment further?' he said.

'No.'

'Why?'

'Because I'm prevented by the provisions of the Official Secrets Act. The type of work I was involved in made it necessary for me to sign it. I'm subject to the penalties provided in the Act if I breach it.'

'If you can't come up with some kind of reasonable explanation or answer,' he persisted, 'it will in all probability be sorted out by court martial.'

'I'm prepared to explain what happened,' I said. 'But only if you supply me with a written and witnessed guarantee from someone with the authority to absolve me from my obligations under the Official Secrets Act, and also guarantee that I won't be charged under the Act. Why don't you approach my superior officers?'

'They have been approached,' the Major admitted. 'But they've been evasive.'

'Well, if my superiors won't talk, how can I?'

He thought for a moment. 'I'll take it up with the others. We'll see about absolving you from the Official Secrets Act. Be back here tomorrow at 1300 hours. I'll give you a leave pass. Do you have somewhere to stay?'

'Yes.'

'Give me an address and phone number where you will be staying.'

'No problem,' I said. 'If I may say something, if I'm absolved from the Official Secrets Act, I'll be able to sell my story to a newspaper or a magazine, so that'll be fine with me.'

That made him look up and think. I got my leave pass and left.

⁓

There were three of them to greet me the following day. The Major had been joined by a Lieutenant Colonel and another Major. My man from the day before opened. 'We have not had you absolved from the provisions of the Official Secrets Act,' he said.

'Does that mean that you can't – or won't?'

'Well, it may not be possible. Is your attitude still the same as yesterday?'

'I have no choice,' I said. 'As I told you, I'm governed by the Official Secrets Act. But tell me, among your documents are there any statements from the local civilians who saw what happened?'

I could just imagine what Lena would have said. 'No, we have no statements from the locals,' was his guarded reply.

'Have you been in touch with Z Special Unit base in Melbourne?'

'No.'

'Well, if you're relying on the 9th Division, they weren't there. And that idiot Major Ditmas only showed up when it was safe for him to arrive.'

'You don't like Major Ditmas.'

'It's not that, but he's an inefficient and jealous person.'

The Lieutenant Colonel took over. 'We'll be discussing this matter further, but in view of the fact that you decline to answer questions, you will be ordered to face a court martial. Your leave pass will be continued, but you are required back here at 1300 hours tomorrow. Is that clear?'

'Yes, sir. May I ask your advice?'

'Yes.'

'Well, frankly I'm between the devil and the deep blue sea. I'd be very happy to answer your questions if the Official Secrets Act permitted it. But because I can't, which is not of my doing, I'm to face a court martial. Is there any reason I can't talk to a newspaper about my current situation? I certainly wouldn't breach the Secrets Act. Perhaps *Smith's Weekly* would like the story.'

Although it's no longer published today, *Smith's Weekly* at the time relished sensational stories and I knew they'd love this one.

'I don't know about that. We'll discuss it and I'll answer you tomorrow,' said the Lieutenant Colonel.

So as soon as I got home I phoned *Smith's Weekly*. They were enthusiastic and asked when they could interview me. I said I'd get back to them the following day. That made me feel a bit better, but I didn't know why. I had a couple of drinks at the Botanical – but only two, because I was determined to stay on the ball.

The following afternoon at 1300 hours I faced the same trio at Victoria Barracks, but they were less antagonistic this time. The Lieutenant Colonel spoke first. 'There have been considerable discussions regarding the allegations against you. We're conscious of your obligations under the Official Secrets Act. The allegations have been dismissed as unfounded. We've been instructed to expunge everything relating to the allegations from all records. This has now been done. We are instructed to congratulate you on your handling of that situation in Sarawak.'

He continued. 'We hope that you won't be looking for publicity.

I'm instructed to apologise for any anguish caused to you. The Major will arrange two weeks leave for you. Thank you.'

He shook my hand, smiling weakly, and made his exit. I went with the young Major, who seemed friendly enough, although he'd never actually been very aggressive.

'What made them change their minds?' I asked him.

'Well, we sought advice about absolving you from the provisions and penalties of the Official Secrets Act, but it was apparently unheard of. Then somehow it reached Blamey's ears.'

I've already described how General Blamey, chief of Australia's armed forces, instigated the formation of our special operations units. Being no slouch, Blamey knew what SRD-Z Special Unit had been up to and it turned out the enquiries should never have been made in the first place.

The Major told me the orders to delete the files had come directly from Blamey. Apparently he went off the planet when he heard about the business and demanded to see the file himself, then instructed that the matter be treated as if it had never happened.

'You must have done something,' the Major said when he'd finished.

I was tempted to say, 'I can't tell you because of the Official Secrets Act,' but I just smiled and said nothing, then thanked him for the two-week leave pass and he wished me luck.

That night I went out with Penny to celebrate. We had a good time, although she didn't know what we were celebrating. I hoped I'd run into Ditmas one day so I could tell him a few home truths and give him a smart backhander or two, but the opportunity never arose.

Two weeks passed and I returned to HQ AMF, for my discharge, on the 11th of April 1946. I'd been on leave for over four months, ever since I'd returned from overseas. So I walked out a civilian again. But I didn't feel very different, probably because my units had never bothered with the yes-sir-no-sir crap that went on in normal regiments or battalions.

My mother seemed more pleased for me than I was myself. We had a drink together to celebrate and she said, 'Come and listen to this. It's a new one to me.' She led me over to her piano and proceeded to belt out 'The Blacksmith Blues'.

'What a character you are!' I laughed with her and gave her a hug. I thought what a lovely woman she was and how lucky I was to have her.

Afterwards I went around to the Botanical for my first drink as a civilian.

First thing the next morning I wrote a letter of resignation to the bank where I'd worked before the war, deciding that if I went back I might get into a rut and stay too long. It had only ever been a stopgap job until I was old enough to go to university in any case. The bank was good to servicemen employees, keeping their jobs open while they were away for the war and making up their pay to what it would've been had they still been working there, which was very generous, but they had plenty of money and it was their contribution to the war effort, I suppose.

Now I could finally enrol at university, this time under the Veterans' Repatriation scheme. But the prospect of settling down to the six-year grind of a medical degree was daunting. Could I possibly do it after the type of life I'd been living these past four years? There was no use in procrastinating or stuffing myself around. I quickly decided that I couldn't buckle down to it, and the following years were filled to the limit with excitement, business, money, property, ladies, sport and controversy. I began exporting goods to Britain, then opened a real estate business with my father keeping the books. I married three times, lived with several other lovely ladies and had three children. There never seemed to be a dull moment and the time flew by. I may write about it sometime.

PART FOUR

Australia: Today

36

Out of the Blue

Life had been marvellous, all I had hoped for. Although memories of my wartime experiences did not dim, my life as it unfolded was always my main focus. I belonged to no wartime associations and didn't go to any wartime reunions.

And not much was said about Z Special Unit over the years. As far as I know, for example, it wasn't until the late 1970s that any mention of the Sleeping Beauty one-man submarines surfaced. I don't think this silence was to do with the Official Secrets Act. I imagine that most operatives, like me, just left their past behind them. More recently there have been a handful of newspaper items about some operations and a couple of books, but I've never read them.

Life can be so unpredictable, however. Suddenly, out of the blue, my involvement with SRD-Z Special Unit was resurrected. In January 1998 I was contacted by Major Jim Truscott, a serving member of Australia's SAS (Special Air Service), who was writing a monograph for the Army called *The Return of the Ant* about the Semut guerrilla operations in Borneo. *Semut*, you may recall, is Malay for 'ant'.

Semut had covered an extremely large area and involved numerous Z Special Unit parties, most of whom operated without any contact with each other. In fact most of us never knew the other operatives at all. I know I didn't. Major Truscott had obtained a lot of information from the Z Special Unit Association. I gave him a short précis of my time with Semut 3. I haven't seen his finished work, but it was nice to know someone had an interest in our activities after all this time. Shortly afterwards an ex-Z Special Unit operative phoned me to say that Bob Reece, a professor of history in Perth, was writing a book on Sarawak under the Japanese. Titled *Masa Jepun*, Malay for 'during the Japanese occupation', it naturally made many references to our operations. Reece had mentioned interviewing an interesting lady in Perth for his book. In 1995 an article about her time as a prisoner of the Japanese in Sarawak had been published in the *Sarawak Gazette*.

'Sounds like the lady you got out,' he told me. 'I'll send you a copy.'

I received it and sure enough, there it was: *More Bitter Than Sweet*, featuring Lena Ricketts. I was overjoyed and excited. But how could I find her? My friend was unable to give me her address or phone number. The Perth telephone directory had nine Ricketts listed, so I phoned them all. They thought me somewhat strange, but none of them was my Lena. It seemed the trail had gone cold.

Then early one evening I came home to find a message on my answering machine. It was a small, musical voice I knew so well: 'Brian, it's Lena. Please ring me.' She left her number and I rang straightaway.

It was incredible. We hadn't spoken to each other for fifty-three years, but now, to me, it seemed like only yesterday. Lena would have had no idea where I lived. Although I was Melbourne-born and bred, I'd long since moved to Sydney. Lena tried to find me through the RSL but couldn't because I wasn't a member. But finally someone in Perth mentioned my name and she was able to get my phone number.

She had stayed on in Sarawak after the war. Then, in September 1963, the nation of Malaysia came into being and included Sarawak and Sabah. People of British extraction were immediately prohibited from working. Lena came to Australia in 1964 and settled in Perth, where she had been for over thirty years.

She had a daughter and two granddaughters. I told her I'd come and see her soon, and it wasn't long before I was on that plane. During the long flight west, memories of my last visit returned to me. The Sleeping Beauty training school, my altercation with the intrepid Alfred R Sleep in Kings Park, the gorgeous Mavis; it all seemed so long ago. I smiled as I wondered what had become of Mavis. She was so beautiful, such a marvellous person to be with.

My reverie was interrupted by the pilot announcing that it was a fine day in Perth and that we were about to land. I dumped my gear at Sullivans Hotel, where I'd booked to stay, and rang Lena. 'Get a cab,' she told me. 'We're waiting for you.'

Well, what a welcome it was! There was Lena, her daughter Vivian and Vivian's daughter Isabella, all waiting for me to arrive. We spent hours talking and enjoying each other's company, but it wasn't until later that night, back at my hotel, that I had time to think and appreciate what some of their feelings and thoughts must have been.

Seeing me would surely have brought back to Lena the horrors she had endured as a prisoner of war. Only she knows the full story of that awful time. I can't speak for her, of course, but if I'd been through even the fraction of her suffering that I knew about, I'm sure it'd haunt me for the rest of my life.

Then there were the probably more pleasant thoughts of our memorable meeting, of the way she survived the Kempeitai officer's orders to murder her and the other prisoners that day. Lena was very resilient. And here she was now with a lovely daughter and granddaughter. At a later stage I told both Vivian and Isabella how brave Lena was, probably the bravest lady I've ever met.

She had lived with those memories for fifty-three years. So had Vivian and Isabella, to a degree, since Lena had told them about the war when they were very young. But all that time they had lived with an unknown image of me. They had no photos of me and they would have had all kinds of mixed feelings when I arrived.

At first they all just stared at me as if I was some kind of exhibit in the zoo. There was nothing in the least rude about this, because these lovely people didn't have a nasty bone in their bodies. They just wanted to see what I looked like, I suppose, which was understandable. Then their welcome was so enthusiastic I felt almost as if they were going to eat me. Straightaway they made me feel part of the family.

It had been a big day. The next day Lena and I were to be interviewed by Bill Bunbury for ABC Radio National about how we had met. A friend back in Sydney, librarian Judy Steele, had contacted them when I told her I was going, insisting that the reunion should be documented. Bill called early in the morning and we breakfasted together while he quizzed me about details he needed for his story. Recording took up most of the morning and when the ABC broadcast it, it received extensive comment and was replayed several times.

I was in Perth for a week and spent every day with Lena and her family. Vivian drove us around all the local sights and often I'd look up to find one of them eyeing me. I didn't know what to do or say, so I just smiled back. On one occasion Vivian pulled up at a service station to get petrol and I said, 'Look, let me pay for this.' She looked into my eyes said, 'Oh no, we wouldn't be here if it wasn't for you.'

A couple of days later we were walking in a national park. Isabella asked me what I thought of the view and I answered, 'Fantastic. It's so good of you all to spend this time taking me around to see all these things.' Isabella gave me the same look her mother had, straight into my eyes, and said, 'You shouldn't say that, because we wouldn't be here if it wasn't for you.'

But it was the third time that really rocked me. I've already mentioned the fierce intensity on Lena's face when I was questioning the Japanese officer at Simanggang. It has stayed with me ever since and I've often wondered what she had been thinking. Well, I found out all right.

I had intended to ask her about it but changed my mind, thinking that the memory might distress her. Alone with Vivian one day, I tentatively asked if her mother had ever spoken about what had happened in Simanggang.

'Oh, yes. She told me everything when I was little. We still talk about it all the time.'

I told her what was on my mind and she said, 'Yes, I know about that.'

'I've wondered all these years what she was thinking about,' I said.

'Oh, she was just hoping you'd kill the rest of the Japanese.'

Vivian couldn't understand why I hadn't realised. What could I say to that? But I had to say something, so I mumbled something like, 'I'd have liked to, they were such rotten animals. But I got into an awful lot of trouble as it turned out, anyway.'

At the week's end they drove me out to the airport.

I had promised to see them again soon, but our next meeting was quite unexpected. The Department of the Army commissioned a documentary on Z Special Unit for training purposes and sale to television. Someone mentioned me to the director, Graham Shirley, while he was attending a Z Special Unit reunion in Tasmania. I agreed to be interviewed, and we filmed at an army base at George's Heights, Sydney, situated on beautiful waterfront land.

The process was all new to me. 'We'll be shooting on the cliff top overlooking the water,' Graham told me. Well, I'd done plenty of that before, but it wasn't the kind of shooting I was used to!

For the next three hours or so I concentrated on looking at the camera and talking. Every so often Graham called, 'Cut!' and I'd have to repeat something – at times twice. If a plane flew overhead we'd have to wait for the engine noise to recede. It was a bit wearing, but I didn't mind because I believe a new experience is usually a good thing in itself. Finally Graham was satisfied with the result, but he had a surprise for me.

'If we flew you over to Perth, do you think Lena would be prepared to tell her story for the documentary?'

'I think so,' I said. 'I'll ring her tonight and ask her.'

Lena agreed, we looked forward to seeing each other again soon and Graham arranged everything. We filmed in Lena's living room, which was turned into a film set. She had considerable memorabilia salvaged from Sarawak. This intrigued Graham, but Lena herself intrigued him even more. The whole crew was spellbound by her story. She spoke with great clarity and detail and I'm sure they learned a lot more than they expected to. I had a very pleasant week, each day spent with Lena, Vivian and sometimes Isabella. And it came to an end all too soon.

I still phone Lena, the Little Rose of the Batang Lupar, every week.

'*Salamaat, kechil rose,*' I say. Hello, little rose. '*Apa kaba?*' What's happening?

'*Salamaat malam. Kaba baik,*' she replies. Good evening. Everything's fine.

She's as lively and vehement as ever. Although born and raised in Sarawak of English stock, there's no doubt Lena is a true Australian in all her thoughts and actions.

EPILOGUE

A couple of years ago I came across army documents which cast some light on my threatened court martial. They were sent to me by Bob Reece, who had dug them up at the Australian War Memorial while researching his book *Masa Jepun*.

I had written Bob Reece a nasty letter over claims made in *Masa Jepun* that Dave Kearney and I were pulled out of Sarawak for ill-treating the Japanese. It was completely untrue, but I don't want to detract from his book in any way. Bob Reece wrote in good faith from sources, which he quoted, but the information in them was wrong. After my very strenuous complaints he apologised and was good enough to distribute an 'errata' correcting his mistake. After our argument was settled, he sent me copies of army correspondence he thought would interest me.

When I saw these documents I was amazed, disgusted and then furious. I had a couple of stiff vodkas and water before my mind settled. I read them again. Although I wasn't named, it was obvious who they were talking about.

The first was by SRD-Z Special Unit's Jumbo Courtney, addressed to 9th Division HQ. It reveals that a General Staff Officer visiting Kuching on the 5th of October 1945 took 'a complaint by the Japanese that the SRD at Simanggang harassed and killed some Japanese who were preparing to move to Bau in accordance with their orders, and incited the natives to attack these Japanese.'

Courtney's report is dated the 9th of October, the day before I was first called to see him at Labuan. Here is his conclusion:

From the native evidence at Simanggang, it is apparent that this particular body of Japanese had indulged in their usual forms of amusement, such as the water cure, sun cure and public thrashings. It is therefore considered that the fact that they were

*not all killed by natives after fleeing to the jungle, shows the efficiency of Capt
Kearney's control over the local populace and conclusively rebuts the charge made by
the Japanese that Capt Kearney incited the natives against them. It is recommended
that investigations be carried out at Simanggang regarding atrocities carried out
by this party of Japanese.*

It was nice to see that Jumbo Courtney took no nonsense and stood up
for his operatives, especially since we'd done nothing wrong anyway.
Although his account is not strictly accurate – he says the Japanese CO
was phoned from Betong, for example – it was certainly not exaggerated.
Three days later, Colonel Wilson of 9th Division HQ acted on this by
recommending that 9th Division's Kuching Force 'investigate subsequent
conduct of Japanese formerly in Simanggang area and reprimand Japanese
Commander for making a false report.'

Kuching Force was led by Brigadier Eastick, overall commander of
Australian forces in Sarawak. On the same day Wilson wrote to him,
Eastick evaluated another complaint collected by the Staff Officer in
Kuching. Four Japanese – allegedly civilians – asserted that while
evacuating Simanggang by boat on the 14th of September their group of
fourteen was 'suddenly and unexpectedly' fired upon. This referred to the
Sea Dyaks and me, although they thought 'no whites appeared to be in
the party.'

The Japanese claimed that no soldiers were with them, that only three
Kempeitai were stationed in Simanggang and that these had already left.
Eastick notes all four were 'emphatic that they did not take any offensive
action and were entirely surprised by the attack.' There was no mention
of their attempt to ambush us. Nor of the fact that all the prisoners we
took afterwards wore military uniforms and carried weapons. They knew
how to use them, too, because they did their best to shoot our bloody
heads off. And all they had to do was surrender, for Christ's sake. The war
was meant to be over.

I don't know how many of them were Kempeitai, but their
commanding officer proudly admitted he was. The locals confirmed it,
too. His ceremonial sword featured Kempeitai insignia and his very
impressive battle flag was inscribed with many of his proudest moments.
He was a little shit.

'As no opportunity for collusion was allowed them,' Eastick continued, 'the story must be accepted as reasonably reliable.' Utter crap. They were together when I locked them up in Fort Alice on the 14th of September and they were still there when I left Simanggang a week later. Eastick himself admits they 'remained in the local gaol until collected by Major Ditmas's party from Kuching.' There was plenty of time to concoct excuses and get their story right. They must have been shitting themselves imagining the repercussions for belting around and maltreating local people over four years.

Although Eastick wrote that 'allegations that Japanese personnel were killed are not substantiated,' in fact some were killed as a result of their decision to open fire and ignore my call to surrender. But he also ruled that 'the evidence taken would also lead to the conclusion that the Japanese were not the aggressors as stated by Capt Kearney. There is no independent witnesses available to verify the veracity of Japanese witnesses.'

No wonder I was amazed and disgusted reading this crap fifty-three years later! Why was there no effort to gather evidence from locals or ex-POWs? Surely they qualified as independent witnesses. Lena and her brother and sister were readily available in the area. In fact Lena stayed in Sarawak another nineteen years without ever being approached for her eyewitness account. I wondered what the locals would think of the commander of the allied forces listening to the Japanese instead of them? How could Eastick have taken the four Japanese 'civilians' seriously when the Kempeitai officer had complained about the same incident? The very fact that he was there proved them liars. Both complaints were in the staff officer's notes, which Eastick's report reveals he saw.

Dave, who was well-versed in staff reports, always said he knew bullshit when he saw it. I'm sure that's what he'd say about this document and I would agree with him. Its author generated no respect from me, only contempt for his naivety.

There was no ill-feeling between Z operatives and 9th Division troops. We did our job and they did theirs. But it was known within our unit that some people in 9th Division's upper echelons viewed our activities with distaste, possibly because they had no control over us.

Records show that Z Special Unit, with a handful of operatives and local guerrillas, killed more Japanese and reclaimed more Japanese-occupied territory in Sarawak than the entire 9th Division, and without suffering a single operative casualty. Maybe this had something to do with Brigadier Eastick's attitude, but only he would know that.

The paperwork relating to Z Special Unit operations was supposedly destroyed years ago. These have only survived because they're 9th Division documents. It's all in the past now, but I was glad to learn more about what had gone on behind the scenes.

I didn't see George Warfe after the war. Later he returned to the army, and during the Vietnam War went over to teach jungle warfare to the Yanks. He died of cancer a few years ago. Dave Kearney moved to Canada.

I often wonder what became of Bujang. A few ex-Semut people, including Ross Bradbury, revisited Sarawak ten to fifteen years ago. Jim Truscott tried to retrace our footsteps while researching Semut 3, but was denied access to a lot of the area. And so much of it has changed. Malaysia has logged a lot of Sea Dyak territory and they've lost vast tracts of their jungle, poor bastards. In some places they haven't got any trees left at all, just mud. Elsewhere in Borneo, Indonesian resettlements have sparked conflict and I've heard that headhunting is back again.

But I see no point in going too far back and I don't want to dwell in the past. Even using a computer for the first time to write this story has opened up a whole new world to me and there are new experiences every day. So I'll just see what's next. After all, life is for living.

ACKNOWLEDGEMENTS

I'd like to thank some people who helped me give birth to this book.

Judith Steele, a lovely lady, librarian and good friend, regularly nudged me over three years to write the book. 'When are you going to start? Have you started it yet?' and so on until I did.

Steven Swan, another good friend, is a computer wiz. I was 101% computer illiterate (I'd never even touched one) but Steve showed me how to operate a laptop. He set it up for me and helped out on numerous occasions, especially with layouts and scans.

David Levell arrived at my unit one day to interview me for the 'Australians At War' Film Archive. I was grilled on videotape for seven or eight hours. I told David I'd written a book and asked if he knew any literary agents. He said he just might.

I thought no more about it, but some three weeks later he rang me to say that if I sent him several chapters he would show them to a literary agent. He wouldn't tell me the name of the agent at this stage, no doubt in case the book was really crook, but he was too polite to say so. He then asked for a copy of the whole manuscript, and finally put me in touch with Selwa Anthony.

Selwa Anthony turned out to be a real treasure (actually, David turned out to be a real treasure also, but I can't and don't call a bloke a 'treasure') and gave me excellent advice. David edited my book and did a marvellous job.

Selwa very promptly 'off-loaded' my book to ABC Books who are, of course, so very professional in what they do. And now the book is born. I hope you enjoy it.

Thanks a lot Judy, Steve, David, Selwa and ABC Books.

Brian Walpole, May 2004